TV News, Urban Conflict and the Inner City

Studies in Communication and Society

Series editors: **Ralph Negrine and Anders Hansen**
University of Leicester

TV News, Urban Conflict and the Inner City

Simon Cottle

Leicester University Press
Leicester, London, New York

Distributed exclusively in the USA and Canada by St Martin's Press

Leicester University Press
(a division of Pinter Publishers)

First published in 1993

Editorial offices
Fielding Johnson Building, University of Leicester, Leicester, LE1 7RH, England

Trade and other enquiries
25 Floral Street, London, WC2E 9DS *and*
Room 400, 175 Fifth Avenue, New York, NY 10010, USA

British Library Cataloguing in Publication Data

A CIP catalogue record for this book is available from the British Library

ISBN   0 7185 1447 5 (hbk)
        0 7185 1462 9 (pbk)

Library of Congress Cataloging-in-Publication Data

Cottle, Simon.
  TV news, urban conflict, and the inner city/Simon Cottle.
    p. cm. – (Studies in communication and society)
  Revision of the author's thesis (Ph. D.–Centre for Mass
Communications Research)
  Includes bibliographical references and index.
  ISBN 0-7185-1447-5 (hbk.). – ISBN 0-7185-1462-9 (pbk.)
  1. Television broadcasting of news–Great Britain. 2. Inner
cities–Great Britain. 3. Sociology, Urban–Great Britain.
4. Social conflict–Great Britain. I. Title. II. Series: Studies
in communication and society (Leicester, England)
PN5124.T4C64 1993
070.1'95–dc20   92-44432
                                            CIP

Typeset by Saxon Graphics Ltd, Derby
Printed and bound in Great Britain by SRP Ltd, Exeter

For

Sam, Theo and Ella .... and Lucy

Lest anyone should underestimate the power of
commercial television:

'Daddy can I tell you about my dream?
It had adverts in it.'

Sam, aged 4

Contents

List of figures

List of tables

Acknowledgements

In recent times the problems of the inner city have periodically found headline attention and, along with many of Britain's outer estates, look set to continue to do so for the foreseeable future. The underlying problems of concentrated urban distress and social marginality referenced by such urban places have, if anything, become further exacerbated in recent years. This study owes a debt of gratitude to two institutions both concerned in their different ways with the public representation of social problems and conflicts.

The Centre for Mass Communication Research at the University of Leicester has for some considerable time been concerned with the public mediation of social problems and political dissent, producing a series of scholarly studies which have become classics within the field of mass communications research. I was fortunate indeed to be offered the opportunity to pursue a PhD study, the origins of this book, at this centre of excellence. Professor J.D. Halloran, the then Director of the Centre, presented me with what can only be seen as an enviable research opportunity while generously declining to stipulate or even delimit the scope of the research. The task of curtailing overly ambitious lines of research inquiry fell to my more immediate supervisor Anders Hansen. Without Anders' good sense and gentle steering touch I would, no doubt, still be up to my eyes in a backlog of VHS tapes. To both my academic supervisors and their colleagues at the Centre, thank you.

The other institution, without whose help and co-operation this study could not have been pursued, is Central Television plc based at Birmingham. It was here that I was granted the privileged access, generous support and facilities to pursue the case study which forms the basis of the research. Over a period of nearly two years when based at Central I accumulated many debts of gratitude, too many in fact to mention everybody by name. However a special thanks must be said to the then Controller of Factual Programmes, Robert

Southgate, whose title in line with the changing structures of broadcasting appears to be constantly under revision. Instrumental in setting up the research opportunity and opening doors rarely traversed by media researchers, this study owes much to his enthusiasm for collaborative inquiry and genuine interest in Central's portrayal of the problems of the region's inner cities. Barry Reeve, Head of Research at Central, has also continued to generously offer me his time, support and considerable understanding of all things television.

I would also like to thank the newsroom personnel for their kindness, co-operation and candid statements freely offered in numerous interviews and impromptu conversations. Both Ted Trimmer, Managing Editor, and Bill Campbell, Programme Editor, conceded to my many newsroom requests over a period of many months and volunteered insights into the regional news process, notwithstanding the sometimes frenetic and pressurized daily ebb and flow in which they were immersed. To them and all their newsroom colleagues who put up with the intruder in their midst, I would like to express my gratitude. So too must I thank other programme makers and senior corporate personnel including Associate Producer Simon Bailey, Documentary Producer Malcolm Frazer, Controller Programme Planning Dawn Airey and Controller Features Richard Creasey. While I suspect none will concur in entirety with the argument presented below and may feel the conclusions somewhat harsh, hopefully none will perceive an instance of uninformed media bashing.

Figure 2.1 showing the Central Television franchise/licence area has been drawn for this volume with ITV Boundaries information for the area based on a map kindly supplied by BARB (Broadcasters Audience Research Board Limited, London).

Approached from a standpoint outside of the professional practices and wider constraints informing the routines of programme production, it is not surprising perhaps that an outside view should come to a different perspective on the world of television. Where a degree of common ground may be found is in the necessity to take seriously the obligation to report and represent the social problems and difficulties endured by so many in the surrounding region. This study, however imperfectly, seeks to address such concerns with reference to the professional practices and surrounding constraints informing programme design, production and portrayal. If criticism is involved this is directed not at individual programme makers but at the wider contexts and forces in which and in relation to which programme makers conceptualize and produce their programmes. A senior executive once quipped that I was criticizing 'base metal' for not being 'gold'; unlike the alchemists with their faith in transmutation, however, I am more concerned with understanding the forces that routinely produce 'base metal' in the first place. Here at least, some overlap of interest may be found between those of the critical researcher and concerned broadcaster.

In addition to the two institutions above and their personnel, the Economic and Social Research Council also helped to ensure that the earlier PhD life of this book came to fruition with its studentship grant. More recently, the support and good advice of my editor Ralph Negrine at Leicester University Press has ensured that some of the excesses of PhD verbosity have been rendered, in this completely rewritten version, into a more readable form. Bath College of Higher Education, as well as providing me with an aesthetic environment in which to teach and work, a million miles away from the urban realities of the inner city, has also kindly contributed to the secretarial costs of preparing the manuscript. Here I would like to say a special thanks to Christine Eden, Deputy Dean of the Faculty of Education and Human Sciences, who has offered kindness and support in what can only be described as a particularly crowded stage of the life-cycle. Part of this crowd – Lucy, Sam, Theo and Ella – also ensured that my feet stayed resolutely on the ground even when seeking more rarefied climes. If the book suffers from a degree of empiricism I can hardly blame them however; I know, in retrospect, that I have much to thank each of them for too.

Introduction: Approaching television

Television and the inner city: contested realities

This is a book about television, principally TV news, urban conflict and the inner city. It is about the way in which the television medium has represented the conflicts centred in and around some of Britain's most socially deprived, economically disadvantaged and politically marginalized urban localities. It is about the failure, and explanations for that failure, of the TV news medium to convey the lived conditions and curtailed life chances daily confronted by those living within run-down areas and marginalized communities. In particular, it is about that part of the television system which might reasonably have been thought to provide the most fulsome representation of local conditions of urban malaise; and how, on any reasonable criteria, including those of the professional broadcasters involved, such has manifestly not happened. It is also about a major social contest over meaning: the struggle to define and publicly engage opposing points of view in relation to the problems and issues of urban distress. Whether concerning Britain's deprived inner cities or the more spatially distant, but socially proximate, outer estates,[1] such urban contests have become part of the contemporary urban scene. They tell us much about the way in which contemporary social relations are ordered and they reveal how forces of social exclusion and inclusion often find expression in the patchwork of city spatial forms. They also reveal how participants to social struggle and contest become increasingly dependent upon the mass media, including the medium of television, in pursuit of increased visibility, wider public understanding and political legitimacy.

Urban conflict, therefore, is not confined to the increasing catalogue of serious disorders in Britain's inner and outer cities finding headline attention across the 1980s, continuing into the 1990s. While such headlines as 'MADNESS!', 'PRECISION PLANNED RAMPAGE', 'FLAMES OF HATRED' or 'RIOT RAMPAGE' and 'THE STREETS OF VIOLENCE' typically position the latest outbreak of disorder as an aberrant event, a dramatic but temporary outpouring of unrestrained violence, urban conflict does not only inhere within these events alone.[2] The mainsprings of urban conflict also inform the contending positions of perspective, political action and response which variously seek to interpret and prescribe in relation to these events, and questions of urban marginality and disorder more generally. Indeed, the effect of, though not necessarily the conscious intent behind, such headlines can already be seen to have entered the contested terrain of inner city politics, preferring a particular lexicon and understanding of such events and not others.

The extensiveness of the problems and difficulties condensed within our inner and outer cities, as much as the depth of individual despair and social dislocation engendered there, demand nothing less than public recognition, understanding and political response. The mass media, and television especially, play a key role here. They occupy a privileged position and perform a crucial function in mediating to a wider public urban conflicts and social contests conducted in and around marginalized places and communities.

This book, then, is above all else an examination of the politics of cultural mediation. It is about the way in which the TV medium has practically and symbolically mediated or conveyed inner city issues and concerns *to* a wider public. It is also about the manner in which television has provided a public platform and mediated *between* contending inner city points of view and perspective. So too is it about mediation in the sense that major conflicts are ultimately informed by the pursuit of resolution, if only *in extremis* the triumph of superior force. Here mediation refers to the way in which TV presentations can become involved in the *management* of public contests, perhaps preferring certain responses, certain solutions to defined inner city problems. Finally, it is about the nature of the *medium* itself and the manner in which, in this instance, established programme forms have impacted upon or mediated in characteristic fashion inner city concerns. It is in these four senses that the term mediation is used in this study, each pointing to a fundamental aspect of television's involvement in the politics of the inner city and urban unrest. To what extent, in what form, and for what reasons the television medium has represented and responded to the challenge posed by Britain's inner cities forms the central inquiry of this study.

The remainder of this introductory chapter briefly reviews existing research approaches to television and situates the present study within this contested field of theory.

Approaching television

The television medium continues to attract academic interest, while its popular appeal hardly needs emphasising. Part of the daily fabric of existence for most people, the television set has for some time embedded itself within the domestic milieu and proved itself to be an indispensable piece of domestic technology, serving a variety of private and public uses and appealing to diverse wants and needs. Its unique features as a relatively new medium and cultural form has attracted critical discussion (Williams 1974; Postman 1987; Ellis 1988). TV has also been recognized as increasingly ingratiating itself into the rhythms of daily, weekly and seasonal life, thereby reflecting and in part helping to constitute those temporal rhythms, routines and rituals of modern existence as experienced between the home and the outside world (Lodziak 1986, 1988; Scannell 1988; Silverstone 1990); this is not to forget its potency as a source of imagery, ritual associations and public memories marking even wider durations of individual biography and/or collective experience (Chaney 1986).

Recently, attention has also been devoted to television as the 'family hearth' around which the play of cultural power and gendered domestic relationships takes place (Morley 1986). Moreover if, in the latter part of the twentieth century, television has rapidly colonized the domestic space and assumed the role of the mass media medium par excellence, in the years ahead it promises to further embed itself into daily existence as a focal point for a much expanded repertoire of domestic uses and communication facilities (Morley and Silverstone 1990). If all these and other characteristics of television approached variously as a distinctive medium, spatial and temporal routine, domestic practice, and indispensable form of social technology are important, they should not be allowed to overshadow the historical and continuing appeal of the television medium as a provider of images and ideas for the most part delivered in programme form.

Television schedules, it hardly needs to be said, are composed of disparate if carefully arranged programmes and programme items, each designed to attract and appeal to a wide audience. That is, they are about 'something', frequently addressing issues and concerns as well as audiences in a manner which is likely to encourage audience interest and continuing viewing commitment. The medium of television, in other words, provides a seemingly ceaseless parade of images and accounts, representations and discourses, structured within and across a spectrum of programming fare. It is here that the principal interest in television, whether from viewers or academic researchers, is found. If popular interest in television also occasionally extends to questions of media effects, and the impact of violent imagery upon children especially, this by no means exhausts the concerns of studies interested in the influence of television as a provider of images and ideas (Halloran 1980; Cumberbatch and Howitt 1989; Gunter and McAleer 1990).

It is television's capacity as a medium of communication that continues to attract most research interest. Indeed, it is this capacity to both reach and appeal to, and in part therefore help constitute, a 'general public' that for some commentators represents its historical potency. 'The fundamentally democratic thrust of broadcasting lay in the new kind of access to virtually the whole spectrum of public life that radio first, and later television, made available to all' (Scannell 1989: 140). If television broadcasting has helped to constitute a new kind of general public, it has also provided a means by which that public could be addressed, persuaded, influenced and, on occasion, mobilized in support of diverse political projects.

Studies which have sought to address the impact of the mass media, including television, as a form of political communication across different areas of public life and policy now include the following: the portrayal of the 'triumphal return' of General MacArthur from the Korean War (Lang and Lang 1953), elections and publicity processes (Blumler 1990), the displacement of the politics of public demonstration (Halloran, Elliott and Murdock 1970; Murdock 1981), the provision of social welfare and the introduction of the Community Charge (Golding and Middleton 1982, Deacon and Golding 1991), industrial relations and the management of the economy (Glasgow University Media Group 1976, 1980), Government policy in Northern Ireland (Curtis 1984), the support of Government war aims (Morrison and Tumber 1988; Cummings 1992; Taylor 1992), the politics of crime and criminal justice (Schlesinger, Tumber and Murdock 1991), and the reporting of social forms of deviance more generally (Cohen and Young 1981; Ericson, Baranek and Chan 1987, 1989, 1991). Each of these, and many other studies, have identified the mass media as a potent source of ideas, images and discourses which variously inform, and therefore to varying degrees and in different ways either enable or disable the politics of active citizenship. They have been conducted in terms of what has recently been termed 'the public knowledge project' (Corner 1991: 268) or 'political aesthetic' view of mass communications (Curran 1990: 146). Though difficult to generalize, it can be noted that questions of power and determination here tend to be focused in relation to the constraints and pressures exercised at the moment of production, and less preoccupied with what happens at the moment of audience consumption.

Such studies have approached the mass media, either implicitly or more often in recent years explicitly, as a central institution of the public sphere, that is, as a realm of social life in which public opinion can be discussed, rationally debated and courses of political action decided upon (Habermas 1974, 1989). While most of the studies above would argue that such laudable democratic ideals have rarely been achieved by the mass media in practice, and provide differing explanations as to why this should be, they tend nevertheless to approach the mass media as a key site in which political information, beliefs and ideologies find wider public representation. Which is not to say, of course, that all political opinions, viewpoints, beliefs and informing ideologies find equal opportunity for media participation. In this sense, such studies may also be seen as conforming, broadly, to what the American cultural theorist James Carey has coined the 'transmission view of communication' in which information is seen as conveyed across space for the purposes of social influence or control (Carey 1989: 43). Carey usefully distinguishes this approach to communications from a 'ritual view'.

A ritual view of communication is directed not towards the extension of messages in space, but the maintenance of society in time (even if some find this maintenance characterized by domination, and therefore illegitimate); not the act of imparting information or influence but the creation, representation, and celebration of shared even if illusory beliefs. If a transmission view of communication centres on the extension of messages across geography for purposes of control, a ritual view centres on the sacred ceremony that draws persons together in fellowship and commonality. (Carey 1989: 43)

Carey's formulation is useful, throwing into sharp relief a dimension of communications which is rarely at the forefront of studies of political communication; it can be criticized none the less for tending towards a form of dualistic essentialism. It apparently suggests that communications can either be approached as a form of information 'transmission', typically construed in terms of negative control, or as a form of collective 'ritual', which tends to be seen in more celebratory terms. It can be countered that mass communications can be approached as both, embodying simultaneously the dimensions of information extension and ritual affirmation. Moreover, the extent to which each may be seen as serving, respectively, purposes of social control or affirming collective identities and needs, is not a question of absolute differences apparently inhering in each, but essentially a question for empirical investigation. There is no logical reason why, for example, ritual appeal cannot on occasion serve a decidedly anti-democratic purpose, while information exchange can equally facilitate collective democratic goals.

Carey's insight into the symbolic nature of communications is none the less profound and deserves, with some qualification, to be taken seriously in studies of political communication. In the British context, such insights have tended to inform the recent profusion of academic interest in popular culture, including television forms, developed within cultural studies. This provides the second major orientation to the mass media and can be termed 'the popular culture project' (Corner 1991: 268) or 'popular aesthetic' (Curran 1990: 146). Here popular cultural forms have tended to be approached as a mediated form of 'negotiated resistance' in which popular tastes, beliefs and pleasures inform, albeit within modified terms, the commercial products of the culture industries (Bennett, Mercer and Woollacott 1986). Gramscian insights into the nature of ideological contest are reworked, where a situation of ideological hegemony is seen as constantly under assault from contending social interests. Here ideology is less a question of the imposition of dominant ideas, and more a question of a hegemonic project continually seeking to incorporate or co-opt the cultural values, beliefs and interests of contending social groups in pursuit of social dominance.

Whether recovering the meaning of subcultural styles (Hebdige 1979), the pleasures afforded to readers of romance novels, and their temporary escape from patriarchal domestic tasks (Radway 1987), the 'regional-popular' significance of working class holidays in Blackpool (Bennett 1986), or the pleasures of melodrama found in popular TV soap operas (Ang 1985), crime and police series (Clarke 1986; Sparks 1992) or TV quiz shows (Fiske 1990), all these, and countless other studies, have sought to take seriously questions of popular pleasure and the appeals of entertainment forms. The cultural studies approach has also contributed to the renewed interest in 'reception studies' where audiences have been found to be far from the 'cultural dopes' sometimes assumed, and are found, in contrast, to be differentiated, discerning and actively involved in processes of interpretation and sense-making (Morley 1980; Lewis 1985, 1991; Jensen 1987; Schroder 1987; Moores 1990). Studies of television reception have indicated that studies concerned with the critical analysis and interpretation of texts cannot assume that the meanings there discerned are in fact the ones communicated to different audiences. Meaning, in such accounts, is typically best seen as an outcome at the interface of text and audience. If the 'public knowledge' orientation of media studies has tended to address issues of cultural power in relation to the parameters and pressures of media production, here cultural power becomes focused in relation to the moment of audience consumption and the varieties of meanings there sustained.

This is not the place to engage with the intricacies and detail of hermeneutic and ethnographic studies of audiences. Two main points can be made however. The first concerns the extent to which media texts have been found to prefer particular interpretations and responses. While these may not always be accepted by members of an audience, the fact that 'negotiation', 'resistance' or even 'opposition', to use the preferred terms of audience studies, can be found to inform viewers' interpretative responses implies that a preferred meaning is prefigured and structured within the text. Moreover, the extent to which certain television forms, and TV news in particular, are characterized by structured forms of delivery, repetitive story treatments and involve prominent thematic presences and silences, suggests that the interpretative resources made available do not avail themselves to open interpretation (Philo 1990). Second, ideas of texts as openly polysemous ignores the extent to which audience members or 'interpretative communities' engage with texts from a limited number of social sites and positions, informed perhaps by the less than comprehensive nature of previous media exposure, which combine to effectively curtail the range of positions for discursive engagement and contest.

This study recognizes that audiences bring to the viewing context a range of preformed beliefs, values and ideas and that viewing takes place within different contexts, all of which are likely to influence processes of viewer engagement and interpretation. It also recognizes, however, that media texts are produced under determinant ideological, institutional, commercial, technological, statutory and professional conditions and arrangements, all of which inform the production, organization and delivery of media texts. These texts do not escape the conditions of their production, and inevitably bear the traces of their professional and socially informed construction. Moreover, to the extent that programme items are mediated by established programme forms, so too are they actively produced to conform to genre and sub-genre requirements – whether programme subject interests, styles of treatment, or characteristic audience appeals and modes of address (see Williams 1985: 180–85).

Questions of cultural mediation are thereby raised, pointing not just to the ideological commitments or discursive alignments thought to inform professional programme makers, but also the professional contexts, routines and practices of programme production which combine to assemble and reproduce established programme forms, the latter of which, once conventionalized, may well exert their own determinacy. This study explores in detail the range and forms of interpretative resources made, or not made, available to a wider public in relation to the contested site of the inner city and seeks to account for why these and not others have found public representation.

Insights and approaches from cultural studies have also begun to be directed at popular and populist forms of news, particularly the tabloids. Here such studies include an examination of the popular TV programme *Nationwide* and its audience (Brunsdon and Morley 1978; Morley 1980), styles of serious and popular radio talk (Cardiff 1986), the *Sun*'s appeal to women readers (Holland 1983), the growth and ideological implications of the human interest story, and its underpinning by commercial goals (Curran, Douglas and Whannel 1980), and most recently a collection of studies addressing a number of aspects of popular journalism (Dahlgren and Sparks 1992). In broad strokes, something of the distinctiveness of popular forms of journalism can briefly be indicated by a number of characteristic contrasts, presented here as a series of oppositions. These involve thematic and stylistic differences, as well as differences of audience mode of address, and projected 'ways of knowing' or news epistemologies.

Whereas serious journalism has tended to be oriented to the sphere of formal politics, social and political elites and the happenings of the public sphere, popular journalism is disposed to reverse such priorities, seeking out the personalities and human scandals behind the formal world of politics and elite happenings, endorsing the ordinary pursuit of private consumption, leisure, family life and sexuality. If serious journalism seeks to inform its readers/audience through the delivery of rational accounts and opinion advanced by elites and experts, popular journalism is inclined to appeal directly to sentiment and empathy, invoking first hand testimony and the individual human interest story. While serious journalism presents its claim to objectivity via the authoritative and detached tones of its news presentation and accessing of expert opinion, popular journalism is inclined to parade its moral commitment and championing of engaged opinion in the name of the people and common sense. Whereas serious journalism presents itself as fulfilling a democratic mission to inform and act as public watchdog and guardian of the Fourth Estate, popular journalism proclaims its entertainment value, seeking to inject fun, spectacle and scandal into the mundane routines of ordinary people, often with an irreverent eye towards elite institutions, personalities and practices.

Such contrasts are, of course, best seen as tendencies within and along a continuum, rather than absolute differences, with any particular form of news journalism constructing its own distinctive character and market appeal. Such oppositions none the less serve to indicate that the 'popular culture project' has much to say of interest when addressing forms of TV news, whether serious or popular, and is likely to throw further light on those studies of political communication conducted within the 'public knowledge project' referenced above. On the other hand, it may have less to say of interest in relation to questions of cultural power as exercised at the moment of production.

In terms of this study and its concern with the televisual mediation of the problems and issues of the inner city, it is clear that its interest straddles both these ways of approaching media communications. Concerned as it is with the way in which television has mediated an important social and political concern, it addresses the manner in which those contending perspectives on the problems of urban marginality have variously found public representation, providing a resource for public knowledge; it is also, necessarily, concerned with the manner in which established television forms, including a popular TV news form, have mediated such a public contest within and through programmes, for the most part, designed and produced to maximize their popular appeal. Clearly, attention can usefully be directed at the way in which established programme forms, each with its characteristic subject interests, forms of audience appeal and projected relationship to its audience, mediate the problems and issues of the inner city.

Recognizing the insights that can be gained from aspects of the popular culture project this study differs markedly from most cultural studies however. Unlike most cultural studies it does not rely on a critical interpretation of textual forms alone, which typically seek to recover the play of contending social interests and discourses found within the wider society. That approach too often fails to recognize the manner in which processes of cultural mediation have been practically and professionally produced, often with decisive impact upon those media products then subjected to critical interpretation. In other words, cultural critics have tended to fall into the trap of 'the problem of inference' where a critical reading of the text is thought to provide sufficient insight to address issues of explanation. When considering issues presented within the news, whether press or broadcasting, such analyses have tended to assume that journalists simply give expression to the play of dominant ideas current within society at a particular point in time: 'television news is a cultural artefact; it is a sequence of socially manufactured messages, which carry many of the culturally dominant assumptions of our society' (Glasgow University Media Group 1980:398), or 'the practices of television journalism reproduce accurately the way in which "public opinion" has already been formed in the primary domains of political and economic struggle, how it has been structured in dominance there' (Connell 1986:140).

While agreeing that television news can be approached as a 'cultural artefact', ironically this cultural studies approach fails to interrogate the manner in which news has been professionally and practically produced and mediated, not just in terms of unconsciously held dominant assumptions, but purposefully according to the known parameters and requirements of an established cultural programme form. In this sense such cultural studies have not really dealt with questions of cultural mediation at all. A more sophisticated version of the cultural studies approach to the study of news has been developed by Stuart Hall and his colleagues (Hall 1975; Hall et al. 1986). Here questions of mediation have begun to be addressed in terms which recognize the practical involvement of journalists in news-making processes via the strategic position they occupy: 'broadcasters and their institutions mediate – hold the pass, command the communicative channels – between the elites of power (social, economic, political, cultural) and the mass audience' (Hall 1975: 124). In accounting for the privileged access granted to society's elites by the media, two principal explanations are advanced: (a) the constant news imperative of working against the clock, and the consequent dependence upon institutional sources for routine news comment and opinion; (b) the professional journalists' claim to impartiality and objectivity which leads them to access authoritative spokespersons who appear to have expert knowledge (Hall et al. 1986: 58). For these reasons the news media are seen to afford privileged access to elites who effectively act as the nation's 'primary definers', providing interpretations of news topics which then ' "commands the field" in all subsequent treatment and sets the terms of reference within which all further coverage or debate takes place' (1986: 58).

This influential formulation begins to advance explanations of news coverage by addressing the practical constraints and practices of news routines and, as such, does not simply rely on the culturalist explanations above where journalists unconsciously give expression to dominant ideological codes and discourses. Moreover, to the extent that it recognizes a degree of differentiation within and between different news outlets, in that each news outlet translates into a characteristic 'public idiom the statements and viewpoints of the primary definers', so too does it begin to address issues of news differentiation as existing cultural forms (1986: 61). It does not, however, pursue such concerns into the news production domain and in any case conceptualizes such differences only to the extent to which they inflect, but do not substantively alter, the relaying of 'primary definitions'. Attention to the impacting properties of the medium thereby remains undeveloped as do the changing, contested and institutionally fractured nature of 'primary definitions' (Schlesinger 1990). None the less, it points to some of the insights which may be gained from attending to the professional journalist's practices and the routines of news production, and also begins to recognize that news is also produced in accordance with established, and differentiated, forms of news provision.

A number of sociological studies of news organization and production have been pursued in more focused terms elsewhere. These have typically addressed the mechanics of news production including its bureaucratic organization, routinized nature and professional dependence upon shared news values, colleague relationships, institutional hierarchies and source organizations (Breed 1955; White 1964; Epstein 1973; Sigelman 1973; Tuchman 1973, 1978; Altheide 1974; Chibnall 1977; Golding and Elliott 1979; Gans 1980; Fishman 1980; Schlesinger 1987; Ericson, Baranek and Chan 1987; Soloski 1989). These studies have contributed enormously to our understanding of the news-making process, and secured insights which simply could not have been sustained from a reading of news texts alone. They throw considerable light on the inside pressures and constraints daily moulding news output. For the most part, however, they have tended to neglect the way in which, though each news outlet is inevitably organized along bureaucratic lines, each manages to produce a distinctive and differentiated news product. Questions of cultural mediation, it would appear, are not exhausted by reference to general newsroom routines, bureaucratic organization, and processes of professional socialization into a shared understanding of 'news'. (For a review of these see Cottle forthcoming (a).)

Similarly, the political economy approach to the study of the news media, though pointing to the informing background of competitive market pressures, prohibitive market entry costs and advertising dependence, has also tended to under-theorize the differentiated forms of the news media (Murdock 1982, 1990; Murdock and Golding 1984). This approach points, none the less, to a wider context of impersonal constraints and pressures which undoubtedly circum-scribe the operations of the news media and culture industries more generally. To what extent economic forces are a necessary though not sufficient condition for explaining media products is a continuing source of disagreement however (Golding and Murdock 1979, 1991; Hall 1983; Fiske 1989a). Interestingly, a leading exponent of this approach has also been involved in an important study in which forms of actuality and fictional TV programmes were found to have mediated discourses on 'terrorism' differently (Elliott, Murdock and Schlesinger 1986). In contrast to those findings from case studies largely confined to forms of national news, the authors admit to being both surprised and exhilarated by finding differing degrees of ideological openness and closure across different programmes and indicate that such work has only barely begun (1986: 284).

Following this brief critical review of approaches to television, it can now be stated that this study also addresses the way in which contending discourses have variously been mediated by existing actuality programme forms, and attends to both the production and the characteristic impact of such programmes upon the display of public knowledge. The public knowledge here, of course, refers to those contending definitions and perspectives on the problems and issues of the inner city. It is to a review of these contending positions that this discussion will shortly turn, identifying key issues and points of view with which to examine television's representations.

1
Urban conflict and the inner city: contested realities

This chapter first considers existing research on the media presentation of the inner city, identifying significant findings as well as research lacunae or silences. A number of these important omissions, including the relative absence of sustained work on TV's production and portrayal of inner city problems, especially in relation to regional television news and other forms of programming, are identified and pursued in this study. Given the contested nature of the inner city as both lived reality and symbol or wider social ills, the discussion then returns to consider how the inner city has variously been conceptualized within public discussion. This includes a review of perspectives on collective social violence which are found to order public debate, official and unofficial public inquiries and political responses to both the events of urban unrest and interpretations of their causation. This usefully identifies the contested nature of the inner city as a site for competing discourses, each defining the problems of the inner city differently. These can then be marshalled in relation to TV's representation of the inner city and its associated problems. Finally, this chapter provides a brief overview of the structure and organization of the book.

Media research on the inner city: findings and failings

With one recent area of exception, the inner city has not been the focus of any sustained or detailed research interest concerned with questions of media representation. This is surprising. The inner city and other margainalized urban areas represent some of the most deep-seated problems of contemporary urban society, visibly crystalizing patterns and processes of social inequality in concentrated form.

'It is not only', to quote one commentator, 'a particular sort of place on the map, but a symbol and summation of the dark side of the whole society' (Harrison 1985: 21). If the problems of the inner city and its associated environs demand public recognition, the manner in which such have been mediated by the mass media also deserve serious scrutiny.

The area of exception here concerns the media portrayal of recent urban disorders. These studies can usefully be reviewed and a number of research lacunae identified, each pointing to departure points for the present study. These studies have generally sought to demonstrate and analyse the ideological alignments and forms displayed within Britain's newspaper coverage (Sumner 1982; Cohen 1982; Joshua, Wallace and Booth 1983; Searchlight 1985; Hollingsworth 1986; Murray 1986; Solomos 1986, 1989; Van Dijk 1988, 1991). In addition, Downing (1985) has concentrated specifically upon the 'elite' press, and Murdock (1984) the popular press with Hansen and Murdock (1985) reviewing across the popular and quality national press and observing how 'news is a field of continual conflict in which competing discourses struggle for publicity and legitimacy' (1985: 255).

These latter studies are interesting in that they distance themselves from any simplistic analysis which maintains a priori that a dominant ideology is likely to be advanced in such news accounts and locate at least a degree of internal differentiation and discursive struggle within and between the main contending perspectives in play. No longer entrapped with a limited and some would say unnecessarily empiricist notion of 'ideology' which distorts from the analyst's presumed insight into the 'real', these theorists have tended to seize upon the insights afforded by a sensitivity to language organized as discourse. That said, these studies have tended to find the generality of riot news reports advancing a perspective on the riots in which conservative themes have been preferred. Graham Murdock's study, following a detailed discussion of press accounts of the Toxteth riots, is representative of this general finding when he concludes:

The major news media . . . presented a highly consistent account of the Toxteth disturbances centred around the image of a 'thin blue line' of police defending the community against an unprecedented wave of violence and lawlessness, and within this view the riots were defined as a criminal rather than a political phenomenon, as street crime on a mass scale, to be dealt with as such, through more effective policing and extended police powers. (Murdock 1984: 78)

Interestingly, while studies of press riot coverage have tended to conclude that a law and order framework of interpretation has dominated such accounts, studies which have specifically sought to contrast the serious disorders of 1981 and 1985 have noted how mediated public responses have varied across these two periods

(Solomos 1986, 1989: 99–121, 160–74). In particular, while the 1980/81 disorders were found to be dominated by themes of: 'race and the enemy within', 'the breakdown of law and order', 'youth unemployment and social disadvantage', and 'political marginality' the mediated 1985 disorders established a linkage between race, crime and disorder much more firmly than in earlier media accounts. Though Solomos's analyses do much to illuminate the possible interplay between ideological constructions of the riots and policy responses, his discussion does not attempt to analyse or theorize the exact mechanisms and role of the mass media within such processes. In other words, the specific contribution of the media to such wider processes of signification and political and policy response remains unexplored and untheorized.

In a novel study, the role of the inner city is seen as providing a central and essentially mythical role in the 1981 disorders (Burgess 1985). This study points to the role of the media in constructing the inner city, symbolically, as a distant and deviant place, observing how 'the newspapers fulfil an ideological role in which a myth is being perpetuated of The Inner City as an alien place, separate and isolated, located outside white middle-class values and environments' (1985: 193). However, like those studies already noted, it does not inquire into the possible explanations that may help to account for such findings. Confined to an interpretation of media portrayal alone, these studies have left in abeyance questions of why exactly such media forms have been produced and remain open to interpretations which favour simplistic, if popular, conspiracy or ideological complicity explanations. Such easy inferences may well fall far short of an adequate explanation, as one commentator at least has recognized.

Contrary to the 'high' and 'low' conspiracy theories favoured by some critics of the news media, the answer does not lie in interventions from on high or in the personal prejudices of journalists and editors, but in the routine business of news production and the practical and commercial pressures which shape it. (Murdock 1984: 78)

To what extent and in what way the routine business of news production has impacted upon riot portrayal and inner city coverage more generally has, to date, remained unexplored. If the production domain and professional practices of journalists have not been pursued in studies of recent disorders and their news mediation, studies of the audience have also been conspicuous in their near absence, though here a social psychological study of six participants and their apparently preformed 'social representations' of the 1980 St Pauls riot in Bristol proves insightful (Litton and Potter 1985).

In addition to the studies of press coverage of urban disorder, two studies focusing specifically upon television coverage deserve comment. The first study, by Howard Tumber (1982), charts the main evening national news broadcasts over the two week period of the

1981 summer of rioting. Adding further confirmation to the general finding advanced by most of those press studies noted above, Tumber's content analysis 'revealed television's preoccupation with law and order as the answer to the problems of the disturbances rather than as a possible cause' and, following a review of this material asks, did the viewer 'understand that the kind of violence that erupted in the inner cities in 1981 was a result of many factors? If there was sublime ignorance among the population and among senior politicians, must not television take part of the blame?' (1982: 51). The study has not gone without criticism however, due to its efforts to refute the 'copy cat' thesis. This idea, frequently aligned to a conservative understanding of the causation of riots and under-pinned by a behaviourist model of televisual 'effects', though also mentioned within Lord Scarman's report (Scarman 1986: 173–5), maintains that the media contribute to the spread of serious disorders by providing a model for others to imitate. It has been argued, however, that to take this idea seriously is to displace attention from the possible social causation of the riots while also failing to pursue more important questions of media involvement and influence (Herridge 1983).

Tumber's analysis makes effective use of traditional forms of content analysis counting frequencies of themes, social and political actors, broadcast durations and so on, on which his interpretation depends. In a detailed textual analysis Justin Lewis (1982) provides a degree of insight and interpretation neglected by the studies above. Attending to TV news treatments of inner city riots as a form of narrative which involve stages of revelation, interpretation and closure the televisual 'enigma' of the Brixton riots in April and July of 1981 are contrasted. Enigma, in this context, points to the implicit, sometimes explicit, frameworks of explanation accompanying the riot news presentations. Interestingly, television news is found to have covered these temporally proximate disturbances in different ways. While the April 1981 Brixton disturbances afforded opportuni-ties for the law and order frame to be undermined by the media questioning both the role of the police and invoking a frame of understanding posing social conditions as explanatory factors, the later July 1981 riots are seen to have been almost entirely subsumed within a law and order framework of understanding. Lewis accounts for such differences by attending to the narrative forms of these different episodes:

We can begin to answer this question by considering the difference in narrative forms: Brixton was the story of an event; Toxteth, Moss Side etc, were all episodes of a continuous saga. The self-contained structure of the news structure was transformed into the episode of structure of a crisis. The repetition of the revelatory sequence disrupted the revelation–interpretation–closure narrative, the revelations interrupting the interpretative stage and subverting any attempts to close the analysis . . . The shift in narrative form created the conditions for the re-establishment of the law and order discourse. (Lewis 1982: 24–5)

This account of the televisual portrayal of inner city disturbances is of note because once again it points to the formal possibility of discursive 'openings' within media treatments. On this account, these may change through time while also indicating something of the inherent and predisposing limitations of news forms when confined to reporting initial (revelatory) events. However, the manner in and extent to which such riot discourses are in fact dependent upon professional journalist practices and news production routines, rather than the narrative form of events seemingly requiring certain discourses and not others, once again poses a series of questions not addressed in such interpretative accounts.

This brief review of media research concerning recent inner city disorders has identified a number of key silences as well as prominent findings. In relation to the present study five major research lacunae can be identified and addressed. First, attention has tended to focus upon the initial reports of inner city riots; while these may well be the most dramatic moment of media portrayal, it is not clear how, if at all, such accounts are supplemented over a considerable period of time. Is it the case that riot portrayals continue, long after the initial events of a riot, to be reported in similar terms? Or do follow-up reports relating perhaps to issues of long-term consequences, or considered responses as to their causation provide a more extensive framework for interpretation? Here the regional television system and its centre-piece of regional news may be thought to provide an important, if hitherto neglected, contribution to the reporting of inner city disorders. If riots temporarily attract the national news spotlight, the scale and drama of such events in regional terms are likely to generate continuing regional news coverage, long after the national news cameras have moved on.

Second, attention has focused in the main upon national press, and to a limited extent national television coverage; such media forms cannot necessarily be assumed to be representative of the mass media generally. To what extent the television news media may be differentiated in important respects, perhaps reflecting different programme forms and audience appeals, is an area as yet relatively neglected in the TV news literature. In combination with the point above, attention can usefully be devoted to the possible specificities of regional TV news and the manner in which such may be found to impact upon representations of the inner city.

Third, attention has not only been focused upon national media forms of riot coverage but so too has it tended to focus upon news specifically, seemingly subsuming other forms and types of media coverage to the generalized conclusions derived from news studies. To what extent current affairs or documentary programmes, to name only the most immediate programme cousins of TV news forms, either reinforce and supplement or perhaps qualify or even contradict news treatments is also in need of comparative investigation.

Fourth, with few exceptions, these studies have advanced their analyses from a close reading of news 'texts' and, as such, have tended to say little concerning the possible parameters and pressures informing the production of such news treatments. As stated above, and whether consciously held by the authors or not, such accounts are likely to lend support to simplistic conspiracy or professional complicity accounts which do less than justice to those complex factors, including professional journalist practices, production routines and programme ambitions informing the production of media portrayals.

Last, it is also noteworthy that the review above has tended to suggest that such studies are in danger of compounding long-standing criticisms of the news media which note 'there is an inherent tendency for the news to be framed in a discontinuous and ahistorical way, and this implies a truncation of context, and therefore a reduction of meaningfulness' (Schlesinger 1987: 47; see also Halloran, Elliott and Murdock 1970; Golding and Murdock 1979). In the particular context of media presentation of the problems of the inner city the event orientation of news may, in fact, be found to be supportive of a particular interpretation of the disorders rather than reducing meaningfulness. That said, the point being made here suggests that media researchers are poorly placed to account for inner city portrayal if reliant only upon those initial reports of the events of inner city disturbances. A similar point, made some time ago in a transatlantic context, repays consideration here.

The Commission's major concern with the news media is not in riot reporting as such, but in a failure to report adequately on race relations and ghetto problems and to bring more Negroes into journalism . . . Disorders are only one aspect of the dilemmas and difficulties of race relations in America. In defining, explaining and reporting this broader, more complex and ultimately far more fundamental subject the communications media, ironically, have failed to communicate. (Kerner 1968: 382)

Twenty-five years later, in the wake of the Los Angeles riots of April–May 1992, as much as continuing inner and outer city urban disorders in this country, it can again be asked to what extent the communications media have managed to communicate those enduring problems of social marginalization condensed within certain localities? In answering that question, it is necessary to look beyond the initial media responses to inner city disturbances and consider how they have treated the problems and issues of the inner city in general.

This study, then, sets out to explore to what extent a major representative of the British television medium has managed to communicate those lived inner city conditions and contested realities found within its region to a wider audience? On the findings of the above, the study deliberately focuses its sights upon one of the 'big five' independent television broadcasters, paying special attention to the professional practices, production routines and programme forms mediating inner city related portrayal, as well as representations of inner city problems and issues broadcast over an extensive period of time. One of the most serious instances of inner city disorder and its television mediation is examined in detail with particular reference to its follow-up reporting. Different programme forms, including news, current affairs and documentary programming are all consulted, but regional television news assumes the focal point of inquiry. This form of TV news has received next to no serious research interest, and yet it is this programme form, more than any other, which claims to routinely address issues and concerns of immediate proximity to regional audiences – including those concerns and problems associated with the region's inner and outer cities. Not only, then, does this study investigate for the first time the manner in which general issues of inner city concern have been addressed by the television medium, it also examines in detail a part of the TV news system which has so far escaped serious critical examination. This it does by examining, in tandem, both the contexts of television programme production and broadcast portrayal of inner city issues.

Urban conflict and the inner city

During the weekend of 10–12 April (Friday, Saturday and Sunday) the British people watched with horror and incredulity an instant audio-visual presentation on their television sets of scenes of violence and disorder in their capital city, the like of which had not previously been seen in this century in Britain. (Scarman 1981)

It is the events of urban conflict that have, above all else, placed the problems of the inner city and the outer estates on the political agenda in recent years. Lord Scarman's notable intervention into the public debate on the inner city provides a useful starting point for this discussion (Scarman 1986). Though his assertion above, that such scenes of violence and disorder are without historical precedent, can be challenged both in relation to forms of collective racial violence (Miles 1984; Fryer 1989: 298–386) as well as violent disorder more generally (Dunning et al. 1987), there is no doubting the fact that these events found unparalleled visibility in the medium of television. For most people the only encounter with these disorders has been via the images and accounts found within the mass media. It is here that such events have become 'publicly known'. The mass media, and television especially because of its capacity to convey 'moving pictures' – both literal and figurative – has assumed a central position in the provision of representations of these newsworthy events, as well as providing the public stage on which the ensuing contests of interpretation and political response could be advanced.

In both these respects the mass media has assumed a pivotal role, providing and organizing images and accounts which either ignore, sustain or challenge particular frameworks of interpretation and political response. A scholar of political symbolization has implicitly drawn attention to the importance of mass mediated views on the inner city when he states:

> The critical element in political manoeuvre for advantage is the creation of meaning; the construction of beliefs about events, politics, leaders, problems and crises that rationalise or challenge existing inequalities. The strategic need is to immobilise opposition and mobilise support . . . It is the language about political events, not the events in any other sense that people experience. (Edelman 1988: 103–4)

From the vantage point of the 1990s, the urban disorders that first sparked Lord Scarman's inquiry at the beginning of the 1980s proved to be only the first of innumerable urban contests, continuing in parts of Britain's inner cities and outer estates to this day (Benyon 1984a; Benyon and Solomos 1987, 1991). A brief roll call of urban inner and outer city disorder across the period makes the point that such events cannot be seen as either rare or confined to only a few localities. The first major disorder of the 1980s occurred in the St Pauls area of Bristol in 1980, this was followed in 1981 by Brixton and Southall in London, Toxteth in Liverpool, Moss Side in Manchester, Handsworth in Birmingham, as well as districts in Sheffield, Nottingham, Hull, Slough, Leeds, Bradford, Leicester, Derby, High Wycombe and Cirencester. Minor disorders were also reported in parts of London and Liverpool in 1982, 1983 and 1984. In 1985 a major outbreak of urban unrest occurred in Lozells, Handsworth in Birmingham, followed by Brixton in London, Toxteth in Liverpool and, later, the Broadwater Farm estate in Tottenham, London. Tensions remained high in some of these areas with disorder again breaking out in 1986 as well as on the North Prospect estate in Plymouth. In 1987 and 1988 disorder occurred in Wolverhampton, Chapeltown in Leeds and Notting Hill in London. Disorders have continued across subsequent years, with serious disturbances on the Ely estate in Cardiff, the Blackbird Leys estate in Oxford and Handsworth in Birmingham, followed by the Meadow Well estate in Tyneside and Elswick area of Newcastle all in 1991. At the time of writing the pattern of serious urban disorders continues, with disturbances on the Brackenhall estate in Huddersfield, the Brookhouse estate in Blackburn, the Stoops and Harner Clough estates in Burnley, the Wood End estate in Coventry, and Hartcliffe and Southmead estates in Bristol, with other disorders also reported in parts of Newcastle, Manchester, Birmingham, Oxford, Stockton, Luton and Salford.

If all these have placed the idea of the inner city – and more recently the outer estates – within the public domain, they have also unleashed a flood of statements and rhetoric from senior politicians and others in some way concerned with the politics of marginalized urban spaces and communities. The following discussion identifies and outlines the contending ways in which the problems of urban marginality have been variously understood within political discourse; these will then inform the the remainder of the study and its examination of TV's representation of these issues.

The problems of the inner city are not new. In his classic study of the conditions endured by the English working class in the 1840s, for example, Engels describes areas of urban squalor which are not unlike many contemporary accounts of the inner and outer city.

Every great city has one or more slums, where the working class is crowded together. True, poverty often dwells in hidden alleys close to the palaces of the rich; but, in general a separate territory has been assigned to it, where removed from the sight of the happier classes, it may struggle as it can. These slums are pretty equally arranged in all the great towns of England, the worst houses in the worst quarters of the towns . . . (Engels 1987 [1845]: 70)

He also lists a number of features characterizing such slums. These too sound strangely familiar: inadequate and overcrowded housing, endemic poor health and high mortality rates, environmental squalor, unsanitary conditions, dangerous working conditions, a noted prevalence of crime, promiscuity and alcohol and narcotics abuse, as well as a concentration of (Irish) immigrants (see Harrison 1985; Seabrook 1988: 26–71). Whereas Engels could point, however, to such conditions as the basis for envisaged 'social war', others, perhaps fearful of the swelling residuum threatening to overspill into respectable Victorian society, could equally point to the necessity for liberal social reform, while yet others sought to contain such a threat and blamed the profligacy and inadequacy of those directly affected (see Steadman-Jones 1971). In other words, the interpretation and understanding of such phenomena appear to depend, in considerable measure, upon frameworks of political judgement and values which are not simply 'read off' from those conditions identified but rather selectively inform and emphasize certain conditions, certain issues and not others in accordance with the political viewpoint brought to bear upon the inner city scene.

Such appears to have altered little in the intervening one and a half centuries. What has perhaps altered, courtesy of the mass media and television, is that whereas the inner city in the middle of the nineteenth century was, for the most part, removed from the sight of those 'happier classes', in the latter part of the twentieth it has been subjected to wider public gaze. Indeed, the way in which the inner city has occasionally found wider public resonance has led some commentators to suggest that it can best be approached as a 'myth' or ideological representation acting as a symbol of wider social worries, and put to work in the service of wider political and ideological projects (Burgess 1985; MacGregor 1991). Mrs Thatcher's celebrated comment of 'we have a big job to do in some of those inner cities' following her third general election victory in 1987 and subsequent policy initiatives, lends support to the view that the inner city has indeed been subject to processes of political appropriation and 'representation'. A recent study makes the point well:

> The 'inner city' is a representation which serves as a focus for politics and policy. It is a public issue which represents a constellation of social worries, to do with urban poverty, squalor, ill-health, deprivation, decay, crime, social disintegration, and social polarisation. The core issue is that of urban poverty. (MacGregor 1991: 64–5)

A persuasive case can undoubtedly be made that the inner city has, in recent years, served to focus issues of politics and policy, though the issues variously placed at the heart of the inner city cannot thereby be assumed to have found equal public representation. It would be a mistake however to thereby construe the long-standing problems associated with such symbolic locations as also a matter of representation and nothing more. The problems of urban marginality, though not confined to and certainly not accountable by their spatial concentration in certain localities, none the less do find noticeable presence within 'separate territories' which, for the most part, are 'removed from the sight of the happier classes'. An impressive array of studies have now documented how processes of social exclusion and urban marginality have found spatial form across a number of diverse concerns and issues. Government inner city policy has for some time addressed issues of spatially concentrated poverty and disadvantage and, with the help of census findings using a number of indicators of urban deprivation, identified many inner city localities as the most deprived areas in the country (Dept of the Environment 1977a, 1977b, 1977c, 1977d, 1981; Begg and Eversley 1986). Demographic and other indicators of concentrated urban decline and change have been the subject of academic interest (Hall 1981; Hausner and Robson 1985; Hausner 1986; Spencer et al 1986; Robson 1988) with the Archbishop of Canterbury's report identifying both outer estates and inner city areas as Urban Priority Areas in need of urgent policy attention (Archbishop of Canterbury 1985).

Sociological studies of the growth of urban inequality have also observed spatial processes of social polarization and patterns of demographic change over a considerable period of time (Elliott 1984), and observed the intricate connections between economy, government policy, unemployment and under-employment, poverty and urban deprivation impacting on living standards and health (Townsend 1991), education (Mallen 1991), and housing (Raynsford

1991). The politics of central government inner city programmes, of which there have been many in recent years, and their deficiencies have also been subject to critical study and review (Sills, Taylor and Golding 1988; MacGregor 1991)

Moreover, parts of the inner city have been identified as areas in which many of Britain's immigrants and ethnic minorities have established communities. John Rex's long-standing concern with Britain's ethnic minorities has documented how certain areas, dubbed 'the inner city's inner city', are characterized by both poor housing and a high density of ethnic minorities (Rex 1984: 192), requiring sociological explanation (Rex and Moore 1967; Ratcliffe 1979; Rex and Tomlinson 1979). Others have also directed their attention to spatial processes of ethnic segregation and residence (Smith 1989; Skellington and Morris 1992: 44–9) and the endless pressures confronted by Britain's black community in such localities (Pryce 1979). Furthermore, in relation to issues of inner city policing and crime, a number of studies have observed long-standing tensions and hostility evident between the police and black youth particularly (John 1972; Brown 1982) with more recent research identifying failures of policing strategy within many inner city areas (Small 1983; Smith 1983; Smith and Grey 1983; Lea and Young 1984; Benyon 1986; Chatterton 1987; Scraton 1987; Cashmore and McLaughlin 1991). Evidence of police harassment and brutality perpetrated against black people, including the targeting of certain inner city localities for special operations, has also been compiled (Institute of Race Relations 1979, 1987). Finally, accounts of inner city life and personal experiences also document something of the human consequences and hopelessness often felt by inner city residents (Harrison 1985; Seabrook 1988: 26–71).

If the inner city, then, has served ideological purposes, the problems and issues referenced by such localities have been found to be, and experienced by many as, all too real. Processes of social polarization and marginalization have informed the urban landscape, with sections of Britain's population consigned to live in some of the most dilapidated, poorly resourced, unhealthy and, often, architecturally inhospitable, places found on the urban map. Those processed by economic insecurity, the administration of welfare, or simply the inheritance of class-based residential occupancy are likely to find themselves segregated, shunted and decanted into 'separate territories' positioned on the margins of society. This has happened to vast sections of Britain's urban poor, including the vulnerable and the deprived, the long-term unemployed and the unemployable, the racially discriminated and victimized, and all those other groups of economically insecure and socially excluded individuals and families who collectively make up Britain's growing underclass, who now find themselves spatially removed from 'the happier classes'.

Wider frameworks of explanation have pointed to the backdrop of deindustrialization and the reorganization of capitalism, shifting the boundaries between, as well as the social composition and relative density of, core workers, part-time workers and non-workers (Lash and Urry 1987; Hall and Jacques 1989). Regional variations in terms of economic decline, restructuring and regeneration point to the wider geography of urban change, while government policy has been seen to exacerbate processes of economic restructuring and social polarization. Conservative Government policies have pursued 'free market' policies and privatization with an ideological fervour unrivalled in the post-war period, reordering public priorities and the administration of welfare with particular impact on the economically vulnerable members of society.

If such forces have effectively imposed conditions of urban marginality upon many of Britain's poor and economically dispossessed, they have also engendered conditions and pressures which are experienced, confronted, endured, negotiated and lived by countless individuals, families and social groups on a daily basis. How such conditions are individually and collectively made sense of, and how such conditions are responded to by those living within their grip is also very much at the centre of processes of urban marginalization.

[M]appings of the arrangements of social differentiated populations in residential locales are important in describing the nature of life in urban industrial cities and have significance because the spatially ordered experience of differentiated reproduction is an important source of social action. (Byrne 1989: 99)

While it would be wrong to over-estimate the extent to which the fragmented nature and differentiated individual experiences of urban marginality can sustain collective forms of solidarity and action, when concentrated in certain urban places, such conditions can contribute to a local climate of despair, group identification and even collective reaction. Such have already been demonstrated, of course, in the most drastic and dramatic of ways. The 'spatially ordered experience of differentiated reproduction' appears to have contributed to recent urban conflicts now experienced in parts of most major urban settings up and down the country, and looks set to continue to do so, so long as some sections of Britain's population find themselves effectively denied full social membership and access to those rights, rewards and opportunities visibly enjoyed by the rest of society.

It is with reference to many of these conditions and issues that the events of recent urban unrest have been variously interpreted. The discussion that follows briefly reviews these, identifying the interpretative frameworks and key concerns informing their respective accounts of urban disorder. Three principal discourses or contending perspectives can be identified. With reference to one of the most serious outbreaks of recent inner city disorder, the Handsworth/Lozells riots in Birmingham in 1985, three responses to these disorders are consulted – two official, one unofficial – and each is found to be informed, to a remarkable degree, by each of the three discourses on social disorder. As may be expected, both the interpretation of the causes of this major urban conflict, as well as the understanding of the inner city and its associated problems, vary considerably across these. To quote Edelman (1988: 3) again: 'There is no politics respecting matters that evoke a consensus about the pertinent facts, their meanings, and the rational course of action.' As will become plain, the inner city has certainly generated a plethora of pertinent facts, meanings and suggested courses of rational action; each being countered by a different set of pertinent facts, meanings and, from within opposing viewpoints, courses of 'rational' action.

Perspectives on social disorder: three different realities

Social scientists, theorists and psychologists have generated a number of theories seeking to account for outbreaks of social disorder within liberal democratic societies, these now constitute a fairly extensive literature and have usefully been reviewed elsewhere (Taylor 1984; Rule 1988). A number of more widely available political perspectives often inform such academic accounts, tending to mould public discussion of, and political response to, forms of social disorder including those of the inner and outer cities. These perspectives have been typically found to assume a conservative, liberal and radical form (Taylor 1984; Benyon 1987). They have also been found to be more socially extensive than organized bases of party political opinion, though often advanced, with the exception of the radical discourse, from within party political positions. They appear, in other words, to be socially available and pre-exist recent urban disorders. In broad terms they also appear to inform responses to other forms of social disorder and perceived threats to the social consensus, whether in relation to the poll tax riots, the prison riots of 1991, disorders associated with various other mass demonstrations and protests, and instances of major industrial conflict, as well as forms of subcultural behaviour including football hooliganism, acid house parties and 'raves' and the so-called New Age travellers. Not confined to interpretations of inner city disorders, such organizing frameworks for political interpretation and action will, no doubt, continue to be heard in the public and mass mediated contests over diverse social and political issues in the future. Here they are considered as organizing frameworks for the public discussion of recent disorders associated with certain urban localities and their causation.

The conservative discourse

The conservative discourse on social disorder is disposed to interpret recent events as illegitimate acts of criminality motivated either by criminal greed, hooligan excitement or political extremism. Those directly involved are regarded as a deviant and criminal minority who, deliberately placing themselves outside of the legal and moral frameworks of society, can only expect and deserve the punitive actions of established authorities. The conservative viewpoint tends to transfix on the criminality and the violence of the event itself, and it is here that the explanation for such disorder is found. That is, in the individual actions and personal culpability of those directly involved.

Typically, an outbreak of urban disorder will be defined and interpreted as a criminal 'riot'. In explaining such lawlessness the conservative discourse relies upon two main categories of explanation: organized or spontaneous criminality, underpinned by the pursuit of profit or hooligan excitement; and the actions of political extremists orchestrating mob violence for their own ends. In such terms the actions of the mob tend to be regarded as essentially irrational, and driven by deep forces whether the conspiratorial intent of organized criminals or political extremists, or the irrational forces of instincts pursuing libidinal gratification.

The nature of the mob, collectively more than the sum of its individual parts, and acting according to blind instinct rather than rational purpose, takes advantage of the temporary collapse of moral and legal constraints and pursues an orgy of gratification, a gratification moreover which is thought to be geographically and socially contagious. Gustave Le Bon expressed such conservative fears some time ago:

By the mere fact that he forms part of the crowd, a man descends several rungs in the ladder of civilisation. Isolated he may be a cultivated individual; in a crowd, he is a barbarian – that is a creature acting by instinct. (Le Bon 1960 [1895]: 32)

Outbreaks of lawlessness and wanton destruction are regarded as a breakdown in the respect for the rule of law, and social authority more generally. This includes the role of parents and the perceived demise of the family structure; the church and the decline of moral teachings; schools and the failure to inculcate responsible behaviour; and those more directly involved in the front line of maintaining and prosecuting the rule of law. Moral degeneration is the flipside to the law and order coin; the perceived 'permissive society', though objectionable to basic conservative canons in its own terms, continues to complement discussions of the 'violent society' which, if left unchecked, threatens to undermine the sanctity and stability of family, home, church and state.

Threats to the established order do not only come from within however, but may also be seen as a foreign intervention from without. Immigrants and ethnic minorities can be regarded as undermining the traditional 'British way of life', including its customs and supposed cultural homogeneity sustained across generations within the territorial confines of the nation. Questions of race, cultural difference and Otherness thus often inform the conservative perspective where 'outsiders' may, in contradictory fashion, simultaneously be regarded as inferior to British stock, traditions and culture and yet able to assume the position of a devious and Machiavellian elite, intelligently exploiting British tolerance and undermining its traditional way of life. If such Others are found to be involved in criminal activity, they are likely to be seen as doubly deviant, in terms of both race and criminal behaviour, and are therefore likely to call forth the most strident calls for punitive measures to be taken.

In summary this perspective identifies urban disorder as essentially a criminal event, perpetrated by a deviant/criminal minority who are responsible for their actions, and who must face a firm law and order response. The apparent simplicity of this interpretation, with its fixation upon the criminal event itself, should not be underestimated however. As an available perspective it can readily be deployed and effectively make sense of – that is, define, interpret, explain and prescribe – in relation to diverse situations of social conflict and disorder. In this respect it is interesting to refer to two key passages in the Chief Constable's Report into the Handsworth/Lozells disorders in Birmingham in 1985.

There is firm evidence to suggest that the disorders were at the outset orchestrated by local drug dealers who had become fearful for the demise of their livelihoods. Similarly, there is evidence that the riots were fuelled and organised by persons who require the supply of drugs to continue their normal life style. (Dear 1985: 53)

I believe that for too long society as a whole, not only the West Midlands, has been persuaded to excuse patent criminal behaviour by groups that have wilfully set themselves apart from the consensus values of society. Of course there are the deprived in society, and I would never seek to minimise the problems of being young, black and unemployed in a decaying inner city environment . . . But they can never be taken singly or cumulatively as an excuse for criminal behaviour or as a retrospective justification for rioting, looting and murder. No group can legitimately justify its cause or actions by averring that some laws are inappropriate to it. By these assertions the members of such a group will surely set themselves apart from the society in which they live and forego the right to make demands for acceptance on an equal basis. (Dear 1985: 69)

A full reading of the report reveals many of those conservative themes noted above. The extracts also indicate a focus upon the criminality of the event itself, the identification of a group of criminal conspirators and the threat posed by such a minority to a presumed shared consensus of values. Furthermore, this group is apparently distanced by involvement within the criminal action of rioting, use of illicit drugs and also, so it seems, by an implicit and racialized conception of cultural difference – why else should such a group 'forego the right to make demands for acceptance on an equal basis'? On the basis of a detailed account and interpretation of the riot, the Chief Constable's report calls for increased manpower, riot equipment and training and the introduction of baton rounds. The explanation of the Handsworth riots, and the problem of the inner city more generally, according to this account, can be summed up in terms of an undermanned and under-resourced police force seeking to foster harmonious community relations in an inner city area in which organized 'drug barons', the general prevalence of crime and – so it is alleged elsewhere in the report – Afro-Caribbean jealousy towards Asian traders, all thwart the best intentions of the region's constabulary.

The liberal discourse

The liberal discourse, while disposed to regard political structures and processes as generally adequate for the representation and pursuit of different social interests, recognizes that such may not always be adequate to meet the needs of minorities and others, especially when confronted by overwhelming processes of social and economic change. While the event of an inner city disorder will also be interpreted as a criminal activity and call forth condemnation, the liberal perspective is inclined to look behind the event itself and seek out possible contributing factors and conditions. Attention to unemployment and widespread deprivation, or perceived and actual instances of individual police harassment or prejudiced behaviour against black inner city residents could all serve, within the liberal framework, as contributing explanatory conditions.

The liberal perspective, like that of the conservative, is also keen to uphold the rule of law and ensure that the police have adequate resources to police inner city areas. It none the less begins to address those informing conditions which help contextualize and make comprehensible patterns of collective social violence. Social violence may here be interpreted as a 'rational' phenomenon to the extent that it gives expression to surrounding social forces and collective perceptions of marginality, but ultimately is seen as an illegitimate and ineffective means for securing social reform, even if desirable. Violence will always be condemned in such a perspective, though the pursuit of social justice by other means will be upheld.

In the immediate aftermath of the Handsworth/Lozells disturbances of 1985, and the Home Office's decision to refuse a public inquiry, an Independent Inquiry Report was commissioned by Birmingham City Council led by Julius Silverman (Silverman 1986). In the light of the above this report proves instructive reading. Contradicting the police report the Silverman Report maintains 'while there was organisation, this was extemporary, and was part of the spontaneous riot' and also refutes the police suggestion that intra-ethnic tensions fuelled the disorders: 'The fact that Asian shops were attacked is simply because the shops were there, and the great majority of shops in this area, in Lozells Road and other parts of Handsworth, are mostly Asian owned shops' (Silverman 1986: 79).

Not placing any store upon a conspiratorial explanation the report seeks to contextualize the disorders with reference to the biting effects of the recession upon the West Midlands manufacturing base, and the disadvantaged community living in and around Handsworth particularly. Moreover the role of the local authority and its failure to generate more inner city jobs through contract compliance is also noted, as is the increasingly constrained provision of local authority services due to the impositions of central government. Accepting that cases of individual police harassment have undoubtedly occurred, Silverman concludes that for the police to maintain that the riots appeared 'like a bolt out of the blue' they must have considerably underestimated the degree of hostility felt by Afro-Caribbean youth, stating: 'I have no doubt that the main object of hatred by these 1985 rioters was the police' (1986: 75). However, it is perhaps the effects of widespread unemployment which appear to assume the principal focus of concern in Silverman's interpretation of inner city malaise:

Unemployment in Handsworth/Lozells is one of the worst in the whole country . . . The social consequences of mass unemployment are well known. It impoverishes the family. It is the greatest source of deprivation. The unemployed person feels rejected, with a loss of self-respect and consequent feeling of humiliation. (Silverman 1986: 93)

The issue of discrimination is also raised, albeit in hesitant fashion when the author states 'racial discrimination and the feeling of being discriminated against is an important part of the social and psychological background of Handsworth' and is 'an essential element in the cause of the riots' (1986: 48). On the basis of these identified conditions, Silverman recommends, in addition to the lifting of restrictions on local authorities by central government, that increased inner city programmes, resources and funds should be made available, stimulating local employment opportunities and leisure facilities. The police should also review their training programme and receive increased riot equipment and vehicles, though the introduction of baton rounds is seriously questioned. It is also considered to be 'necessary to promote greater consultation with, and participation by, local people at the neighbourhood level' (1986: 103).

In summary, this inquiry report demonstrates a remarkable affinity with the liberal discourse above. A series of informing conditions are noted as the backdrop to the disturbances, while a sense of social injustice and exclusion, both perceived and real, are placed at the heart of the account and seen as fuelled by economic and social distress, notably unemployment but also compounded by racial disadvantage and discrimination. This last factor however, as subsequently amplified by two dissenting voices involved in the inquiry, was felt to have been considerably underestimated (Patton and Shaw 1986). The Report is also remarkably similar to the Scarman Report into the Brixton disorders of 1981, raising similar arguments and positioning its interpretation, for the most part, within a liberal framework of explanation and prescription (see Scarman 1986).

The radical discourse

The radical discourse is disposed to regard the occurrence of a 'riot' as more or less inevitable, historically necessary and politically meaningful. Pointing to historical precedents where violent actions have been harbingers of social change, collective social violence can be regarded as a necessary means to a political end. The political ends in such a schema may be far reaching, calling for radical changes including societal reorganization and even revolution. Contrary to the conservative discourse transfixed on the criminality of the event itself, and the liberal discourse content to invoke a degree of contextualization and prior conditions, the radical discourse embraces the need for fundamental change within a much expanded historical perspective. Regarding the liberal's pursuit of informing conditions as, analytically, not going far enough, the radical discourse is inclined to question the very foundations of liberal democracy in which forms of social inequality and discriminatory practice appear to be entrenched. These are not regarded as temporary aberrations in need of reform, but as the outcome of a profoundly inegalitarian social order requiring radical overhaul.

The report *A Different Reality*, sponsored by the West Midland's County Council on recommendation of its Race Relations and Equal Opportunities Committee, sought to provide an interpretation of the Handsworth rebellion by providing an account of black people's experiences and grievances prior to and following the Handsworth disorders (Ouseley et al. 1986). Racism is not seen, however, as an added ingredient to a volatile mix of forms of deprivation and disadvantage, but as inhering within diverse institutional sites and racialized social practices. Not confined to individual 'prejudice' (Dear 1985: 69), or 'perceived' and 'felt' discrimination (Silverman 1986: 48), racism is viewed as deeply embedded within British society and is daily confronted by black people.

No matter what the Government may state or the media write about Black people as part of their rejection of racism's existence, nothing can remove the indelible stain of British injustice being meted out to Black people; no lies or distortion can alter the way Black people experience the harsh realities of life for them in Britain's inner city areas. It is an experience of relative poverty, institutionalised discrimination, denied opportunity, denigrated pride, devalued culture and state harassment. It is an experience that is real and cannot be denied or wished away. (Ouseley et al. 1986: 9)

The report methodically sets out to highlight patterns of oppression and disadvantage, the imposition of a law and order response to black resistance, to challenge the myth of large sums of money going into inner city areas, and examines the reasons why black people lose out in local authority programmes and other schemes designed to improve opportunities and facilities in inner city areas. It also details the manner in which local housing, health, education and social services have all tended to further disadvantage black people. Concerning police–community relations the report maintains 'the police are viewed by a substantial proportion of Handsworth residents as an ill-disciplined and brutal force which has manipulated and abused its powers in dealing with the black community over a long period of time' (1986: 63). As well as focusing upon the negative and oppressive nature of the black inner city experience, the report also seeks to outline the positive role and vibrancy of self-help and community projects developed, controlled and run at a grass-roots level.

In summary, the report calls for a 'real community involvement for the usually excluded groups of people in the inner cities' which will enable 'poor white people and Black people' to 'determine for themselves their own destiny' (1986: 89). The focus on black youth as the principal actors in the Handsworth disorders, noted in the reports above, is challenged to the extent that it ignores or distances the active presence of black women and wider community support. Though the exact nature of the relationship between the state, economy and political process in regard to pervasive 'institutionalised racism' remains unclear the report tends to indicate in terms of the radical discourse outlined above, that existing structures and author-ities of power will have to be engaged, hence its forceful conclusion: 'violent resistance is now permanently on the agenda while the oppression and denial of rights and resources continue' (1986: 77). Though sharing a concern with forms of social injustice and gross inequality, the analysis tends to see these as considerably more embedded than the liberal viewpoint, and argues stridently for resistance and struggle. The themes and tenor of the radical discourse are plain to see.

The discussion thus far has indicated that the three reports into the Handsworth disturbances of 1985 have followed, in considerable measure, the major and contending organizing political perspectives on social disorder. Each has identified a range of concerns and issues, which are placed at the centre of inner city conflict, simultaneously taking issue with those competing 'realities' offered within alternative political perspectives and accounts. As such, they have usefully served to identify a wide array of issues and concerns variously informing competing perspectives on the inner city, and problems of urban marginality more generally. Whether the problems of the inner city are addressed, essentially, as a problem of spatially located crime, criminality and deviance requiring a law and order response; or a problem of concentrated urban deprivation and social malaise in need of massive governmental intervention and enhanced local democratic participation; or whether understood as a problem of systemic social injustice, institutionalized racism and/or political marginalization requiring grass-roots struggle and concerted political action, the informing political frameworks of interpretation and prescribed response underpinning each are clear to see. In short, this example of urban unrest has been characterized by a political contest over definition and meaning. To what extent, in what form and for what reasons each of these contending discourses has found representation within TV's portrayal of the problems and issues of the inner city, forms the basis of the inquiry pursued throughout the study.

Outline of the study

On the basis of the discussion above, this study focuses on the way in which part of the TV system has represented problems of urban distress. It concentrates on the regionalized part of the ITV system and the manner in which regional factual programme forms have mediated to a wider public those marginalized conditions of local and regional hardship. Regional television programming, so far at least, has failed to attract serious critical inquiry, despite its long-standing contribution to the mediation of major public issues and concerns across news and other forms of factual programming. Moreover, to the extent to which public issues and concerns may find heightened relevance and audience interest when focused in relation to the geographical proximities of the region, in contrast to the more removed or generalized appeals of national networked programmes, so regional programmes may exercise a particular interest for regional viewers. The importance of this area of programming is not confined to questions of geography however.

The ITV system as a whole continues to proclaim its regionalized basis, producing and broadcasting a proportion of its programmes specifically for its fifteen separate regions, while separate ITV companies seek instant recognition on the basis of a regional identity and corporate regional commitment, a commitment daily rehearsed most visibly perhaps through regional news programmes. If the regional news programme serves as a flagship for corporate identity and commitment to regionalized programming, it also represents a long-established, distinctive and popular form of TV news programme which, from a prominent position in the prime-time schedules, broadcasts daily to a mass audience. How this popular form of TV news does in fact mediate pressing regional social concerns will be examined in considerable detail. Not only does this provide an opportunity to investigate an area of TV news that so far has failed to attract the consideration it deserves, it also permits a rare opportunity to explore the manner in which a TV news form is routinely produced, fashioned and inscribed with popular appeal. This raises issues of wider theoretical interest in relation to existing studies of TV news production, and questions of media theory more generally.

Though critical attention is focused for the most part on this as yet largely ignored area of TV news broadcasting, other regional factual programmes and their contribution to the representation of regional social ills are also considered. The contention, often advanced by professional programme makers and others, that current affairs and documentary programmes offer a complementary area of programme provision to the necessarily more compressed and cursory treatment of news is put to the test. The study provides, then, for the first time a detailed and inside look at part of the regional television system, focusing particularly upon the production and presentation of regional news but also addressing, comparatively, other areas of programming and their wider determinants.

For the purposes of this study, a case study approach was adopted. A leading independent television company, broadcasting to a region in which many of the most deprived and conflict-prone urban localities can be found, is subjected to detailed examination. In this way, it is possible to observe at close quarters the daily practices, professional routines and organization of programme making as they impact on the production and consequent portrayal of the problems of urban marginality. The wider and changing context of commercial television is also considered however. This is brought into focus to the extent to which increased commercial pressures, technological developments and changing frameworks of statutory regulation have been found to impact on corporate operations, the organization of programme production and 'programme visualizations' pursued by TV professionals. The case study approach also permits a comprehensive and systematic review of some of the main regional programmes and their voluminous output, amongst which can be found representations of the inner city.

Based at the Birmingham studios of Central Independent Television plc for a period of eighteen months, the study draws on over forty interviews with newsroom journalists and reporters, and a further twenty-five interviews with current affairs and documentary programme makers and senior corporate decision makers. During this period newsroom routines, professional journalist practices and the daily production of the regional news programme was observed at close quarters. News, current affairs and documentary programming relating to the inner city and broadcast over an eight year period was also systematically examined, with many selected programmes and news items subjected to in-depth analysis.

The organization of the study is presented in three parts. Part I concentrates on the production of television news with particular reference to how, and in what manner, problems of urban marginality have been subject to processes of professional mediation, and structured in terms of established programme forms and ambitions. Chapter 2 discusses further the regional basis of ITV and provides evidence for the popularity of regional programming and the regional news programme in particular. It then begins to situate the specificity of the regional news programme as an established popular TV news form. Here its characteristic subject interests and popular ambitions are examined with particular reference to the professionals involved, their routine practices and informing programme visualization or shared understanding of the conventions and appeals of this distinctive news sub-genre.

Chapter 3 begins to detail, on the basis of newsroom observations and professional statements of intent, how the regional news programme has in fact reported and mediated problems of concentrated urban distress. Here the discussion attends, in turn, to each of those major concerns already found to order contending viewpoints on the inner city problem whether crime and law and disorder, social deprivation and disadvantage, or questions of race and minority ethnic discrimination.

Chapter 4, also based on newsroom observations and a number of case studies, then details how newsroom processes and professional practices have impacted on the accessing of inner city voices and viewpoints. It also pursues the way in which presentational news formats have either constrained or facilitated the public display and engagement of contending inner city views, and the professional and practical considerations informing their use.

Part II is concerned with the overall patterns and forms of broadcast inner city portrayal, complementing the findings and discussions of Part I. Chapter 5 details how exactly the regional news programme has portrayed the problems of the inner city over an eight year period. The analysis examines, with the help of numerous examples of news inner city portrayal, how the problems of the inner city have variously been mediated according to existing programme priorities and preferred news treatments. This includes attending to how each of the three contending perspectives of the inner city and their respective concerns have found differing prominence and forms of news representation. The discussion also examines the systematic patterns characterizing both the use of differing news formats and accessed voices found in relation to inner city news portrayal.

Chapter 6 then examines in some detail, and with the help of a complementary set of narrative, verbal and visual analyses, exactly how the Handsworth/Lozells disorders of 1985 were mediated by the regional news programme across a full twelve month period of news and follow-up news reports. Once again, questions are raised and answered in relation to the interpretative resources publicly made available across this extensive period of reporting, and the manner in which these can be considered to be either supportive or sustaining of each of the three principal ways of interpreting and responding to outbreaks of urban disorder.

Part III of the study widens the field of vision, both substantively and theoretically. Chapter 7 attends to regional current affairs and documentary programming and the manner in which these may be seen as complementing news representations. Once again, questions of programme mediation are raised and evidence produced for the manner in which different professional programme visualizations impact, often with decisive result, on the portrayal of inner city issues. In recent times, however, these programmes have themselves been forced to adapt in the face of wider pressures for change. Such changes are documented in relation to current affairs and document-ary programmes and the changing corporate context informing both in-house and independent programme producers. How these ever widening circles of constraints and influence – commercial, techno-logical, statutory – reach down, via corporate restructuring and the organization of programme production, to affect the professional pursuit of adapted programme visualizations and, ultimately, the treatment of regional social issues is considered.

Chapter 8, finally, provides a brief conclusion. Here some of the principal findings are reiterated and implications for the study of news and general media theory underlined. These more general observations return the particular empirical findings of the case study to wider questions and debates of media theory.

Part I

TV news production

2
Regional TV news: professionals producing populism

Regional TV programming has been identified as being of possible interest in the representation of local and regional problems of urban distress. If national TV news cameras have been found to provide, at best, a fleeting and fragmentary response to such concerns, typically attracted to the latest outbreak of violent disorder before moving on to the next national and international story, the regional television system holds out the promise of more in-depth and extensive coverage of inner city conditions and concerns, sustained perhaps over a longer period of time. Charged with a statutory responsibility to provide news and other forms of programming produced in, for and about the region, regional television is an area of broadcasting deserving of serious attention. If this is so in relation to the particular interest of this study, the fact that this area of broadcasting has, for the most part, gone without serious study in the TV literature is in need of immediate remedy. This applies to all the regional programmes, whether news, current affairs and documentaries or entertainment and other programme forms.

The regional news programme, the centrepiece of regional television, is long overdue for considered attention. This established and popular TV news programme occupies a prominent position in the prime-time schedules and continues to command audiences that match or exceed audiences watching early evening national news broadcasts. On grounds of audience size alone, then, this form of TV news cannot be considered of marginal interest to students of the news media. Moreover, to the extent that it exhibits a characteristic programme appeal organized through established programme news interests, conventionalized story treatments and projected relationship to its audience, it can also tell us much about the way in which popular forms of TV news journalism mediate issues of public concern. This is a necessary corrective to those studies which continue to address questions of TV news as if all TV news forms simply replicate BBC1 and ITN national evening news broadcasts – programmes long noted for their projected stance of detached, formal and authoritative reporting.

In a period of proliferating TV news provision these 'exemplars' can no longer be assumed to be representative of TV news in general. The advent of breakfast news provision over a decade ago, and TV-am in particular with its pronounced populist appeal, as well as the distinctive, if more analytic programme stances of BBC2's *Newsnight* and Channel Four's *Channel 4 News*, all point to the increasingly varied nature of TV news provision. In addition, processes of change well underway are set to impact on TV news both at international and at local levels. The arrival of satellite and cable news services, including Sky Television (1989) communicating news from Europe and beyond, and the development of new technologies including multipoint video distribution services (MVDS), capable of broadcasting to local communities, indicate that future changes are likely to continue to reorder the TV news landscape. Within this terrain the regional news programme has long been an established fixture, providing a distinctive form of popular news programming. As such it can throw considerable light on the forms and appeals of popular TV journalism and help map the rapidly changing field of TV news – a field increasingly characterized as much by popular as by serious forms and styles of news broadcasting.

Before embarking on a detailed case study of regional news and other forms of factual regional programming, it is first useful to outline something of the regulatory frameworks and structures informing regional television provision, as well as its evident popularity.

Regionalism and popular TV

In a period marked by technological advance, political deregulation and increased competitive and commercial pressures, broadcasting is currently undergoing a process of radical reorganization and change. This is evident in changing programme schedules, the expansion of terrestrial channels, proliferating satellite communications and the recent changes in the regulatory frameworks structuring the operations of the broadcasting systems. The ITV system has been regulated since 1972 by the Independent Broadcasting Authority (IBA) and, following radical restructuring in the wake of the Government's White Paper *Broadcasting in the '90s: Competition, Choice and Quality* and subsequent Broadcasting Act of 1990, was replaced in January 1991 by the Independent Television Commission (ITC). As a regulatory body the ITC, unlike the IBA, has lost the power to preview programmes and approve programme schedules in advance. It continues to police programme provision however, and has a range of sanctions, from a warning letter and fines to revocation of the licence, in the event of a company failing to honour its licence pledges and (remaining) statutory obligations.

The commitment to the regional basis of ITV (Channel 3) continues however, with both the White Paper and the Act laying down an express duty on ITV contractors to provide 'quality regional programming, and regional news produced within the area for which it is produced' (Broadcasting Act 1990: 16(d)). Such requirements are in addition to the long-standing obligation placed on broadcasters to report with due impartiality and accuracy, and to demonstrate sensitivity in relation to matters of public taste and decency. The commitment to regionalism and regional programming was also incorporated into the ITC's guidelines given to all prospective licence holders which stated that the ITC 'considers that the provision of a strong regional service is an essential part of the licensee's responsibilities' and 'an applicant will be expected to demonstrate a thorough knowledge of the region he intends to serve and, through his programme proposals and related activities, a strong commitment to meeting the needs and interests of people living there' (ITC 1990a: 26). The amount of regional programming required by the ITC varies for each of the fifteen licensees, with the minimum weekly requirement placed on Central Television across its three sub-regions in 1990 totalling 18 hours and 49 minutes, while Border Television was required to produce only 5 hours 33 minutes (ITC 1991:30).

If the commitment to regional programming none the less persists, the content and schedule placing of that programming is no longer subject to regulatory control, with the dictates of commercialism and the pursuit of advertising revenue increasingly influencing both. To what extent such factors have already been found to impact upon non-news forms of programming and their forms of inner city portrayal will be examined in detail later. Here it can be noted that regional news continues to be the flagship of the regional TV system and individual corporate identity, and looks relatively secure for the foreseeable future. Its prominent position is clear when looking at the overall proportions of different types of regional programming broadcast across the various regions. A review in 1988 found, for example, that a total of 6,374 hours of regional programming was broadcast within the fifteen ITV franchise regions, over half of which was accounted for by regional news programmes (3,845). The remaining forms of regional programming comprised the following total hours: documentaries (916), sport (405), entertainment (334), current affairs (302), religion (213), arts (138), farming (113), information (77), education (31) (Johnson 1989: 13). Compared to programming networked throughout the ITV system, regional programming plays, in proportional terms, a relatively minor part. This should not be allowed to overshadow, however, its continuing popularity and, in the case of regional news, prominent schedule placing.

Eighteen regional news programmes are produced by the fifteen regional licensees which currently comprise, with ITN and GMTV (the new contractor for ITV breakfast-time programming), the ITV (Channel 3) system. The additional news programmes are accounted for by Central Television which produces three news programmes for each of its sub-regions, and Meridian Broadcasting (replacing TVS) and Yorkshire each producing two programmes for their sub-regions. Broadcast at the beginning of prime-time (6 pm or 6.30 pm), the regional news programme occupies a strategic position in the schedule which is designed to attract and build audiences, and in turn advertising revenue, as well as programme commitment and channel loyalty. The so-called 'inheritance' factor, though in danger of being over-emphasized, is also a consideration well known to schedule planners, who note how some members of the early evening audience will stay with that channel first selected. This competitive fight for the all-important early evening audience has led ITV companies and the BBC to reschedule programmes and deploy their main offensive weaponry of prime-time soaps, whether *Eastenders* and *Eldorado* or *Neighbours*, in the fight to either secure or win back prime-time audiences. Regional news programmes, though not unaffected by the pull of soaps, have none the less generally maintained significant audience viewing figures over recent years and look set to continue to do so (Hetherington 1989: 249–57). Audiences for regional news, though subject to seasonal and daily variation, comprise in absolute terms considerable numbers of people. To take just one example, across its three sub-regions Central Television News regularly attracts an audience of over a million and a half viewers.

Recent research also indicates that professed audience interest in regional news is strong. Over two-thirds of a representative sample of people throughout the UK claimed to watch an early evening regional news programme (69 per cent) and later evening regional news headlines three evenings a week or more (64 per cent). Almost half (48 per cent) claimed to watch early evening regional news programmes every night, with relatively few claiming to never watch regional news (13 per cent)(ITC 1990b: 11). Furthermore, nearly two-thirds of people (61 per cent) claim that they get most of their news concerned with neighbouring counties and districts from regional television news (1990b: 9). This interest in regional TV news finds further endorsement across gender, age groups(16–34, 35–54, 55+) and social class (ABC1, C2, DE) with regional news stated as the most popular form of regional programming by over 90 per cent of all categories (ITC 1990b: 14). If regional news is watched regularly by large audiences, ITV regional news appears consistently to win a larger share of the regular regional news audience (56 per cent) when compared to viewers of BBC regional news programmes (41 per cent) (ITC, 1990b: 11).

Such findings suggest that not only is regional news regularly watched by large audiences, it is also regarded as an important source of regional information and, by the vast majority of people, as the most popular form of regional programming. Clearly, regional news is of considerable interest to many people and routinely secures large audiences. Its flagship role in promoting a sense of corporate and regional identity, and channel loyalty has also not been lost on the various companies that comprise the ITV system. These basic findings point to the established presence of regional news and its continuing popularity with audiences; they also point to the necessity for further inquiry into the nature and organization of the programme's popular appeal. To the extent that regional television may bring home to viewers issues of wider public concern, but with the heightened interest or impact based on a sense of geographical or social proximity, is a further reason why this news form should be taken seriously. With these general observations in place, the study now turns to a detailed case study of regional programming and the portrayal of the problems of urban distress. The study first examines the context of regional news production and its informing conceptualization by professional journalists, before focusing on the production of news concerned with problems of regional distress.

The case study: Central News West

In order to pursue the processes and practices of cultural mediation at close quarters, the study focuses on one of the major 'big five' independent commercial television companies in the country, Central Independent Television plc, and examines in detail its programme production and representation of inner city issues. Situated within the former industrial heartland of Britain, the Central Television region includes many of the most deprived inner and outer city localities in the country, as well as including areas that have erupted into major urban unrest. Central News West particularly, the major sub-region of the regional licence, incorporates Birmingham and the whole of the West Midlands – areas identified to be especially hard hit by recession and including numerous localities identified by central government and local authorities as 'extremely deprived' (see Figure 2.1). How this particular news programme has mediated, both professionally and practically, this extensive urban plight to its general viewers forms the basis of the inquiry.

Based on newsroom observations and interviews with news-workers and senior corporate decision makers, the study details how the regional news programme is conceptualized by the professionals involved, and practically reproduced on a daily basis as a matter of routine. The examination begins by outlining the newsroom organization and resources informing its operation, followed by an overview of the professional roles, daily routines and sources informing the news production process. The second part of the chapter then pursues questions of news culture and the specific character of the

Figure 2.1 Central Television franchise/licence area showing the West and East sub-regions of the Central franchise region prior to 1989 (a third South sub-region was introduced after 1989)

Note: The regions indicated on this map are based on a map kindly provided by BARB

regional news programme, its conceptualization by the professionals involved, its aims and appeals, and populist strategy for viewer engagement.

Newsroom organization and resources

Central News is transmitted simultaneously from the main production centres at Birmingham, Nottingham and most recently Abingdon, serving respectively the west, east and south sub-regions of the regional franchise area. Daily bulletins of approximately five minutes duration are transmitted throughout week days at (during the time of the research) 9.55 am, 11.35 am, 1.20 pm, 3.25pm and 10.30 pm with a major Central News programme of approximately half an hour duration transmitted each weekday evening, with occasional programmes of one hour transmitted on Friday evenings. In addition, weekend bulletins are also transmitted from Birmingham for the whole area over the weekend. Approximately five to six hours of news programming is produced by each of these centres each and every week throughout the year. No other programme even remotely approximates the amount of broadcast programming generated by these news teams; news can be taken as a major corporate and programming commitment. As a news editor remarked 'a major documentary is an hour, runs for a maximum of an hour and half, they're prepared over six months of continuous work; we produce five to six hours each week!'.

Collectively producing this considerable amount of routine output involves about forty technicians (studio crews, sound and vision engineers, tape and film editors, transmission controllers) at each of the main centres, with about twenty at Abingdon; three teams of journalists, involving about twenty-five each at Central West and Central East and twelve at Abingdon; five video camera units at each centre and over fifty freelance correspondents or 'stringers' throughout the region. In addition to the main production centres, news offices manned by reporters are also based in Stoke on Trent, Leicester, Derby and in the House of Commons, while at Swindon and Gloucester studio facilities are available for live contributions to the Central South news programme. Pictorial coverage is also supplemented by eight freelance cameramen in towns across the Central region, while occasionally Central's outside broadcast units can be called upon for the live transmission of major events.

Each centre also involves the services of sports teams and four specialist politics journalists, two of which are based in Birmingham and two at the House of Commons for the politics current affairs programme *Central Lobby* and *Central News*. Occasional features and regular inserts into the main programme produced by freelance production units such as the crime watch insert 'Police Five' also supplement the news production effort. Major regional news items are frequently transmitted by ITN, with one or two major regional news stories finding their way into the national news every week, and occasionally international news via satellite. Microwave radio links and British Telecom lines facilitate the exchange of items and pictorial material with other ITV news stations. With the introduction in January 1988 of a fully computerized news system, 'Newstar', the flow of communication both within and between the main Central production centres has recently undergone considerable change. With each journalist and reporter writing their copy directly into the system, not only is it easily accessed by other news personnel for further editing but it is also automatically timed at average reading pace and delivered to the autocue for final presentation by the news presenter. It is anticipated that individual reporters, each carrying a portable computer terminal, will soon be able to write their copy and access existing copy while on the road. Regional news represents a major corporate commitment, is increasingly dependent on advanced communication technologies and is closely integrated into the wider communications news grid. The resources placed at its disposal, both professional and technological, are clearly considerable.

Professional roles, daily routines

The above has indicated something of the complexity and effort which routinely accompanies the production of Central's regional news programmes. Central News West generally assigns five or six reporters to follow-up daily stories or stories for future broadcast, with each reporter producing one to two stories each day. The reporters are each backed up by a camera crew and the team of journalists in the newsroom – managing editors, editors and sub-editors – who comprise, on average, a further ten to twelve people directly involved in the editing processes. This is not forgetting, of course, the considerable retinue of technicians, secretaries and support staff who also populate the newsroom, as well as incoming stories already prepared and packaged by other Central News centres (on average one or two per week). Central News West, as the largest Central News operation, provides more stories to each of the other sub-regions than it receives.

A structure of command and decision making informs this production both in corporate terms (Figure 2.2) and within the newsroom itself (Figure 2.3). Working to the director of programmes, the controller of factual programmes has overall control of the production of regional news programming and is instrumental in setting the broad contours of programme policy and orientation. At an intermediate corporate managerial level, the managing editor, editorial manager and heads of news each perform various functions including arranging staff contractual matters, the co-ordination and implementation of new technology and projects, and the supervision of independents and responsibility for various general policy areas. In terms of the day to day running of the news programme however, it is the programme editor who is in overall charge of the programme both in terms of the traditionally conceived input aspects of news gathering and production as well as news processing and final output of broadcast material.

The programme editor, therefore, is in overall charge of the programme, implementing and carrying out on a day to day basis the general programme remit outlined by the controller, while also responsible for maintaining statutory requirements on impartiality, balance and good taste and ensuring legal considerations are not

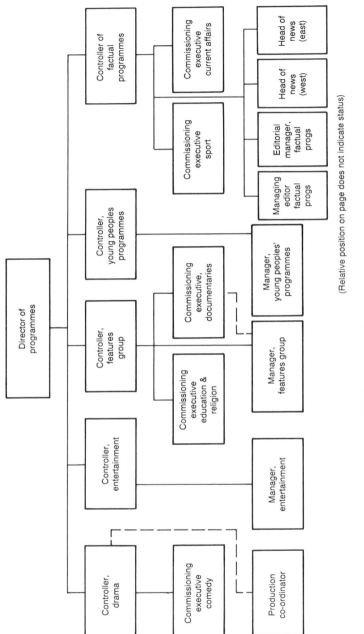

Figure 2.2 Central Television and corporate programme management
Note: This figure is based on findings at the time of research.

(Relative position on page does not indicate status)

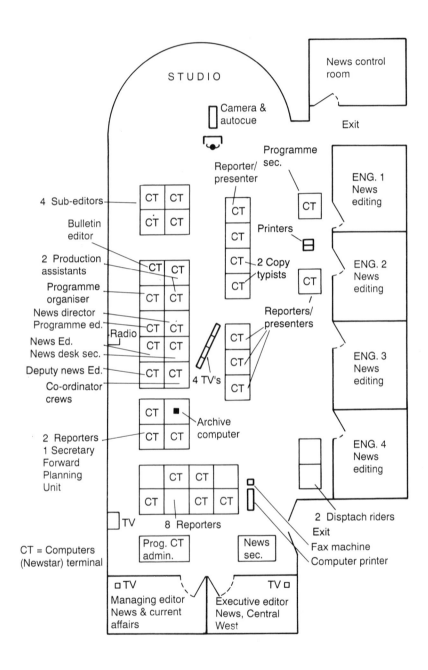

Figure 2.3 Central News West: newsroom layout and personnel

infringed. The news editor works directly to the programme editor, and is mainly involved in news gathering: finding out about the stories that are breaking on the day; assigning and organizing reporters, news crews and dispatch riders; generally checking out stories and ensuring that major stories are in fact covered; while also compiling the 'prospects list' for the following day's stories. The deputy news editor and desk number three, or stand-in reporter, also man the newsdesk and assist this general news gathering and co-ordinating process with the assistance of the camera crews' co-ordinator. As well as a team of reporters including presenter/reporters working to the newsdesk, a forward planning team of two reporters and a secretary are also involved in a constant process of sifting through incoming mail and ensuring future 'diary stories' are logged and brought to the attention of the news editors.

While these positions are the nub of the news gathering process, the programme organizer, bulletin editor and a small team of sub-editors work to the programme editor, and are responsible for editing and packaging the gathered news material into the final news programme and bulletins. Attending to scripts, link pieces and visual elements the programme organizer and bulletin editor literally construct the programme into a split-second schedule which orders the final presentation technically implemented by the news director from the news control room. In addition to these various positions, production assistants, secretaries, copy-takers and film and video editors all populate the newsroom in varying degrees of frenetic, occasionally frenzied, activity reflecting the rhythms of the news production process and approaching transmission deadlines. With the above providing a brief overview of the key personnel found within the newsroom, the general rhythms and temporal processes of news production can also usefully be sketched.

At 7 am the early sub-editor arrives and consults the hard diary (a folder of press cuttings, forward planning memos, notes, public relations' handouts) left by the late reporter and sub-editor from the previous night. This provides details of running stories, as well as new stories of likely programme interest. The newsroom computer system, Newstar, is also consulted and the provisional prospects, compiled by the news editor on the previous late afternoon, summoned up onto one of the many computer terminals positioned around the newsroom. Check calls are made to the police and fire services, and the feed in system to Newstar by the Press Association is also continually monitored. At 7.30 the news editor arrives and begins to monitor various news sources – TV, radio, press, Press Association – and make adjustments to the prospects list. With the arrival of the early reporter at 8.00 and the deputy news editor, bulletin editor and sub-editors at 8.30 and programme editor at 8.45, the newsdesk progressively comes alive. By this time editors are busily preparing early morning bulletin scripts, typed directly into the Newstar system, as the ring of telephones begin to fill the newsroom and compete with the sound of overhead televisions (tuned to other channel news programmes).

The early morning news services of all channels are constantly monitored as are the local radio bulletins. With the arrival of the latest local and national daily newspapers all these sources of news are attended to through a growing smog of cigarette smoke and endless cups of coffee. The banter of updating running stories, discussion of 'breaking' and diary stories begins to mix with the general cacophony of 'news' now permeating the newsroom as the programme editor and news editor arrange the prospects for the day's programme. This early morning frenzy and sense of purposefulness continues through-out the day, only occasionally lapsing into periods of relative calm immediately after the midday news bulletins and main evening programme.

Following the early morning bulletin, copies of the prospects are printed and handed out to assembled reporters, sub-editors and newsdesk personnel for the morning conference. The news editor briskly runs through each two line summary, with comments and discussion usually confined to questions of logistics, availability of camera crews and anticipated news developments. Occasionally some discussion concerning the news story itself and possible differences of treatment are broached by those assembled, but in general an unspoken consensus appears to reign with reporters and editors seemingly in accord about the priorities and appropriate regional news treatments of different news stories. The programme editor oversees this daily process, only occasionally intervening with a gentle steering touch, and this usually involves those stories which may prove either controversial or legally sensitive. Some of the day's reporters, usually about five in total, are likely to have been assigned the previous night and already on their way to different news locations, with the rest assigned and equipped with story briefs at the morning conference. With an average of ten to twelve news stories in each news programme, which includes newsdesk reports written by sub-editors and a very occasional story 'down the wire' from one of the other news centres, news reporters typically pursue one, sometimes two stories each working day. These occasionally include stories that are placed on the shelf for future use.

Throughout the day the newsdesk constantly monitors news sources and updates stories, checking the progress of reporters' assignments by phone and radio phone. The newsroom is character-ized by different tasks and activities but all pulling in concert: sub-editors prepare their scripts, running orders are printed, bulletin presenters rehearse their delivery from autocue, voluminous post is opened and the bulk of it is consigned to the waste bin, editors and the forward planning section confer, the crew co-ordinator and deputy news editor jiggle the schedule of the crew roster on the wall, ENG ('electronic news gathering' or video) is delivered to the newsroom from location by dispatch riders, bulletins are transmitted, reporters return to write their scripts direct into the Newstar system and edit their ENG material as running times are dictated by the programme organizer. And so the newsroom day typically runs its course accompanied by ceaseless telephone calls, humorous banter and occasional heated exchanges. With a lull after the midday bulletin, the pitch of activity reaches its peak after 4 pm as the remaining news items are finally prepared and packaged into the final programme. The news editor prepares the next day's provisional prospects on Newstar and a hard diary replete with comments, newspaper cuttings and forward planning details is assembled for the late sub-editor. Following the early evening national news, the news editors and remaining reporters file into the cramped office belonging to the head of news and sit back to watch their collective efforts with the live broadcast of the main evening Central News West programme. With an eye for technical detail and general appearance the substance of the programme's items generally calls forth less comment from those assembled than does an inappropriate still (accompanying photo-graph), wrongly placed caption or weak presenter's link piece. The late reporter/presenter may watch the programme with special interest as selections for the late evening bulletin are considered, while the rest of the assembled company invariably indulge in quips and merriment at each other's expense.

This daily cycle is repeated each weekday though the level of intensity and activity can vary from day to day, depending on the occurrence of late breaking news, the availability of news stories on the day, numbers of available journalists and the duration of the programme to be filled. Once a week a forward planning meeting is held on Thursday mornings in which the senior forward planning reporter submits possible diary stories to the programme editor who then discusses these with the news editor, crew co-ordinator, and sports editor. These are then finalized as definite news items, possible items requiring further investigation or possible 'fill ins' for sparse news days, or discounted entirely for a variety of reasons. This organizational accomplishment is summarized in Figure 2.4.

As Figure 2.4 indicates, while news may well commonly be taken to be the latest, up-to-the-moment happenings and events, it can none the less be the result of a protracted, prepared and routine production process which can extend from anything up to a year in preparation. Certainly the forward planning unit and news editor, given the constant pressure to fill the programme and make the best use of available resources on the day, are constantly in search of news items that can be 'placed on the shelf' and 'hard diary' items prepared and/or anticipated in advance of the day's transmission. However, if news can involve considerable pre-planning and preparation over a period of time, the process also allows for flexibility with last minute and even 'on air' changes to the computerized running order and script sent to the autocue.

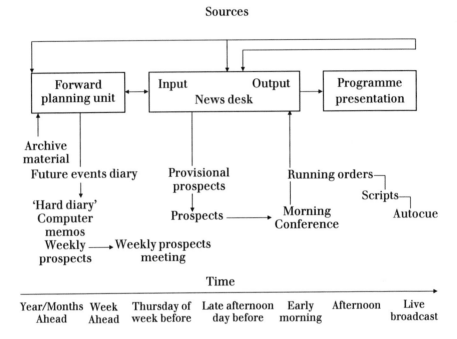

Figure 2.4 Central News West: the regional news process

Sources

If the organizational processing of regional news assumes a highly routinized form, newsroom dependence upon certain news sources is also a prominent feature of news production and evident in the daily round of check calls and other sources contacted as a matter of course. A review of all broadcast items and their respective sources across a sample period of two weeks confirms the highly organizational and institutional character of the majority of source interventions (see Table 2.1). With nearly half of all broadcast items originating from outside sources, the newsroom appears indebted to sources approaching the newsroom or routinely making themselves available, as in check calls, with a regular supply of stories. If nearly half the programme items are found to result from outside approaches to the newsroom, a further fifth of all news items, excluding sport, derive from other media sources. The original source of such stories is therefore lost from view though the news 'immersion' (discussed below) as a general newsroom culture and practice finds its rewards in the amount of stories gathered in this way.

With less than a fifth of all stories actually originated by newsroom personnel the golden days of investigative journalism referenced by the old school of journalists, if based in fact, appear well and truly superseded by the techniques and requirements of fast news processing. Moreover, given that the vast majority of all these newsroom related sources originate from freelances or stringers who, in the main, are undisclosed journalists working for the region's local newspapers, the number of news stories actually originated by Central West reporters has been found to be little more than 2 per cent of all broadcast items. With the remaining sources difficult to determine given the presence and development of 'running stories' already within the news domain, it is apparent that the main source of stories originates from external contacts.

If 'general sources' are further broken down into their different organizational and institutional sites, it is apparent that certain organizations and institutions appear routinely to provide the basis for regional news stories (see Table 2.2). With press releases often couched in terms designed to appeal to known programme interests, such sources routinely gain entry to the newsroom with items frequently processed for final programme inclusion. Local administration and services are found to originate numerous items, followed

Table 2:1 *Regional news items by source, over two weeks*

Sources	Number of broadcast items	%
General		
Press release	22	
Organization call	14	
Routine (check) call	5	
Individual call	3	
Individual letter	0	
sub-total	*44*	(46.8 %)
Other media		
Central South	7	
Central East	6	
Newspapers	4	
Press Association	1	
Television	1	
Radio	0	
sub-total	*19*	(20.2 %)
Personnel		
Newsroom freelances	13	
Newsroom personnel	2	
Central personnel	2	
sub-total	*17*	(18.1 %)
In the news domain		
Follow-up item	8	
Running story	5	
Multi-source	1	
sub-total	*14*	(14.9 %)
Total	*94*	(100.0 %)

Table 2:2 *General news items by source*

Sources	Number of broadcast items	%
Local services/Administration	13	29.5
Business/Company	12	27.3
Pressure group/Community group	7	15.9
Police	6	13.6
Trade unions	3	6.8
Fire service	2	4.5
Individuals	1	2.3
Total	*44*	(100.0 %)

by successful business source interventions, with some of the innumerable pressure and community groups found across the region also finding some presence as a source of regional news. Noticeably the police, though only one institution amongst countless others, represent a news source presence which is comparable to all pressure and community groups combined.

At this organizational level it is apparent that the originating sources of successful news items are themselves partially responsible for 'producing' news items of potential interest to the newsroom. However, a degree of caution is called for lest this should be interpreted as a linear and one-way involvement of sources. The 'news culture' discussed below cannot be assumed to be monopolized by practitioners and producers, but is also monitored by readers and viewers, some of whom regularly seek to intervene from their respective organizational settings, framing their interventions accordingly.

The descriptions above clearly reveal that the production of regional news is a routinized organizational accomplishment. It would be misleading to suggest, however, that the news programme simply reflects such organizational features and the reliance on certain institutional sources. To do so would be to underestimate the creative involvement of news professionals in such processes while tending towards a form of functionalist explanation in which news is approached simply as the outcome of bureaucratic needs. Though organizational and institutionalized features undoubtedly play their part in facilitating, and guaranteeing, the daily production of a news programme, such features also permit more variation in the forms of news produced than is sometimes conceded.

Journalists and news makers work within routinized processes and rely in considerable measure upon organizational contacts. They also, however, practice their craft according to a professional ethos in which canons of journalistic practice and the pursuit of a generalized set of news values also play their part. This professional subscription to a general news culture thus informs their daily practice and, importantly, also permits important variations on the theme of news.

Though all news operations are likely to be underpinned by a division of labour, bureaucratic routines and reliance upon institutional sources it remains the case that such can produce a variety of news forms. A closer examination of the professionals involved in the manufacture of the regional programme reveals how journalists purposefully fashion their particular variant of TV news according to a programme visualization or collective conceptualization of the programme form. It is this which gives the programme its distinctive character and popular appeal, and it is this which mediates in such characteristic terms issues of wider public concern.

From news culture to regional news: fashioning TV populism

On the basis of newsroom observations and interview findings three general observations can now be outlined which are of particular relevance to this study. These observations, while intimately connected to the immediate vicinity of production and professional routines, none the less begin to go beyond those descriptions above which have identified the professional hierarchies, formal routines and institutionalized source contacts daily informing the production of regional news. Important as these are, they remain insufficient as an account of the character and forms of the regional news programme. Attending to considerations of news culture and professional practice the discussion that follows considers the immersion of news makers within an impinging news culture; the degree of role flexibility and interchange evident within the newsroom; and, relatedly, the populist nature of the news product collectively pursued and inscribed into the programme as a professional 'known result'.

News culture and news immersion

The production of regional news is not carried out in a regional news vacuum. Rather, the immediate working environment in the newsroom is totally enmeshed within a much wider news net. Facilitated by advanced technology, as noted above, the news net is also informed by a wider culture of news. Constantly impinging into the centre of the newsroom, national and international as well as regional and local news permeates the journalistic atmosphere in a ceaseless tide of breaking news and updates on running stories. 'News' within the Central newsroom, in other words, is not confined to the packaged outcome of this particular production process but represents a total working environment suffused with the collective outpourings of other news centres. This news immersion, constantly plied by incoming media sources – the day's newspapers, radio and television news programmes, regular updates from the Press Association – combine to produce a sense of 'news' as an impinging reality.

Confronted by, and engaged with, this incoming tide of news it is understandable that the journalist's sense of news as an extrinsic world of happenings 'out there' has often been found to be so unshakable. Though intimately involved in processes of news manufacture which involves selecting, focusing/inflecting, interviewing, scripting, visualizing, editing and packaging news stories, and heavily reliant upon a number of news sources who have already done the same in relation to incoming 'news stories', journalists maintain a sense of 'raw news', simply waiting to be reported. In the context of the newsroom it is easy to forget, perhaps, that such incoming news has already been subjected to various bureaucratic routines, organizational processes, and informed by the practices of other professionals each serving their particular goals and institutional aims.

This immersion in the wider tide of news is both expected and pursued by all the journalists within the newsroom. Such is the professional commitment to keeping up with the latest developments, both work and non-work time appears to be geared to the endless monitoring of news. Many of the journalists spoken to quite freely admit to having something of an obsession for news, filling their leisure hours as well as working environment. The programme editor makes the point: 'If you're a journalist, you're a journalist and you accept it, I expect people to keep themselves up to date and keep themselves immersed'.

This feature of the news operation is important because it locates the production of regional news within a wider media news environment which, though differentiated, none the less constantly affords a reference point in which the specificity of the news product produced can be situated and defined, and which furthermore ordinarily has no need of recourse to external criteria of justification or validation. All the journalists and reporters interviewed had had past experience on local and/or national newspapers and tended to define their understanding of regional news in terms of different types of newspaper journalism.

A news editor stated, for example, that he would like the programme to be 'not as grand as the *Washington Post*, but like the old *Daily Mirror* under Cuddlip', while a forward planning journalist will refer to '*Daily Mirror* type stories', and the head of news, in response to an open question seeking a definition of the regional news programme, declared 'we're sort of around the *Mail*, the *Express*, perhaps approaching the *Sun*, perhaps impinging on the *Telegraph*, I wouldn't say that we're near *The Guardian* or *The Times*, and we're certainly not as awful as the worst parts of the *Sun* and the *Star*'. The programme editor for his part maintains that the programme 'has to be somewhere between the *Mirror* and the *Daily Mail* with a little bit of the *Telegraph* chucked in as well, we'd never go as far down as the *Sun*'. Constant reference to newspapers, though perhaps a useful shorthand for self-definition, simultaneously locates the journalists' understanding of the programme within a wider and differentiated news environment. Journalists producing the regional news programme are not hermetically sealed, therefore, from wider professional understandings of 'news', but fashion their particular TV variant in relation to 'this wider news culture.

Role flexibility

If the regional newsroom and journalistic enterprise is constantly immersed within a shared news culture, within which and in relation to which regional news programming is fashioned, the collective understanding of the regional news programme is further reinforced by the high degree of role flexibility and interchange evident within the television newsroom. As the programme editor remarked:

You need flexibility here and people are paid accordingly, it's that part of the job that is valued very much in all the agreements that have been made. The subs will act as reporters, the reporters will act as subs, the reporters might also sit on the newsdesk and act as news editors, the programme organiser will act up as news editor when the editor is away. All this sort of thing goes on a lot and it also provides more interest and more variety in their working lives and it also gives the reporters the opportunity to learn how to present by doing a bit of it on the main programmes or by doing bulletins; so it's something they can enjoy and get something out of it. It's far better for people to see it's a continuous process from beginning to end and to understand having to relate.

While the high degree of role flexibility, based on the pursuit of improved efficiency and controlled costs, undoubtedly 'oils the wheels' of production through better understanding and appreciation of the overall process, it also helps to ensure that the collective effort pulls in a similar direction with a common understanding of the nature and form of the regional news programme daily produced. As the programme editor observes: 'people in the newsroom know the general trend of what is expected by a general consensus, and by the fact that the editors preach the same message constantly over a period'. The fact that recently appointed controllers and programme editors are known to have built news teams based on the personnel they have previously worked with also helps to ensure uniformity of collective purpose and programme consistency. It is commonly acknowledged, for instance, that: 'Any news editor, any news producer is only as good as the team he has around him'.

This aspect of engendering a collective understanding of the form of news product, while open to fine grained studies of journalist socialization, suggests even at this general level that while production routines and working arrangements exert their own form of determinacy upon the news product, they may also act to further the shared consent and understandings of the specific form of news product collectively reproduced. The following statement by an experienced reporter is revealing in this respect.

You're all working to a known result which is this particular programme. We know the way it works, so we're sort of working to a format formula, which might sound dreadful, people will think that's formulated news. It's not. It's simply that you couldn't go out and see how the mood takes you, this might be a five minute discussion on Islam, or it might just be a two minute piece on this demonstration. You have to go out because of the constraints of time to set the thing up, you have to go out with some idea of its shape.

This statement provides a double insight into the nature of news production. It indicates that the general process and constraints of news production impose certain conditions upon news journalists who must, in the face of daily deadlines, work to preconceived ideas. It also indicates that such preconceptions are tailored by the specificity and collectively understood requirements of the particular programme form. It is this which is daily reproduced as a 'known result'. For these reasons the distinction that has sometimes been drawn in the news literature between 'news gatherers' and 'news processors' following an early study of specialist correspondents (Tunstall 1971), is not helpful in the context of regional TV news.

Working to a shared and common understanding of the specific news form, processes of news processing are inextricably involved in processes of news gathering. The distinction artificially blurs the extent to which both newsdesk personnel and reporters share a common framework of understanding and programme aim. It also ignores the extent to which newsroom specialism has increasingly given way to flexible journalist involvement across the variety of tasks and responsibilities involved in newsroom production. Role flexibility, as observed above, can serve different purposes, but most importantly perhaps engenders a shared sense and common pursuit of a standardized and differentiated news product. From the initial selection of the stories to be covered by senior newsroom personnel to the filing of story briefs and the assignment of reporters, and from the focus of reporters' questions to the visuals sought and shot by camera crews, and from the final sub-editing process to the programme juxtaposition of different news stories, 'news processing' guides the news production process throughout.

What informs this complicated process of manufacture, of course, is a shared understanding or programme visualization of the news programme, its conventions, appeals and characteristic news treatments. The production of news is not simply accountable with reference to processes of socialization into general news values, much less a question of individual or even collective journalist attitudes; rather, the professional production of news is infused with a shared understanding of the specific news product and its requirements. Rapid career moves in and out of different forms of journalism require journalists to adopt and reproduce the character-istic forms and appeals of the news product that they currently serve. If we want to try and understand why certain issues find or do not find news representation within and across the different news outlets, and also account for the news treatment they receive, it is important to understand something about existing programme forms. This in-cludes attending to those in-built appeals and news conventions ordering the manner in which social issues and concerns find characteristic news mediation. How exactly this professional 'known result' of regional news is conceptualized by the journalists involved and inscribed into the final news product, can now be considered.

Professionals producing populism

This last discussion pursues the professional understanding of the regional news programme and its characteristic bid for popular appeal. The discussion first identifies the wider corporate view before focusing down onto the newsroom visualization and the way in which this is pursued on a daily basis. Here wider institutional pressures assume a more muted aspect, with journalists 'filling out' the corporate ambition for a popular regional news programme in a manner which is deemed to be in accord with their professional aim of producing a 'respectable' popular news programme. The pro-gramme is produced according to a professional visualization in which populist themes and appeals are routinely and deliberately inscribed into its news mix, story treatments and modes of delivery. These are seen as necessary ingredients to achieve a successful and popular news programme. However, populism is capable of assuming various forms, with news forms being no exception. On the basis of a long-standing disagreement within the newsroom, something of the specificity of this particular variant of news populism is then elicited and subjected to consideration.

The corporate view: ratings, advertisers and politics

The regional news programme has been previously identified at the heart of regional programming and corporate identity and endeav-our. It is interesting to inquire in the first instance, then, how the programme is viewed at this wider institutional level, before examin-ing how newsworkers see the regional news programme. Clearly, much can depend on who you ask, or, more precisely, the corporate role and responsibility held by the interviewee in relation to news programming. The controller of programme planning, for example, is quite clear about the importance of the regional news programme as a 'schedule tool'.

The news programme is very important as a building block in scheduling terms, because the evening news programme gets a very, very good rating to take viewers through the night, so it's actually very, very important as a scheduling tool.

In terms of the audience sought within the prime-time schedules, the controller of programme planning is equally up front about the pursuit of a prime-time mass audience.

We want a very large share of the audience, if you get that large share of the audience you will get the elusive ABC1s that the advertisers cry out for. But remember advertisers aren't just selling brands to that, they're selling housewife brands too. The bottom line for all ITV companies is to get the largest share of audience, available audience at any time, and within that you will be able to sell to ABC1s too.

Similarly, the controller of factual programmes is equally candid about the role of the regional news programme in corporate affairs.

You want to get your audience in the early evening and hope they don't switch over. It's terribly important. Yes it's a ratings grabber the regional news programme and always has been . . . The first thing that you look at every week is the rating for the programme. You have to. If the programme satisfies my ego but doesn't produce the rating, then the programme isn't very worth while. No, we're very conscious of the rating and always have to be. It's the early evening hook, get them in at 6 o'clock if you possibly can and put them through the rest of the night or at least the early evening.

If such a statement points to the impinging economic imperatives informing the operations of a commercial television company, the recent opening of Central's third sub-regional news service also indicates that news programming can serve other corporate uses. The controller of factual programmes made this comment:

There we would hope to persuade people that we are providing them with a better local service than anything they can currently get from HTV or anything else. That's one statement. But the other statement was a much bigger political statement, saying that if you are a very large company you can none the less discharge your regional and local responsibilities, no matter how big you are, providing you can separate out lots of different news regions. And that was a major political statement we made, and are still making to the government: that we can reduce the number of ITV companies down from fifteen to six or seven. If they all behave as responsibly as Central does in setting up news regions you can still do all your local programming.

The regional news programme, on these accounts, could be approached as simply a corporate ratings 'hook', and/or as a means of winning political favour and pursuing general commercial goals of conglomeration. Further grist to the mill of the 'political' understanding of the corporate role of regional news is apparent from the following observation from the head of news, a long serving news producer.

It's always been a ship that can earn you higher ratings, it's always been that and it's also usually a regional identity of the programme company. So there's two interests in it: one's the ratings the other is the fact, which may disappear, is that regional news suddenly becomes the flagship of the entire operation. When it comes to renewing the contract the board proudly start talking about regional news.

At first sight these frank observations from senior news personnel endorse either a political economy understanding of news production and forms, or a more instrumentalist and political explanation of existing news programming. Whereas the former approach is inclined to delve into those wider economic determinations propelling media organizations to seek out large audiences and advertising revenue by providing middle-ground programme fare, the instrumentalist understanding is apt to see regional news programming simply as a means to further corporate political aims and ambitions. While each approach can find support in statements such as these, they do not provide much insight into the particular nature and characteristic forms and appeals professionally underpinning the regional news programme. Programme ratings, though constantly monitored by senior corporate personnel and ultimately crucial in determining the programme's long-term viability, do not appear to inform the professional practices or preoccupations of senior programme makers on a daily basis. As one programme editor put it:

It's not a matter of pressure, its a matter of your aim . . . It's professional pride. Of course, if the ratings were to fall to what the company felt was a danger level commercially there would be some pressure then; but we're not in that boat at all.

For the most part, newsroom reporters and journalists were found not to be well informed about or even to be particularly interested in questions of audience size and social composition at all. In terms of the immediate proximities of programme production and conceptualization, then, questions of ratings and overall corporate goals prove, on their own, to be too blunt, and on a daily basis, too removed from the actual practices and preoccupations of news producers to offer much in the way of explanatory insight into the production of regional news as an established cultural form. In order to understand the differentiated nature and characteristic appeal of this news programme it is instructive to turn to the professional conceptualization which grounds its production in the newsroom.

The newsroom view: 'it's a popular people led programme'

If implicated within general corporate strategy as well as ultimately dependent upon commercial and economic success, regional news also assumes a particular cultural form, addresses certain issues and concerns in a particular way while appealing to its audience in a characteristic idiom. In these terms, the task of analysis has only just begun when wider commercial imperatives and political contexts are raised. How then is the programme conceptualized by key news producers? Asking the programme editor to describe what he would consider to be a typical regional news programme on a 'good' day, the following programme visualization was offered.

This programme on a typically good day would have a very up-to-date breaking hard news story at the top of it, whether it's crime or whatever, something that grabs the attention of the viewer without being in any way sensational. So obviously a very good story at the top which is a straight forward actuality story. I would also want to see in the news mixture a lot of people led stories; it's a popular people led programme. So you would want stories that would touch the viewer through involving an individual, being based on an individual – whether it's a granny whose involved in a mugging, or whether it's somebody who can't find work despite all sorts of enormous attempts, whether it's a child that's turned up on the doorstep of a hospital and there's a hunt for the mother. All that sort of story which is very much news linked which has preferably happened on that day which will have enormous appeal for the viewer.

Now having gone through all that sort of thing there will be pictures as well. There will be stories that take us out into the region. That get us around the region and reflect the attractions or the problems of the region to the viewer. There will probably be a bit of sport towards the end of the programme before we get to the weather broadcast and so on, the pure public service area. I think it's always quite nice to have a bit of leavening on a day that's been full of very morbid and very hard news, whether it's from courts or road crashes, fires or whatever it's quite nice to have something, a sort of personality type piece, a bit of humour as well, a bit of humanising.

This professional programme visualization provides, in compressed fashion, a reasoned description of the general character and popular constitution of the regional news programme, and serves as a statement of programme intent. In summary terms, a number of regional news ingredients can be noted, all of which are likely to be recognized by regional news viewers. These include a programme predilection for crime news which, like 'actuality' forms of news generally, is taken to be beyond interpretative disagreement, simply being 'reported' by the news programme. The popular ambitions of the programme – 'it's a popular people led programme' – are also uppermost in the programme editor's account, where ordinary individuals are sought for prominent news inclusion. Relatedly, stories of individuals that 'touch' the viewer, that is which engage the viewer emotionally as much as they convey information, are important in the programme's bid for audience appeal. Of obvious interest to this study, the programme is also said to 'reflect the attractions or the problems' around the region. Sports news and 'pure public service' information are also seen as part of the regional news programme's brief. Finally, the editor emphasizes once again the sought popular appeals of the programme by underlining the search for humorous and personality-based stories with which to offset the more serious news items in the programme.

To what extent these characteristics have been found to impact upon news portrayal of the region's inner cities will be scrutinized in detail later. Here it is interesting to pursue a little further the nature of this popular ambition, and the manner in which it is professionally inscribed into the regional news programme. An acting news editor says:

We are an unashamedly popular programme, we go out of our way to be popular, we mean to be popular. We don't mean to be a shadow of the Radio 4 programme *Today*, we don't really mean to be a reflection of *News at Ten*, we set out to be, I dislike the word 'down-market' intensely, it's redolent of class snobbery and bias, we're not down-market we don't do any sleaze, we don't do any dirty divorce cases, we don't do anything the tabloids do except that we do look very hard for the human interest story. Something mum and dad and the nippers at home can watch in the safety of knowing they're not going to get either bad language or appalling people doing appalling things. They can have a giggle over some of the silly things people get up to in our region; and I think that's nice. And I think that's why we're watched because people know they're safe, that they'll get a giggle and they'll sit through the serious stuff as well.

Once again we find that the professional news producer's programme visualization tends to be situated within a wider view of the news media in general, while also seeking to distance its mass appeal from derogatory understandings of mass popular culture. Categories of class are actively eschewed as an organizing basis of appeal, replaced by a particular understanding of 'the family' and its domestic concerns. The programme also, or so it appears from this account, adopts the role of moral guardian, safeguarding 'the family' from some of the worst excesses of the outside world: 'Something mum and dad and the nippers at home can watch in safety'. Indeed, 'the serious stuff' is felt to be an intrusion, perhaps necessary for a well informed democracy, but essentially a bitter pill that has to be endured before the silly stories, the 'funnies', are handed out as a pleasurable reward. The professional pursuit of a variant of populist TV news finds further endorsement in the following:

As journalists we say, this is important you really ought to pay attention to this. But our sort of contract is, OK we're not going to give you half an hour of this, you're going to get three minutes, stick with us because there's a nice little story coming on about a 12 year old boy who's become a circus clown . . . You see we have to tell people so many horrible things about murders and deaths, tragedies and so on, and if you give them a diet of that you are going to lose them. Nobody wants half an hour of depression, sitting there with their fish fingers and chips. As I was saying earlier on, the human interest story, the comical story is very important, very very important . . . It's actually very important I think, and that people actually know it's coming. You know, 'hang on, hang on there's going to be a funny at the end of this'.

This professional view of the regional news programme articulates a relational view of news. Adopting a position of friendly gatekeeper, the professional newsworker administers news in doses and in a form that are thought to be palatable: too much, or too unvaried a diet would, it is supposed, lead to chronic indigestion with long-term repercussions on future news consumption. The 'contract' envisaged is clearly of a particular kind and implicitly works with a restricted idea of an imagined audience – an idea which bears little, if any, comparison to the widely heterogeneous audience actually watching the programme. How this imagined audience is conceptualized by the professionals can be further gauged from the way in which it is addressed.

Populism as mode of address

The regional news programme as a popular cultural form appeals to and addresses its imagined audience within distinctive terms. Here the role of programme presenters is revealing. Though expected to modulate differing modes of address in line with the running order of different stories, the characteristic mode of address generally sought by regional news teams is that of the familial friend. The head of news, as a long-standing regional news journalist who also has a special responsibility for programme presentation, is in no doubt of the special role played by regional news presenters.

It is the feeling that the presenter is broadcasting to an audience of one, and that's what he (*sic*) wants to feel, he's not broadcasting to a huge audience. A good presenter is aware that he is a friend in the living room. He is broadcasting to people watching the set, and not to a public gathering or a large audience, he shouldn't feel that he is addressing a large audience. When he goes on, he goes to talk and relate in a friendly way and try to communicate easily with the people in front of the television. And they do, they strike up a relationship. People do stop and notice when they smile and say I like that, I like him or I don't like her . . . The regional presenters are having to switch from hard news, ie the IRA blowing up the barracks at Shrewsbury into a soft item, say a John Swallow item about holes in the road in Birmingham, that newscaster has got to change pace and emphasis and in a way prepare the viewer for what he is about to deliver. So by his facial expression and the fact that he can relax, he actually relaxes the viewer to accept that he is coming to a softer item and that's pretty skilful stuff . . . your regional presenter, in my view, forms a closer relationship with the viewer, and needs to, or else there is a danger of getting a cold product.

This general familial stance is further confirmed by a regional news presenter:

They always say when you are looking into the camera picture someone familiar in place of that camera, I think the nicest one to think about is the little old lady, sat at home for whom seeing Fred Bloggs on Central News is important to her because they are people she can identify with. And so you think of them sat at home, and you imagine that you are talking to them, that's the thing which makes it more human, that's the key to it.

In short while regional news presenters are expected to command a sense of credibility and authority, itself vital in the authentication and objectification of 'news', so too are they expected to assume a familial stance, ingratiating the audience into its friendly ambiance by 'humanizing' the communication process. The popular ambitions of the programme thereby find a further opportunity to appeal to its imagined audience.

Variants of populism: newsroom dissent

The extent to which pronounced populist appeals should be allowed to inform the programme as a whole is not beyond newsroom dispute however. Though the news programme, as indicated above, is generally orientated via senior news editors and the controller of factual programmes as a 'people's programme, about people, for people', the extent to which this should assume even more deliberate inflection, with an emphasis upon entertainment is a matter of professional disagreement. Forms of popular journalism can assume various forms; TV forms are no exception here.

A division of opinion was found between the 'old school' of regional news journalists lamenting what they see as the passing of the old-style popular 'magazine' news programme, and a new school of journalists who declare themselves keen to firm up the programme and establish a respectable journalistic hard news programme. The controller of factual programming clearly champions a hard news view of regional news programming: 'They were very very soft magazine programmes when I came, and under my ethos I said "this is news, get rid of all that, it all goes, I don't want any set dressing at all, I want a news programme" . . . And that was the shake-up I gave it, to say "you will become news oriented and will be driven by news, driven by the events out there" '. Working to the general directions of the controller of factual programmes the editorial manager was employed to implement just such a shift of professional judgement and programme direction.

If one goes back, say ten years ago to local news programmes, they were more or less that, they were what they call 'magazine' programmes, and it was the pop star in town today, bit of news bit of that. The policy which I was asked to implement, and therefore lay down, and a policy with which I agree, is that we are a news organisation. And therefore our job is to provide a news programme.

If the above is representative of the new breed of 'informers', and further endorsed by the present programme editor's claims that 'this is first and foremost a hard news programme', the following statement from a specialist arts reporter represents the considered views of the old guard of 'entertainers'.

On a 6 o'clock news programme nobody is really watching, the kids are screaming for tea, the cat's fallen over, all hell's going on, nobody's actually sat watching so if you don't grab their attention and then hold them by entertaining they are not going to watch anyway . . . People will put up with the hard news, I'm not exaggerating, if they know there is going to be a Swallow or a Maycock [humorous presenters] or a something on the way. If you start to take it away, they won't put up with you hammering, hammering with boring news. They need to be entertained, it's dead simple. You can go on about duty to the community and informing and all the other crap but if they are not fucking watching you're not going to tell them.

If these two positions represent the old magazine school of the entertainers and the new hard news school of informers, both appear to have consolidated into something of a newsroom mythology, in which opinions appear more polarized than the present constitution of the regional news programme permits. That is, elements of both informer and entertainer ambitions continue to be purposefully built into the present regional news programme, as evidenced in discussions below, suggesting that in so far as some changes have recently been implemented these have not been as decisive as either of these two groups would like to claim.

Regional news: middle ground populism

The regional news programme is characterized by more stability and continuity than either of these two newsroom mythologies are apt to concede. Senior news producers recognize as much when arguing for and implementing their particular conception of the news programme which can be seen as a 'middle ground' form of populism. That is, it appears to incorporate both the informers' mission to report major events and happenings in line with generalized news values and the pursuit of a 'respectable news effort', but it also works with the entertainers' predisposition for populist appeal, deliberately seeking to engage viewers through affective, as much as informative, involvement; purposefully fashioning stories in such a way as to heighten their human interest appeal; and consciously seeking to incorporate the views and experiences, hopes and fears, of ordinary people, that is non-elites, within the programme. This is not the populist excess of certain tabloid forms of journalism, or even past forms of TV news (i.e. TV-am), it is a form of populism none the less.

I think we set out to make an entertaining and informative programme at 6 o'clock in the evening which has its own limits. A different editor might have more features on arts than the present one, another editor might want more sport. At the end of the day we're pretty much the same sort of animal though. (acting news editor)

The middle ground of popular television journalism is therefore taken to be a fairly consistent terrain occupied by the regional news programme which deals in questions of information *and* entertainment.

There's an old maxim that says television news has to inform, educate and entertain. I think a mixture of all three is found in a typically good regional news programme. The first job is to inform people as quickly as possible about the main events in their area on the day . . . the hard news events they just demand attention and you give it to them . . . There's a little bit of education to be done as well and that's something we have to help our viewers with . . . Obviously a lot of the educating and the explaining will be done on the national news, but we'll still have to fit it into the regional picture a bit, to apply it to them, lead them through it a little bit. And the entertaining part of it is not to throw people such a morass of heavy, stodgy, indigestible material that the whole lot becomes grey. You need a bit of lighting here and there, a little bit of humanity here and there, which needn't take you into the realms of being silly, or into pure entertainment as such, but just help to relieve the gloom a little bit for them, that little bit of reassurance that there's a little bit of humanity at the bottom of it. (programme editor)

While the Reithian ethic that television should seek to inform, educate and entertain applied to the entirety of television programming, when applied specifically as a news ethic inscribed into the heart of the regional news form, the character and indeed general purpose of news appears to undergo a radical shift. No longer seeking to simply inform and explain, albeit perhaps within an entertaining mode of delivery, the purpose of the regional news programme appears to be to actively engage with the sympathies and emotional sentiments of its viewers. When a hard news programme attempts to 'relieve the gloom a little bit', and seeks to offer 'that little bit of reassurance that there's a bit of humanity at the bottom of it', the programme appears to be actively embarked upon a form of social massage relieving the anxieties, worries and hardships of private existence.

At the heart of the professional programme visualization therefore, is an attempt to produce a popular-based programme which appeals directly to the experiences, interests and emotional sentiments of its imagined audience. The pursuit of human interest, in other words, is not confined to those so-called 'soft' news stories in which eccentrics and unusual individuals and happenings typically bring up the rear of the programme, but appears to be professionally pursued and inscribed into news items more generally via an attempt to 'personalize' stories.

People who sit at home need to identify with what they see on the screen to maintain their interest, and the best way to do that is to provide examples of situations which are affecting people so that they can put themselves in their shoes and at least be interested enough to at least take in the story. We're selling the story really, we have to do it in a way that is acceptable to them, and in a way that they appreciate, a style. I don't regret saying anything like that to you at all, because I really believe it. As far as I'm concerned it's a peoples' programme for people by people and the issues are brought out not as a 'by the way' but here it is in microcosm and explain a little bit more around it . . . the more you do personalise things the more memorable they become to the viewer. (programme editor)

This style of regional news inflexion is recognized by regional news journalists – alongside other news attributes more widely sought after within the news culture – to be a key ingredient to regional news, and is intimately bound up with the programme's ambition to appeal to a popular mass audience. This appeal, as stated repeatedly by regional news journalists, consists principally of an attempt to engage viewers directly. To go straight to the ordinary person and engage their immediate preoccupations, concerns and aspirations, to invite human interest and affective response, to privilege the experiential account over the expert's dry rendition or the analysis of the wider view. To appeal to commonalities of human experience, rather than indulge the differences of ideological division. This is the politics of populism which, denying that it is political at all, appears to transcend the politics born of collective difference, in the name of 'the people', 'common sense' or perhaps universal human values. As the controller of factual programmes has said 'we're here to represent the punters, not the institutions'.

It would be wrong, however, to emphasize too strongly this aspect of the populist appeals of the regional news programme. Though definitely pursued and often inscribed by those professionals involved, regional news journalists, as noted above, also work within a wider journalist mission to report, inform and impart. Though apparently high on the agenda of regional news priorities, the human interest inflexion is not always sought, nor necessarily found in all forms of regional news treatment. That said it remains, according to the journalists, a prominent programme ambition.

There are several elements that go into making up a good story, and probably the common strands are its appeals to the kind of audience that you are trying to reach, and to do that it's got to be immediate, it's got to have just happened, it's got to be very fresh, it's got to have an element of humanity, of human interest – an ill-used term – running through it, something with which people can identify to a large extent, and quite often a good story will have a degree of conflict within it as well. (programme editor)

If asked what the principal responsibility of the regional pro-gramme is, news producers are apt to say that it should 'reflect the region'. The controller for factual programmes maintains, for example, that: 'The news programme is to reflect what is happen-ing in the region, it is dominated by the region'; and the programme editor has said above that news stories will 'reflect the attractions and the problems of the region'. Such statements represent a laudable ambition in sympathy with the liberal democratic ethos held by many journalists, and which grants the profession the privileged role of guardians of the Fourth Estate. To what extent such professional claims have found regionalized confirmation in relation to the reporting of an important social concern and political contest can be examined in detail in later chapters. Here it can be surmised that the popular ambitions of the regional news programme, as declared above, appear set to impact selectively upon the way in which the problems and issues of the region's inner city have found news representation. To what extent and in what manner will be explored later.

Summary

This inside look at the production of regional news has found that the news programme is situated within a wider corporate and commer-cial context in which it is expected to support a variety of roles and corporate ambitions: corporate flagship, franchise/licence winner, schedule tool, mass audience builder, ratings grabber, advertiser attraction, revenue earner. At the level of programme production and delivery such aims have assumed a more muted aspect, though undoubtedly informing in the longer term questions of programme viability. Attending to organizational routines and resources, profes-sional hierarchies and institutionalized source contacts the produc-tion of regional news is clearly an organizational accomplishment which is likely to bear, in part at least, the traces of such organiza-tional features. However, it was also suggested on the basis of observations and interview testimonies that the regional news programme is actively created by journalists and other professionals collectively working towards a 'known result'. This takes place within an organizational setting and impinging news culture in which the specificity of regional news programming is creatively and purpose-fully fashioned on a daily basis according to a shared 'programme visualization'.

Here the pursuit of a popular-based news programme, 'a people's programme for people by people' to quote the programme editor, finds characteristic expression in terms of programme interests, forms of news treatment and styles of news delivery. This characteristic form of regional news programme has been identified as occupying a middle ground position of TV news populism, keen to purport to be a responsible provider of hard news while simultaneously seeking to engage with the immediate interests, preoccupations and sentiments of ordinary people. How this middle ground form of TV news populism has mediated the issues and concerns of the region's many inner city localities and communities can now be examined in detail.

3
Mediating the inner city: TV news production

The last chapter outlined an inside view of the production of regional news. Attending to the routinized practices, professional roles and institutionalized source contacts underpinning this organizational endeavour, it was also observed how features of a generalized new culture were purposively fashioned by professional journalists into the 'known result' of a popular-based regional news programme. Building on these general insights, this chapter examines the way in which news of the inner city is processed within this complex web of organizational routines and professional practices. The discussion is organized in relation to the news treatment of those key inner city concerns previously identified as central to the contending discourses on the inner city. Thus, particular interest is directed, first, to the production of crime news and issues of law and order within an inner city context; second, to those multiple problems of social deprivation and disadvantage; and, finally, to the systematic inequalities and processes of discrimination affecting the region's minority ethnic communities. How each of these becomes the subject for regional news inclusion and is then framed and inflected according to regional news requirements is observed within the newsroom setting.

First it is useful to consider how practising regional journalists regard the contested site of the inner city as a possible source of news interest. What, if any, is the perceived role of the regional programme in relation to the problems and issues of the region's inner cities?

I don't do inner city stories, I'll do a story on bad housing which may be in Aston, it may be an Asian family, it may be a West-Indian family, it may be a white family . . . So I tend to go for types of stories rather than inner cities . . . I don't go to do inner city area stories, except when some minister or opposition spokesman, or prime minister says this is an inner city area problem and I report it as a news story. I would rather, and I think we do, cover important stories which affect people's lives . . . I don't think our policies towards the inner cities per se have changed because we've always done stories about problems that affect people. (former news editor)

This statement, and others, indicate that as far as regional news journalists are prepared to admit, the inner city has been largely eschewed as an organizing concept for regional news reports. A deputy news editor stated, for instance, 'inner cities is a vogue term isn't it?'. And, in a sense, this can be agreed with to the extent that the semantic site of the inner city has been mobilized within competing political discourses and does not therefore refer to a stable or uncontested referent. However, if the inner city may hold little attraction for regional news journalists as an organizing concept, the range of issues and problems frequently referenced in relation to the inner city are very much at the forefront of proclaimed journalistic interests.

We don't think in tag terms we think in, may be if we do a story about a particular issue, it doesn't matter that much where it is, the story is the story as the journalist would say, and an issue is an issue. Most of our area now that Central South has been taken away is an inner city area more than most places in the country. So what ever we do should reflect the area, and all those things come out. (programme editor)

On such accounts the existing net of regional news reporting is thought to be adequate to the task of reporting those various issues and concerns associated with the region's inner cities because they are part and parcel of the region which, it is often stated, are reflected in the regional news programme; hence, according the deputy news editor 'we've been doing inner city stories for donkey's years'. In relation to such concerns, then, regional journalists are professionally disposed to maintain that their responsibilities remain confined to the general reflective role of impartial journalism.

We have no responsibility as such, we are not solvers of problems, we are reporters and reflectors of states of affairs which is why we exist. So if you ask me whether we have a particular responsibility to that area any more than any other area I would say no, except that large numbers of people live in those areas with whom we should concern ourselves and they are also a very fruitful source of stories and news reports for journalists. So yes, we've got a general reflective role I think, not to allow stories that are difficult to report slip us by . . . we've got a responsibility not to ignore social ills generally, and in this area there are plenty of them. (programme editor)

To what extent, in what manner and for what reasons the multiple 'social ills' associated with the inner city have been reflected in the regional news programme in line with stated professional goals can now be examined in some detail.

Reporting the inner city: crime news

As the programme editor and others have indicated above, the operation of general news criteria is deemed sufficient for the reflection of the problems and social ills of the inner city. Interestingly, however, though the concept of the inner city is said not to inform the production of regional news stories, in general conversations and interviews it became clear that the idea of the inner city was entertained by newsroom journalists, albeit defined within particular terms, and typically identified as a source of crime and criminality.

Former programme editor   So it's a problem of definitions I find. And I find people could actually say 'You're not doing enough on inner cities', and I would say, 'Yes we do stories on the inner cities, we do stories of great interest to the people who are living there'.

Editorial manager   Well I don't think that could be levelled against us, because I think we do a hell of a lot, because most of our programmes are dominated by the major conurbations. If people are living together, they run each other over, they shoot each other, they kill each other, they burgle each other more so than they do elsewhere.

Former programme editor   There's obviously more crime.

As this short exchange begins to illustrate, not only is the inner city tending to be identified as a place of crime and criminality, but so too is an underpinning framework of news values revealed which clearly centres crime at the heart of regional news interests. The programme editor is also in no doubt of the major problem associated with the inner city, though this is presented less as a problem for the inner city and more as a problem for adjacent populations. Commenting on the prevalence of general regional news crime stories he suggested:

It's perhaps an old cliche but it's a sign of the times, people are more and more worried about crime these days. Sociologically speaking it gets into everywhere these days, into everybody's area now. Criminals are less inhibited; they go into areas where they never went before. We carried a story yesterday for instance, about a raid on a house in Knowle in Solihull which is a white ghetto, but not only that, very middle class, very exclusive and normally an enclave of the rich totally untouched by all the nastiness that might go on in the outside world. And yet there, people were being threatened by armed people . . . It gets everywhere, the abduction of a school girl from our own area in Shropshire not long ago shows that crime is spreading out from the inner city areas where it was traditionally dominant.

What is interesting about this position is that in offering an account of the prevalence of crime news in the regional news programme as a whole, the inner city is indirectly referred to as a traditional site of crime and from which crime is thought to spread to other areas. Clearly, an implicit identity between inner city areas and crime is assumed and informs journalist thinking. However the general prevalence of inner city crime news, detailed later, cannot be accounted for by such attitudes alone. It has already been noted how, for example, the regional news programme is underpinned by production routines and institutionalized source contacts. These story sources can be said to be institutionalized in the double sense that not only do they typically involve large organizations and institutions, they also represent routinized and habitual newsroom practices resulting in newsroom dependence on certain sources.

In part this can be explained by the daily pressures of securing news. Reporters and journalists frequently remark to the effect that the programme represents a void, a chasm daily confronting the newsroom. A former news editor observed, for instance: 'We're constantly under pressure to try to build as much up as we can because you know it will help take some of the pressure off the days coming up', and was overheard to say while viewing the live transmission of a one hour programme 'God, this one hour programme doesn't half gobble up news'. More graphically perhaps, a reporter described the daily quest for news as 'a constant battle to fill the programme, it's a great yawning chasm in front of you which has to be filled up every day'. Such practical concerns have engendered an organizational response, in which as many of the uncertainties attending news production are eliminated. In recent years this tendency is recognized to have become more pronounced.

I think what we have become is almost a mini *News At Ten*; we're treating the news in a very hard way, we're working off the diary more than we used to, in other words the courts, the councils, the political questions, Westminister reaction. We're not doing so many of the features which reflect life in the region . . . The idea is fast response news gathering which is all very well but if we're not careful you can end up with a head count of death. You can end up giving the viewer a distorted view of life . . . really pretty tough, and the streets are dangerous and that everything is going wrong everywhere. (head of news)

In so far as this position appears to suggest that fast-response news gathering has reduced the amount of 'features which reflect life in the region', so this can be seen as of likely impact on the reporting of the region's concentrated problems of urban distress. More directly, it can be seen as prompting organizational source dependencies which, in so far as they involve the police and the courts, will undoubtedly lead to a prominence of crime and policing stories. This bureaucratic response which seeks to tame the news environment and routinize the unexpected leads to newsroom reliance on certain sources while diminishing the capacity of journalists to either originate or pursue news stories not based around established institutions. On this basis, contending inner city discourses are likely to find differing opportunities for news representation to the extent that they are associated with and advanced by major institutional or organizational sites.

As far as the inner city is concerned, then, two of the most prominent sources of news stories, the police and the courts, are set to find routine presence within regional news portrayal. It was observed earlier how the newsroom make routine 'check calls' to the region's police and fire services throughout the day, while court lists are also consulted regularly to ensure cases of particular news interest are reported. In addition, incoming calls and press releases from the region's police constabularies are also a routine occurrence. While this relationship between the news producers and the police is not always harmonious, as will be documented later, it is likely none the less to exert considerable impact on the agenda of inner city issues and concerns which find, and do not find, regional news interest.

It has already been indicated, however, that organizational factors cannot be discussed in isolation from prevailing news interests, nor can these be discussed without reference to the specific programme ambitions and news appeals pursued in the regional news programme. If the news culture with its underpinning news values is generally recognized to be attracted to issues and events involving conflict, deviance and negativity, that is, events breaching established social conventions and thresholds, crime news is likely to be a prime candidate for news inclusion, especially if involving acts of violence. When coupled with an organizational response to the exigencies of news production which results in the privileging of certain institutional viewpoints as well as the prevailing newsroom assumption that locates the inner city as a site of crime and criminality, this potent mix of factors helps explain the pronounced news representation in which the inner city becomes centred as both source and site of criminal behaviour.

However, while the news interest in crime appears to be pronounced it by no means runs unchecked within the established ambitions of the regional news programme. Unlike the popular tabloids, for instance, the more sordid, sensational and sexually related crimes available for news treatment are tempered within the middle ground populism of regional news.

Crime is by its very nature sensational, for example last week we had a father who murdered his baby, we've had people who have conspired to murder somebody's husband, this sort of thing. We don't run them at great length. We only run them at perhaps 25, 30 seconds with maybe one picture. We don't do them long because we're aware that people are sitting at home and they don't want to be depressed by endless reports of rapes or indecent assaults; very rare that we run those stories. But those stories about a murder of a child or whatever, we think have an intrinsic interest and I think if you look at every newspaper in the country they too fill their pages up with crime, particularly the local evening papers. (acting news editor)

Though the Central News West area is recognized by news producers to be an unusually 'newsy' area, given its large conurbations and metropolitan characteristics, the extent and types of crime news actually reported appear to reflect as much upon programme ambitions to provide a rounded and 'safe' regional news programme as much as the availability of crime items provided by the courts and the police. None the less, it is apparent that regional news interests and professional practices are structured in such a way as to bring the problems of the inner city to the fore in relation to the key concern of crime and law and order. Newsroom dependency on the police, as both source and participant in inner city related news stories, will be demonstrated in the following chapter. Here, the discussion moves on to consider the production of other news stories which, in the terms of the professional journalists, seek to 'reflect the region's social ills'.

Reporting social deprivation: reflecting social ills?

Unlike crime stories, the reporting of news stories relating to questions of social disadvantage and urban deprivation more generally are frequently planned in advance. The reporting of serious regional crimes, with the exception of court report follow-ups, typically seeks to capitalize upon the drama and immediacy of the event itself, often incorporating eyewitness accounts and immediate police responses, and are reported on the day in question, or the following day at the latest. Stories relating to aspects of social and urban deprivation, on the other hand, are more likely to be planned over a longer time period. This is reflected in the organizational arrangements of regional news production. Here the weekly forward planning meeting is a key point in the decision making process, and provides an opportunity to observe how such issues are typically viewed by programme producers and selected and framed in line with programme ambitions.

This is attended by senior editors including the programme editor, news editor and deputy news editor, crew co-ordinator, programme organizer and sports editor as well as the forward planning editor who presents possible news stories to the team for consideration. The forward planning editor is responsible for drawing up a weekly prospects list for the assembled team and presents approximately five to fifteen possible news stories for each day of the following week's news programmes. These are introduced by an identification term or 'slug' and a brief two line description. A number of these prospects' entries are included below as originally written, and the ensuing comments from the assembled team transcribed. Each of these stories, while illustrating something of the speed with which decisions are made and possible journalistic 'frames' put in place, also reveal some of the most pressing journalistic values organizing regional news and its portrayal of regional 'social ills'.

WARM –   Birmingham's campaign to keep the old folks warm.

Forward planning editor   WARM – Birmingham's campaign to keep the old folks warm. They've got Father Christmas going round delivering copies of a booklet printed in about nine different languages.

Crew co-ordinator   Do they burn well!

Forward planning editor   It's telling them how to keep warm in the winter. We haven't done anything on that at all, have we?

Programme editor   Well let's have a sniff around the subject and see if there's more to it; it might make a peg for us to do something else but in itself it's deeply boring.

Forward planning editor   Yep, yes.

Programme editor   They print almost everything in Chinese and Vietnamese these days, I don't think there's anything in that. That's a maybe thing.

As well as the extremely compressed and fleeting consideration advanced towards possible news items, this exchange alerts us to a number of factors influencing the selection of possible news stories – remembering that these prospects are themselves already the result of previous selections made by the forward planning team. The forward planning editor identifies three elements which might enhance its attraction as a possible news item. First, the fact that Birmingham City Council, a major institution, has launched a campaign to help old people keep warm; second, given the Christmas season they have enrolled the services of Father Christmas; and third, the fact that the leaflets are printed in about nine different languages. The crew co-ordinator's cynicism/humour, frequently found to attend journalist discussions, is passed over, and the forward planning editor emphasizes via a rhetorical question that 'we haven't done anything on that have we', producing a further possible reason for its inclusion. Remaining unconvinced, the programme editor considers the item as a possible 'peg' on which a different story could be hung. The story is thought to be 'deeply boring' however, and the variety of languages and ethnic diversity of the region's elderly seen as of little intrinsic interest.

LONELY –   25th anniversary of the YMCA's Christmas Day Campaign.

Forward planning editor   LONELY – it's the 25th anniversary of the YMCA's Christmas day campaign, they build up the campaign, how they look after people over Christmas, how they feed them, the work that goes into preparing Christmas day; they've got pictures, slides, etcetera, and we can talk to people about how they prepare for looking after people at Christmas.

Programme editor   Well that's possible, as we're getting nearer to Christmas.

Forward planning editor   I'll run some checks on it.

Programme editor   If we do that it's going to have to be widened out; we're going to have to get on the streets and track down the lonely and all the rest of it.

Forward planning editor   Yes I'm sure they could help us do that, if we're interested in doing that.

Programme editor   And presumably there isn't a cardboard city in Birmingham is there?

Forward planning editor   No I don't think there is.

Programme editor   There's too many hostels presumably.

Forward planning editor   There's that old dear who lives in the doorway down by Newstreet Station.

Programme editor   mmm

Forward planning editor   She even has her milk delivered now.

Programme editor   Yes, it would be interesting to find out, because even if we don't do it, then we might want to know where they are, a bit nearer or around Christmas. So we can do that sort of *Upstairs–Downstairs* piece.

This possible item reveals other features of the regional news programme disposition with its possible celebration of the YMCA's 25th anniversary. It also demonstrates how news sources, increasingly well versed in the needs of the news medium, have come forward with a number of aids to encourage and assist the desired publicity of this particular organization and its concerns. Perhaps the most illuminating aspect of this exchange however, is the manner in which the plight of homeless people can be rendered into a seemingly annual ritual where the rehearsed '*Upstairs–Downstairs* piece' can once again be deployed and help structure the news treatment. This refers, intertextually, to a popular ITV drama series in which the lives of servants and their social superiors are focused in relation to a particular household. The tendency to personalize wider collective realities also informs the suggested news treatment. Here the forward planning editor's knowledge of a homeless 'old dear' who 'even has her milk delivered' is offered as a way of enhancing the news interest. As such it provides further insight into the disposition of regional news and its search for an individual, humanizing, focus.

YOUTH –   Drive for Youth, charity formed to find jobs for unemployed youngsters, starts 10 day tour in Birmingham.

Forward planning editor   YOUTH – it's a drive for youth, it's a charity that goes round the country that tries to get kids jobs. They've started a ten day tour from Birmingham on Monday. It sounds very dull. But I'll give them a ring.

Programme editor   Well again it's something to humanise, you need to get hold of individual unemployed kids.

The forward planning editor anticipating the programme editor's response, seeks to salvage the story, declaring that he's going to find out more about this particular story despite the fact that 'it sounds very dull'. The programme editor, always keen to inflect such stories in terms of the popular appeal of the regional news programme, immediately suggests that it's 'something to humanise' by finding 'individual unemployed kids'. It is apparent that the issue of youth unemployment informing the charity's efforts is not of focal interest here, which is regarded as 'very dull', but rather the possibility of finding human interest via unemployed individuals. It is this, and not the overall problem of youth unemployment or, indeed, the actions of the charity involved, that will determine its eventual news inclusion.

COUNTRYSIDE – Conference on Crisis in the Countryside. The plight of the rural poor at Aldridge.

Programme editor COUNTRYSIDE that needs a bit of exploration, it sounds terribly worthy at the moment, plight of the countryside and all that.

Forward planning editor Yeah, what they're saying you know, they're saying all about the inner cities this and that other, there's a lot of poor in the countryside, but I mean it sounds very dull.

Programme editor Well let's explore it a bit before we chuck it, to see if it comes to anything.

This item is also considered 'terribly worthy' and 'very dull'. In itself, the plight of the rural poor appears to be of little news interest, though the forward planning editor relays the organizer's attempts to link the issue to the public debate over the inner city. That is, a possible variation on an established theme is offered as increasing the unusualness of the news item and hence its regional news value. The programme editor, not holding out much hope for its inclusion, however, defers the final rejection decision just in case the story develops further lines of news interest.

DIRECTORS – Duke of Gloucester and Eric Forth, Minister for Inner Cities at Institute of Directors Conference on Making the Most of The Midlands.

Forward planning editor This sounds fairly boring. The Duke of Gloucester and the Minister for the Inner Cities at the Institute of Directors conference which is a sort of morning to lunch time one, but it sounds desperately boring.

News editor It could be very boring.

Programme editor It sounds as if there will be very boring people there.

In line with the programme's populist inclinations, political and social elites are not guaranteed routine access within regional news programming by virtue of their status alone. In this sense, the deliberations above represent a typical regional news response to a ministerial visit or political statement. A general antipathy to the formal world of politics and politicians, which is regarded as 'boring' unless of major national prominence and/or immediate regional impact, militates against the inclusion of such items. This is notwithstanding the fact that a minister for the inner cities is present at a conference which addresses possibilities for business development and expansion in a region in which such developments are desperately needed by the region's unemployed. Though other stories have gone on to be considered if a human interest angle can be found, it is noticeable that this story does not even merit this consideration from the news producers.

Taken together, these selected examples of decision making illustrate a number of features of the news producers' programme aims. Each impacts upon the selection and non-selection of inner city news items as well as their form of eventual news treatment or inflexion. These include: a revealed antipathy to the formal world of politics; a pursuit of stories which also include 'good' pictures; the quest for popular appeal via stories with either intrinsic, or which are capable of sustaining, human interest; and, relatedly, a tendency to focus stories through an individual viewpoint. In such terms the programme, contrary to professional claims, does not appear to be unduly concerned to 'reflect the ills of the region'. Rather, it has been observed to be principally concerned to pursue its popular ambition via human interest, an ambition which indirectly displaces the wider realities of inner city conditions and experience.

Regional news producers have sought to inscribe human interest by focusing upon a particular individual, preferably an unusual individual, around which a story can be shaped. The tendency of regional news journalists to think in such individualized terms, and the limitations of such an approach when approaching the collective realities of the inner city, was further illustrated by a regional reporter below.

People having problems with their rent, damp houses and things, there's so many of them. Unless they are exceptional they'll never make it, maybe the local paper – I mean the very local paper. Like the *Redditch Indicator* for instance would do the story about a Redditch person perhaps, but it wouldn't really be any good for us at all unless there was something astonishing about it.

Contrary to the professional position above, it can be countered that it is precisely the ordinary nature of urban distress, involving collective problems with rent and damp houses and all the other generalized ills of urban and social deprivation found concentrated in the marginalized environs of the region, that is astonishing; in other words, that needs public representation and explanation. When viewed in collective terms it is these widespread problems and difficulties which characterize an important part of the inner city situation, and yet it is this same reality which is likely to be passed over unless an exceptional individual case can be found to make it newsworthy. The limitations of such an individualized approach to the problems and difficulties confronted across the region are apparent.

The pursuit of human interest, then, has been found to be a core ingredient of the programme's sought popular appeal. In the context of inner city reporting this has frequently assumed the form of the pursuit of 'personalized troubles'. To borrow a distinction from C. Wright Mills, it is the 'personal troubles of milieu' and not 'the public issues of social structure' which are forefronted in the journalistic imagination of regional news producers, though even the milieu is likely to find sparse news attention (Mills 1975: 14). As such, the politics of collective struggle and contending views tends to be displaced from public view. The following statement by a former programme editor, in which a number of past regional news stories and their characteristic form of news treatment are described, confirms the general tendency to 'personalize' important public issues.

We're in television, we're not *The Sunday Times* that's got a whole page to do it. So we have to do two things: we've got to impart information in as fair a way as we possibly can, but we've got to tell it in quite a short time in visual terms. So therefore, to give you a perfect example, yesterday a unit which looks after children with heart troubles in the whole of the West Midlands is being reduced quite severely. We could have just told the story as it was, or we could tell people that it's being reduced and the effect it has is THIS. So you always look for the consequences of the story. So you a get a family whose child has been told it can't have the heart operation. You find a bloke in Handsworth who says he's been badly beaten up by fascist thugs for instance. We did a story on the police opening up an anonymous telephone line for people who were victims of racial attacks rather than just go and have a boring black councillor talk about it, and turn people off, because they're just not interested. We found a woman from Wolverhampton who had been subjected to nasty telephone calls and she taped them. So there we had an example and we say to people 'Here's a new telephone service to stop racial attacks, it may not seem much to you, but this is the effect it has on people'.

The examples offered by the former programme editor illustrate the way in which journalistic treatments may typically seek to inflect a news story, appealing to viewer empathies and sympathies by personalizing the issue in hand. The former editor accounts for this particular journalistic style by indicating that it is a response to the restricted time available for the delivery of separate news stories. This, however, is not strictly accurate with news items delivered in anything between eighteen second news reports to features running up to eight or nine minutes – durations that are relatively generous by TV news standards. The manner in which such items are treated, journalistically, could also be very different if conforming to a different set of programme conventions and appeals. However, it is the tendency to structure news items around the personal accounts and experiences of individuals, as opposed to the elaboration and involvement of wider social viewpoints and issues, that is of particular interest here.

It is maintained above, for example, that the story of the cut-backs in a child heart unit could have been 'told as it was' or the effects could be given added poignancy by 'finding a family whose child has been told it can't have the heart operation'. This technique threatens to displace the issues by concentrating upon the human plight of an individual family, failing to contextualize such an event within the wider political debate and contest surrounding the funding of the National Health Service. To focus on a particular family involving, perhaps, the anguished and emotional appeals of those immediately involved, does not automatically raise the issues. What it does do is conform to the programme's populist ambitions to 'touch' the viewer, appealing direct to human sympathies and empathy.

Similarly, to 'find a bloke who says he's been badly beaten up by fascist thugs' though drawing attention to the individual experience of violent attack, does not explore the wider context and issues known to inform patterns of inner city racial attack. Relatedly, the 'boring black councillor' may be exactly the person to provide an informed overview of the frequency, patterns and possible motivations of racial abuse and attack. As it is, the appeal to empathetic understanding does not illuminate the wider patterns and collective realities behind such individual occurrences. The 'boring black councillor', if asked, would probably have been able to provide exactly the sort of wider overview unavailable to the individual attack victim, and now, by default, denied to the wider public. It also remains unclear why the editor should assume that racist telephone calls 'may not seem much to you', though it is unlikely that a wider understanding of the contours of racial tension, harassment and violence experienced by many inner city residents is likely to be communicated with reference to one individual's experience.

Taking these examples as offered by the senior news producer, it is apparent that the pursuit of human interest has frequently individualized the portrayal of serious social issues and realities experienced by groups of inner city residents, and has thereby failed to reflect the collective nature of such social ills. When combined with the regional journalist's lack of interest in the plight of the elderly, unemployed youth, the poor or even a ministerial visit to a depressed inner city region because such are perceived in regional news terms to be boring, dull or worthy, the prospects for detailed and serious news representation of the region's social ills look poor indeed.

Reporting 'race', racial discrimination and social injustice

Problems of racism and racial disadvantage have previously been identified at the heart of the radical discourse and its interpretation of many of Britain's inner city disorders. This discourse, more than any other, points to the systematic and structural nature of inner city inequality and the manner in which processes of racial discrimination have marginalized certain minority communities. How the regional news programme practically produces news concerned with the region's ethnic minorities is therefore of considerable interest. Outside of the programme's noted predilection for inner city crime and law and order news, issues of 'race' do not figure prominently within the newsroom's priorities of news interests. Where issues of 'race' and minority ethnicity have found a degree of professional regional news interest is in line with the programme's bid to celebrate cultural diversity and spectacle. Consider the following forward planning meeting discussion.

DIWALI –   Hindu new year starts today.

Forward planning editor   Right, we had some dancing which we didn't do earlier this week on Hindu, we just put it back to say 'the Hindu Diwali new year, starts on the 9th'. Whether there's anything going on I don't know.

News editor   All the temples are decked out, it's a massive event, I mean bearing in mind there's about half a million of them in the patch.

Programme editor   Well, we're going to have to find something worth shooting aren't we?

Forward planning editor   Yes.

News editor   Usually there's the big temple in aah . . . it's the biggest centre in the country, very colourful.

Sports editor   Handsworth High Street, Soho Road are normally quite pretty, decked out with fairy lights and things.

Programme editor   What we need to do then is check on Tuesday night, I think we should do it.

News editor   It helps with the old IBA gravy train doesn't it.

Though the forward planner appears to have little knowledge or understanding about this event, the news editor stresses the fact that 'there's about half a million of them in the patch' prompting the programme editor to declare 'we're going to have to find something worth shooting'. The comments of the editors, couched in terms which stress the pictorial quality of the piece, suggest the central appeal of the item while the concluding comment by the news editor, delivered half in jest, also indicates that a felt obligation towards the reporting of the region's minority communities and cultures, though occasionally implemented on regional news criteria alone, is also motivated by a wider climate of institutionalized concern, though this may not be entirely welcome. Significant numbers, pictorial quality and a climate of multi-culturalism, institutionalized in IBA requests for ITV contractors to be 'socially responsible', combine to ensure the eventual inclusion of this news item.

WALK –   5,000 walkers expected on 10 mile hike from Handsworth Park to B'ham City centre and back in aid of Jamaican hurricane disaster appeal.

Forward planning editor   WALK – apparently they're expecting 5,000.

Programme editor   That's a bit better than normal.

Forward planning editor   Yes it's a 10 mile hike from Handsworth park, it's in aid of the Jamaican hurricane disaster appeal.

Programme editor   Now I must say, we've had a lot of phone calls from people locally about this Jamaican disaster fund, it was first of all people worried about relatives because the Foreign Office were playing silly buggers. I think it's a good idea to cover it, obviously there's a lot of interest, there's a lot of relatives.

Forward planning editor   Yes, they've got Cyril Regis walking and they've got Bunny Johnson the boxer, he's walking and there's several others, they're hoping to get several other black superstars to do the walk.

This brief discussion is also revealing in a number of respects. Once again the anticipated numbers of people on the walk cannot be ignored. The amount of response already encountered by the programme editor and the numbers of local people indirectly affected by the hurricane also point to a sizable constituency of interest within the region. In addition, attending public personalities also grants the story further regional news appeal. Together, these afford enough news interest for the programme editor to readily accept the story.

If such items are found to offer one of the few means for minority representation within the regional news programme, other than crime and disorder news, the antipathy held by regional news producers towards the formal world of politics observed earlier also impacts upon the reporting of issues of 'race' and racism. The pursuit of a popular based programme is found to displace issues of formalized politics traditionally thought to be at the heart of serious forms of journalism, and the profession's self-proclaimed informing democratic mission. Rarely are political questions and issues pursued in terms of the formal arrangements of political parties and local administration in regional news. This can be accounted for in terms of the perceived 'boring' nature of formal politics, already hinted at in some of the transcribed comments considered earlier, with politics and politicians tending to be seen as too distant, too removed from the mundane concerns and circumstances of ordinary people and offering little opportunity for indulging the programme's predilection for human interest. Referring to local government the programme editor maintains, for example:

It's a difficult subject to make attractive to anybody, whether it's newspapers or anywhere else. Unless there something of interest to our viewers there's no point in attempting to tackle a lot of subjects. We've got to do stories that are of general interest enough, or can be personalised to make them of general interest enough to be interesting to the whole of the region.

In the context of news reporting of issues of 'race' and racism this programme silence has a particularly detrimental impact. Issues of local decision making, democratic involvement and community control have often been placed at the centre of radical critiques of the inner city problem, with minority communities seen as effectively disenfranchised from democratic processes and decision making fora. Moreover, the extent to which the changing relationship between central and local government has had a pronounced effect on inner city communities, altering the amount of public funds and services that can be locally administered to the benefit of such localities, is also set to be under-reported by existing programme news priorities and interests.

Recognizing that formal politics is not prominent within the regional programme the programme editor and news editor have observed 'there are other vehicles for that anyway. You've got *Central Lobby*'. Clearly, given this general programme antipathy to formal politics, as well as the routinized production, as opposed to investigative pursuit of news stories, the centrality of politics within the inner city contest appears destined to find little expression within this particular programme form. To what extent and in what form regional current affairs programmes have, in fact, addressed the political chasm of regional news will be considered later.

A recent development within the organization of regional news production, however, holds out the promise for improved minority representation and news visibility. This concerns the initiative of a newly appointed programme editor in which two newsroom reporters were given the special responsibility for establishing source contacts with, and generating stories about, the region's Asian and Afro-Caribbean communities. Newsroom journalists, though tending to specialize informally in relation to certain types of stories, whether arts and culture, health and education, agriculture and countryside, or comic relief and so on, have not generally assumed the position of exclusively specialist reporters. Given the changing dictates of the roster, staffing levels and constant career moves of personnel as well as sought flexibility built into the organization of the news process itself such specialization has not characterized the newsroom operation to any prominent degree. This most recent development, then, is novel and was prompted by the latest programme editor's identification of a serious programme void. Keen that the programme should reflect the region's diverse cultures and minority groups, the editor outlined his initiative as follows:

So what I'm going to do is pull some of the more seasoned reporters off the roster and send them down there to make contacts with people. And maybe, as you find with all journalism, once you start to do one or two stories people come out of their shells a bit more, and you tend to do more. So there's a definite gap there, a definite gap that needs to be filled.

Though recognizing the need for such a development, it is interesting to note that the programme editor tends to distance, spatially as well as culturally, the region's ethnic communities to some other place, 'down there', and seemingly implies that the lack of minority news visibility is in considerable measure based on the communities' own reticence to 'come out of their shells'. This fails to appreciate the extent to which existing regional news interests, daily displayed in the regional news programme, may be regarded by some sections of the region's communities as an unlikely vehicle for adequate representation. That said, a programme void has none the less been identified by the programme editor and some newsroom reporters.

If you look at our output, they're generally white stories about the white community, you've only got to look at the programme over a few weeks, and I think most people would say that's true. And there are huge community areas in the cities of Wolverhampton, Coventry, Birmingham that are predominantly Asian, or Afro-Caribbean. They've got good stories too, that we don't necessarily hear from them. But I'm not talking about positive discrimination, I suppose I'm just talking about being aware of stories coming in and wanting to do them. (specialist reporter)

The inherent risk that such an initiative may result in merely further extending established regional news priorities, interests and appeals under the rhetoric of increased programme representativeness, is a possible scenario already intimated in some of the observations offered by senior news producers. In accounting for this recent development, for example, the acting news editor has observed:

I think we are seeking bigger and bigger audiences, we make no apologies for that. If all of a sudden, I don't know how many people of Afro-Caribbean origin there are in the region, but it must be getting on for a quarter of a million, half a million. And if half a million people out there took up knitting over night, we'd do articles on knitting. It's no different. And we'd also cover knitting in its full range of stories, from people being murdered by knitting needles to people knitting 25 foot long scarves. The absurd and the serious, and I think that's exactly what we want to do by looking at these communities. To do the nice stories about the festivals, the holidays, the success stories about the kids doing well, the black businessman who has come from Handsworth who's now employing twelve other people besides himself, as well as the hard luck stories of which there are probably an inordinate number. You know, social security, immigration. If you're not careful you end up by doing those all the time, and that just gets depressing for everybody concerned. It doesn't reflect all the aspects of community life.

Informed as much by the pursuit of increased audiences as a proclaimed mission to 'reflect the life of the region' the statement demonstrates, amusingly, how regional news pursuing both the serious and the absurd is poised to selectively appropriate and inflect such stories in line with established programme interests. Indeed the editor supplies a list of just such 'representative' stories envisaged of likely appeal and future involvement. It was such stories as these, already encountered above and systematically detailed later, that can be seen as providing little in the way of informed insight into either the daily difficulties and problems encountered by inner city communities, while the pursuit of the exotica and spectacle of cultural difference represented within the 'steel bands, saris and samosas' approach to minority ethnic cultures can be seen, at best, as a superficial response to questions of regional ethnic diversity and difference. Once again it can also be observed how the statement points to the regional journalistic tendency to reduce the collective nature of social problems to an inordinate number of individual hard luck stories. These, in any case, are thought to be best left for sparing coverage given their depressive effect. In short, the professional journalist's pursuit of established regional news interests and appeals portends badly for any hoped for improvement upon the representation of the region's minority communities, their ways of life, collective aspirations and responses to common difficulties.

Producing disorder news

The discussion cannot end without also addressing the events of Handsworth/Lozells 1985. These major disorders, like others around the country, have helped place the inner city on the public agenda. In regional news terms, the Handsworth riots of 1985 (as these events have become generally known) represent a major news story. The drama and scale of these events continue to be remembered by those newsroom personnel involved at the time and continue to inform current news reports on Handsworth. One seasoned reporter stated unequivocally that 'Handsworth was the high point of my career'. In terms of news value, of course, the Handsworth riots represented a dramatic and visually compelling outbreak of serious social conflict and disorder – all key ingredients to a good story. To return to the programme editor's words above, not only does a good story include 'immediacy, and freshness, with an element of human interest running through it', it must also have:

a degree of conflict within it as well; opposing points of view are always an attractive option for a journalist looking for a story. Controversy is something that's going to grab someone's attention rather than something which is a more passive experience. News to my mind, is about hitting people between the eyes and saying 'hey look'.

The Handsworth riots on all these counts was, of course, a good, even spectacular news story. A story moreover which promises to constantly return to inform present news items relating to Handsworth. Clearly conflict was at the heart of the Handsworth riots, though the extent to which the contending viewpoints in play gained equal access will have to wait until the detailed analysis presented later. Interestingly, the regional news predilection for more positive news features manages to inflect even the most serious of urban disorders. Keen to celebrate and affirm as well as report and inform, the pursuit of 'happy news' informs the regional news programme and is deliberately sought by reporters.

In this regard the Handsworth riots and subsequent Handsworth stories are apt to involve either a 'trouble' or a 'happy news' frame. Immediately prior to the 1988 Handsworth Carnival for instance, a newsroom reporter related how a memo was sent to all reporters to wear their bleepers 'in case of possible trouble'. The morning prospects list compiled by the news editor also confirms the continuing legacy of the Handsworth riots on Handsworth reporting; though conflict and violence was absent from the carnival, the event continues to be informed in such terms none the less (see Halloran, Elliott and Murdock 1970).

HANDSWORTH –   One quarter of a million enjoy themselves over the weekend at Handsworth. No trouble, biggest and best yet.

Though the possibility of trouble always looms large on the journalist's horizon of interests, the regional news pursuit of more 'happy' stories involving liberal doses of human interest can also inform the professional appropriation of inner city events and activities.

It's nice to get to the stage where you are not just on the hunt for the problems. The obvious thing here is to go down to Handsworth and see if there's any more trouble brewing. Which isn't really a very rewarding brief to be given, it's just a sort of trouble shoot. It's much more interesting to take the thing over a longer period of time and say we'll meet people in a calmer mood and talk to them about what they are doing, see perhaps what the city council is doing to try and help the young Afro-Caribbean kids – they've got a scheme which I'm interested in which is where they are taking some of them back, they are being taken to their parents' or grandparents' roots and learning certain skills in the West Indies. It might be carpentry or whatever and that's a lovely project to get involved in and have a look at. So those stories would be nice to do, and they've got a nice vehicle on Central News to put them out on. (specialist Afro-Caribbean reporter)

Summary

It is now apparent that two regional news orientations inform the production of inner city related news stories. The first is attracted to those major events and happenings breaching societal norms and involving drama, immediacy, conflict and controversy. When brought to bear upon the problems and issues of the inner city we find, perhaps not surprisingly, that crime news and news of serious disorder provide the recurrent ingredients for major news interest. Furthermore, in so far as conflict involves violence and trouble such elements are of themselves newsworthy, and do not necessarily call forth attempts at either contextualisation or explanation.

The second regional news orientation, based within the programme's bid for popular appeal, permits an occasional wider view, going behind those events reported in the hard news stories, and producing features concerned with the lives and activities of ordinary people in a 'calmer mood'. Though features may hold out the promise of a more 'reflective' and even analytic stance to some of those inner city issues and concerns, the pursuit of popular appeal via human interest appears to typically individualize issues which can best be approached as of collective impact and concern.

Clearly it cannot be maintained that news producers should be invested with the omniscient responsibility of disclosing the nature of reality, though frequently the journalist's claim to 'reflect' things as they are can sometimes appear to offer just such a possibility. What can be maintained is that the regional news programme, by the declared ambitions of the professionals involved, should seek to represent the major problems and social ills of the region. From the observations above, such has not been found to be high on the list of regional news priorities. Rather, the journalists involved have sought to select and inflect inner city news stories according to their perceived contribution to the programme's popular appeal. This appears to have impacted differently upon each of the three contending inner city discourses and their principal identified issues and concerns. Though issues of crime, and law and disorder more generally, appear to resonate with news value and are found to be underpinned by organizational routines and institutional source dependencies, such cannot be said of either issues of social deprivation or racism and ethnic minority disadvantage. Here the pronounced tendency to seek out human interest via personalized accounts and experiences, has been found to distance or entirely displace the wider view. The collective realities of inner and outer city existence, socially and spatially marginalized in the region's 'separate territories', have not been at the forefront of journalists' concerns.

To what extent, and in what form, different inner city voices have found access to this news portrayal and managed to advance their contending viewpoints forms the subject matter of newsroom observations in the next chapter.

4
Mediating the inner city: producing inner city voices

Intimately involved in the public contest and debate surrounding important issues are those voices which seek to define the nature of the 'problem' and the correct interpretation and response required. The problems and issues of the inner city are no exception here, of course, with an array of contending voices seeking access to the wider public via the TV media stage. Clearly, 'what gets said' or, equally as important, 'what doesn't get said' in relation to the inner city contest is likely to depend in considerable measure on 'who gets on'. This examination of journalist practices and professional judgements seeks to provide an insight into why certain inner city voices, and not others, have found a prominent public platform from which to advance their particular point of view. Based around three newsroom case studies, the chapter first observes the way in which regional news priorities and practices have impacted upon the accessing of police voices, community voices, and minority ethnic voices. The second part of the chapter then pursues the professional practices and decisions behind the use of different presentational news formats, a further important feature in the public display of contending points of view.

Considerations of access cannot be separated from those journalistic processes in which a 'good' story, that is, a story replete with news value and regional news appeal, is originally conceptualized and pursued by professional journalists. In the first instance this may or may not involve the accessing of others, but it is the initial selection and conceptualization of the story itself which is of primary interest to working journalists. This informs the selection of 'appropriate' voices, and is also implicated in the professional journalist's view of impartiality and objectivity. The programme editor, for example, is in no doubt where the 'truth' resides within a story, and is equally clear about the subordinate role of accessed voices.

The truth is in the sum of the parts, the overall appearance, the overall story. It's not within what one particular person said, even though he (*sic*) might be speaking the truth and speaking very much so right down the line, but in the general overall account . . . and the interviewees are put in as representative of the various points of view, and we're very careful to tag people to whatever point of view, both in terms of editing but also in terms of getting a reasonably clear account/reflection of what they are about, so that people can make up their own minds about whether they are biased.

While positing the news producers in a position of seeming neutrality *vis-à-vis* this 'truth', notwithstanding its dependence on the journalist's understanding of the story and its requirements, the role of accessed others is clearly subordinated to the requirements of the story. Given the previous discussion of the established conventions and appeals characterizing the regional news programme it would be surprising if these did not also colour the professional pursuit and final accessing of inner city voices.

What makes a good interviewee is someone who knows what they are talking about, that's the first thing; they've got to be relevant. So like the fire I was talking about it's got to be the neighbour who fought his way in, or the eyewitness who saw something happening and can say something vivid and relay the passion and the excitement of the moment, and that's quite enthralling. As far as issues are concerned we want someone who knows the issues very well, who represents a clear point of view and who can express themselves properly . . . Now, it doesn't rule out the vox pop, the man in the street, that's a different category and entirely different way of saying things, that's a way of getting reactions to issues, or 'funnies' or whatever. That's giving the ordinary viewer a chance to have their say as well, and to feel that they are being represented. (programme editor)

A good interviewee must, according to this account, be relevant, which in the context of regional news is construed in terms which reflect the programme's bid for popular appeal, typically involving the professional pursuit of immediacy, drama and general human interest. Accessed voices must also be articulate and 'represent a clear point of view'. However, whether a point of view is deemed clear is liable to be influenced by one's own perception and understanding of the field of views in play which, in the search for representative views, appears to be at risk of being polarized into positions of simple opposition. Interestingly, the use of vox pops, to be discussed below, is also mentioned and again it is apparent that such a form of involvement is in accord with the popular ambition of the programme granting the ordinary viewer 'a chance to have their say' and, perhaps more importantly, 'to feel that they are being represented'. At this general level, questions of access can be seen to be intimately related to the overall conceptualization of the regional news programme as pursued and embodied within individual stories.

However, following previous discussions of newsroom routines and organizational practices, it is also the case that institutionalized contacts and dependencies existing between the newsroom and other sources of news are also implicated in the processes of accessing outside voices. The routine reliance of the newsroom on organizational sources, most notably the police, courts, local authorities, large businesses and corporations as well as other media and organized pressure and community groups, has been observed earlier. Here the organizational tendency to routinize the contact with certain institutional news sources has been found to inform regional news production as much as any other large news operation. However, even here the form that such institutional contacts can take is likely to vary according to the professional ambitions for the programme as a whole, and in consequence can generate conflicts and tensions between the aims of the news producers and those of the institutions.

You mustn't get the wrong idea about institutions and journalists; journalists are very suspicious about what they are told by them and try to find out if they are telling the truth. They know, for instance, the West Midlands Police Press Office is pushing out guff all the time, propaganda, they come on the phone with it, they put it on the fax machine, through the post, they contact this man, that man, it's a huge propaganda exercise that's on. We're amazingly wary about that and dislike it intensely. And anybody else who tends to come too far over the top at us we stand a long way back from them. It's easy for a journalist to have a soft option in going for regular calls to the fire brigade and all the rest of it, that's part of your job to do that, that's how you find out that something's been happening that way. Journalists are there not to represent the institutions but the punters. (programme editor)

This populist view of 'representing the punters' is echoed throughout the newsroom and by senior managerial positions. It is all the more surprising therefore, to find that the bulk of unsolicited, solicited and successful source interventions (see Chapter 2, Tables 2.1 and 2.2) do in fact emanate from large corporate and institutional organizations. While a routine reliance upon certain sources is evident within newsroom routines and arrangements this often produces friction and resentment, especially if sources seek to unduly ingratiate themselves within or manipulate the professional practices of news production. Organizational requirements as well as the professional understanding of news pursued can lead to a situation where professional claims to journalistic independence are found, on occasion, to be compromised.

Relations with the police, in particular, cannot necessarily be assumed to be organizationally cordial or, more importantly, as productive of a shared framework of understandings as some commentators have tended to suggest. In other words, while an undoubted reliance upon the police does exist, this can be as much a source of tensions as incremental acceptance of a police-led perspective upon the world of crime, criminality and general policing matters. Referring to the relations with the West Midlands' and other of the region's police forces, the inherent friction and resentments found to characterize such source dependencies are openly admitted.

We can't do anything without them, they keep us at a distance and stop all their officers below Chief Constable from talking to us unless the press office has approved. It's an astonishing way to go on. That's their problem, their 1984 situation of their own making, we work around that as best we can. Other forces are more average: Warwickshire are reasonable to talk to, but quiet, so we don't have a lot of contact; West Mercia, the relationship is a little better; Staffordshire has decided to open the doors a bit more. (programme editor)

Though the day to day relations with the police may not always be as cosy as commentators have sometimes assumed, the fact remains that the police can and do regularly appear within the news and, as documented later, news of the inner city especially. Established regional news interest in crime and policing matters, then, places the newsroom in a position of potential dependence which, in turn, can lead to a situation where the news organization is highly susceptible to police misinformation and propaganda. Numerous examples of organizational reliance upon the accounts and views of the police could be detailed. Here one case study is included which illustrates in the most dramatic way the costs of such a relationship in an important inner city story. Contrary to the ideal of the news story described by the programme editor above, where representative views are found and positioned within an overall account produced and presented by an independent news team, the story is found to be totally framed within and dependent upon the official police perspective.

Case study 1: death in the inner city – police voices

When Clinton McCurbin, a member of the Wolverhampton black community, died from asphyxiation by an arresting police officer's arm lock round his throat the organizational reliance upon the police, as both source of information and contending protagonist within a major news story, granted the police privileged news access. This enabled them to establish an uncontested framework of interpretation while manipulating the media as a conduit for its particular views. The full transcript of the initial news report of this incident is included below, as broadcast.

News presenter   Violence broke out in Wolverhampton this afternoon after the death of a man who'd been arrested by police. There were running fights in the town's main shopping streets involving one hundred youths. Several policemen were hurt, one seriously. Two hundred policemen are patrolling the streets but the town seems to be calm. From the scene, Peter Brookes.

Reporter

The violence was a direct result of the death of a 22 year old man in this town centre boutique early in the afternoon. Police say two officers were called to the shop where the man attempted to buy clothes with a stolen credit card. As they tried to arrest him a scuffle broke out and the man collapsed and died apparently from a heart attack; police say he'd been taking drugs. The two officers tried to revive him with the kiss of life but to no avail. Shortly afterwards fights broke out up and down this street, six people were injured and ten arrested. More than two hundred police officers are now in Wolverhampton town centre.

News presenter

And the police have just announced that an officer from an outside force has been called in to investigate the man's death.

[Rest of programme news . . .]

News presenter

We're going back now to the story about the disturbance in Wolverhampton involving a hundred youths. Several policemen were hurt, one seriously. It happened after a man collapsed and died soon after being arrested. A short time ago West Midlands Police explained what happened.

Supt.Martin Burton

Soon after this man had been arrested a large number of people collected outside this shop. It was quite remarkable where they came from but within a short space of time a large number of people, probably as many as seventy five to a hundred appeared – the word had got round very quickly. The atmosphere was not a very nice atmosphere to say the least. Soon after the ambulance arrived to take the body of the dead person away a senior police officer also arrived because the situation up to that time was deteriorating. Because of the action taken at the time that situation was defused and the ambulance managed to get away. But the people who had congregated spilled out into the surrounding area and disorder did take place. A number of shops were attacked, some looting has taken place and some police officers have been injured; an inspector has had a rather nasty injury to his eye and has only just been discharged from hospital, though I haven't got further details of that at the moment.

News presenter

We will of course bring you more details on that story as it happens in our news later tonight.

This first news report of the death of Clinton McCurbin is revealing. The dependence of the news producers upon the police interpretation of the events in question clearly reveals how a framework of understanding is placed within the public domain which essentially locates the violence as the ensuing disturbance with youths and the serious injury of a police inspector, though on the police account itself this officer had already been discharged from hospital in a matter of hours. The violence which has framed the event, and caught the attention of the news producers, thus appears to be the street disturbances and *not* the violence which has caused a man to lose his life while being arrested. Indeed, the deliberate misinformation, later conceded as expedient to the purposes of the police, concerning the claim that Clinton McCurbin had died from a heart attack probably related to drug abuse, and relayed by news personnel was later found to be entirely without foundation. Importantly, it is also noticeable that at no time in the report is it indicated, either verbally or visually, that the man who has died is black. In the wider context of documented instances of police abuse, harassment and a number of black deaths in police custody as well as local tensions between the police and the black community, such an omission is significant.

If considered carefully, the indebtedness of these news reports on police information and the direct accounts presented by the police themselves clearly leaves little room for alternative or opposing views to be formulated. Why exactly so many youths should feel compelled to congregate and engage the police in disorder is a question which fails to be posed in this news report, which simply accepts the police version of events. To say, for instance, as the reporter did, that the violence 'was a direct result of the death of a 22 year old man' is to postulate a partial understanding of the violence involved in the afternoon's events while also making a causal link which apparently requires no further explanation or contextualization. With constant reference to police statements and accounts as well as the introductory link statement, 'the police explained a short time ago what happened', presented as a matter of fact, is to totally subsume the news report within the interpretative framework established by the police.

The organizational dependence upon the police as a source of information clearly reveals the costs of such a relationship when the police are central protagonists, as they invariably are, within major law and order stories. The subsequent career of this story also indicates how such a reliance is supplemented by the limited foci of regional news interests. Indeed, the subsequent reporting of developments and revelations relating to this major inner city story illustrate that, while the newsroom is not disposed to champion the cause of the police, its repertoire of news interests none the less frequently fails to interrogate such events with an informed awareness of some of the contending perspectives in play. Over subsequent months the McCurbin story was reported in terms of a mass demonstration following in the immediate aftermath of Clinton's death, the coroner's inquiry and verdict and police training methods in unarmed combat. As the programme editor observed at the time of the coroner's inquiry: 'We're fascinated by the armlock and all that sort of thing. And I've got Peter to phone up the police and get them to demonstrate their unarmed combat training, which is a little story in itself, but it's hard to see where the story can go from there. It's a case of waiting.' A newsroom reporter similarly perceived the story:

I think it was basically following on from the outcome of the inquest. And the job then was to get the official Police response to the inquest ruling and also, as we did, we got the mother's reaction and the solicitor's reaction outside the court. So all those flowed very naturally . . . It just happened and you report the story as it is. I don't think the shape of it was altered or it wasn't shaped in any specific way . . . You just report the facts as they are.

Following on from the first news report and its police-led account, the story moves to the official coroner's proceedings and becomes focused upon the question of police training tactics. The principal voices finding access, then, are the police, relatives and their representatives and the coroner. Once established as an important regional news event, the conceptualization of the story determines who is able to speak while ruling out other voices who do not fit into the established frame of reference. This is not to say that the frame of reference is static, indeed the constant search for novel developments or new twists continues to afford different possibilities.

You've got to find somewhere to take it, there was obviously still a lot of public interest about this story still going on today. As a news programme we have to try and find a lead, or something to follow up the next day to keep the story going because people want to know more, that's the assumption you always work with, to make it fresh, to make it interesting again. You look for something which is different, and today it was police training, because that has come under police criticism as well. OK, how exactly are officers trained given that the Police force admitted that the officers were not trained to cope with the situation? (newsroom reporter)

Though the story could have been developed in a number of different ways, no attempt was made to question why the death of Clinton McCurbin should have caused so much street conflict and antagonism. Thus while a camera crew and reporter were consigned to the night streets of Wolverhampton (known in newsroom banter as 'the riot patrol') following police anticipation of further trouble, nowhere was the possible cause of such widespread community tension raised and pursued. Asking the programme editor why this wider question was not broached with members of the Wolverhampton community, the programme editor stated:

No, no it hasn't, and that's difficult to tell. To get that side of the story, ummm you've got to make sure the people you are talking to are representative, and are more than, you know one man with an axe to grind, ummm we'll get that eventually, but that sort of story it seems to me has to tell itself a bit as well. There's got to be a reason for doing that other than the, aaa, I think we did the on-the-day thing alright, aa (sigh) what we might do eventually is we might just sort of sit around umm go out for a day, and sort of follow around one of the community guys and try to film them. The interplay between the two is a hellish difficult thing to try and do. You've got to hide the camera terribly to do that. You've got to eavesdrop to get any flavour of that. It's easy to tell in radio, it's easy to tell in newspapers that story, but in television it's one of the toughest things to do.

While it would be unfair to interpret the editor's loss of normal fluency in the face of such a direct inquiry in any particular way, I think it is fair to surmise that this side of the story was not at the forefront of the programme editor's or wider newsroom's interests, nor was it likely to be pursued in the future. This case study is illustrative of the way in which an organizational dependence upon the police initially helped the police to place a particular interpretative frame upon the McCurbin incident which displaced alternative accounts and frameworks of interpretation. This was achieved by both the relaying of police accounts and also the direct accessing of a police spokesman. However, while this interpretative frame was gradually challenged, with the role of the police officers involved and also wider concerns of police training subjected to a degree of media questioning, at no point was the wider context of this incident explicitly pursued by the news programme. The surrounding context of community suspicion and anger, fuelled by past encounters with the police and general conditions of inner city deprivation, did not find news representation. Rather, following the initial report, the news interest shifted to the unarmed training methods deployed by the West Midlands police force and the possibility of further trouble.

The story indicates that the police are not entirely immune from critical news attention, notwithstanding their continual presence within the news as both source and subject of news stories. It also indicates, however, that such critical investigations tend to be framed within the limited professional horizons of regional news interests. The McCurbin story and its subsequent news treatment provides a dramatic instance of the way in which organizational dependencies *and* professional journalist understandings of such stories fail to look behind the epiphenomena of conflict and tension to their underlying social roots. Contrary to the reporter above, therefore, it is possible to say that the McCurbin incident was shaped in a particular way, and that the inner city voices gaining and not gaining access were instrumental in this.

If the police appear to find privileged access to the news making process and represent an institution of considerable regional news interest, politicians fare less well within the popular appeals of the regional news programme. A typical reaction to a press release received through the post by the programme editor, for example, and concerning a ministerial visit publicizing a governmental inner city initiative, 'Action for Cities', received speedy dispatch to the waste bin in the following terms.

This is part of the free publicity for Government Ministers doing nothing in particular campaign, so we won't be covering that, Norman Fowler doing something intensely boring.

However if the programme's construction of the popular finds politicians and politics removed from the mundane concerns and preoccupations of ordinary people and therefore 'boring', the sought popular appeal permits increased opportunities for the accessing of ordinary people – that is non-elites, people who do not talk for an organization or institution but who represent ordinary individual experiences, 'no-nonsense' common sense, and the sentiments and preoccupations of mundane existence. The value placed on professional experts and ordinary people by the regional news programme is contrasted in the following terms by the programme editor.

Experts we use sparingly, some experts are articulate and can say things succinctly and they're ideal for us, because obviously we don't want everyone looking at this professor, or whoever he is, going on and on about something which is alright but it's not all that riveting. It's far better to get people who are involved, and people who are sitting at home being able to understand someone else's experience, it's all part of keeping your viewer involved in what's going on . . . Experts we use sparingly because often they are not very interesting, because we tend to use speech in bites, that's the style of it all. And the same applies to ordinary people, they're cut down to the bone as well, keeping the better bits of what they say, the more lucid bits of what they say, and that's all part of the skill of editing and putting it together in an intelligible way. The experts are often cut down in what they say to make it more punchy and more to the point.

While the regional news programme does appear to be disposed to access ordinary people it is also apparent, as discussed earlier, that this tends to privilege the experiential dimension over the analytic, the individual experience over collective situation, and frequently appeals to a privatized realm of consumerism rather than the public realm of political citizenship. The reliance upon professional spokespeople, though facilitating the fast production of news and providing the news reporter with his or her required 'sound bite', is none the less a feature which is carefully monitored by regional news producers. This is so, given the programme's ambition and professional pursuit of popular appeal.

What makes an interesting story is something that is happening which basically touches people isn't it? If it's a good big story like a plane crash everybody is interested in that, or a disaster; but if you are talking about a slightly more manufactured story, it seems to me that it's human interest. It's people that are interesting. And I'm not talking about that other thing, 'spokespeople', there seems to be something of an obsession about professional spokespeople. Because they are very easy to interview, you don't have to edit them very much, you edit them in 20 second clips and say 'great !' – it's not very riveting. There's nothing like a good local person, that's why vox pops, you know out on the street with a microphone up peoples' noses, because people give better reactions. A good human interest story with genuine people talking, not spokespeople, I feel makes a very good story . . . On occasion you have to use a spokesperson because of time really, you've no choice. But it's nice, if you are aware of that, to at least try and also speak to members of, well like you and me, members of the public. (newsroom reporter)

The classic way of accessing ordinary, in contrast to elite, voices has been through the use of the 'vox pop' (*vox populi* – 'the people's voice'), the impromptu responses and reactions recorded from members of the public, typically gained on the street. Are these a means by which a differentiated public has managed to find access to the TV stage in relation to the contending viewpoints on the inner city? The first observation in this regard is that vox pops, in the main, tend to be relegated to certain subject areas, and not others.

We obviously do meet a lot of ordinary people particularly on human interest stories; vox pops still seem to be mainly found in silly stories, you know, 'Do you wear socks in bed?', 'How many times do you make love to your wife?' rather than, 'How do you feel about community relations in Lozells?' You're less likely to go down Newstreet and ask people that, I admit. (reporter)

According to a news editor vox pops perform two functions: 'They're a good fast way of getting a straw poll as well as involving your viewers on the programme. So, you know, they can say "yes, that's my daughter" or whatever'. Issues of representation within this professional view become subservient to the programme's bid to involve and engage ordinary viewers, rather than providing a means of genuinely representing contending public views. Vox pops are less concerned, then, with representation, in any meaningful sense of political participation and debate, than with re-presenting members of the public in a highly orchestrated fashion – a public moreover, which is actively assembled and edited to fit the news journalist's story requirements. The claim that vox pops can and do serve a genuinely representative function continues to be made by journalists, however, as this reporter demonstrates:

I think it's a good idea, I think probably this is the best indicator of how the community actually feels, because you're grabbing people unprepared and you're probably getting their true feeling. And you're picking people at random, and you're obviously looking for a balance of viewpoints. You know you could have spoken to ten people and got the same thing so may be you look for a balance so in that respect perhaps a bit of selection.

This curious state of affairs where the vox pop is seen both as a means of 'getting a straw poll' and a 'true' insight into the feelings of the community, as well as the means by which the journalist can find his or her sought 'balance' of views, is a logical contradiction not readily recognized by practising journalists. The case study below demonstrates how community voices can be actively sought, not as a means of representing the extent of collective feeling and opinion but rather as a means of balancing a story, of making it 'stand up' in line with journalist preconceptions. Here the possibility that such professional practices do not only fail to adequately represent collective opinion, but effectively misrepresent community opinion become all too apparent.

Case study 2: vigilantes in the inner city – community voices

When the American group of self-proclaimed vigilantes the Guardian Angels arrived in Handsworth, Birmingham, a political storm erupted with the local MP, Jeff Rooker, leading a campaign for their return to the United States. The story was of great interest to the newsroom and reported at some length. However, the problem remained, contrary to the claims of the Angels themselves, that nobody could be found from Handsworth who would support their arrival and intent to combat street crime. The following newsroom discussion at the morning conference illustrates the journalistic imperative to find a 'balancing' community point of view with which to justify the news attention afforded to the Guardian Angels.

News editor   Yes, a reporter's trying to get a line on this, this morning.

Programme editor   And we must try to get some comment from a community group that will say they want them here.

News editor   The problem is Rooker, who's been in contact with all the community groups in Handsworth, says nobody wants them here. None of the community groups have said they want them here.

Reporter 1   What about getting comments from the street. We've got comment from local 'worthies', police, politicians, what about getting some reaction from people on the street.

Reporter 2   We had a vox pop in that piece yesterday. The 'community' is different from Joe Soap on the street, I'm sure if we could get some reaction from someone in a local street saying 'I'd like them at the end of my street'.

Programme Editor   Yes OK, I can have a certain amount of that stuff but we must find someone who is prepared to say they asked them here.

News Editor   When they were in London six months ago some diverse Asian group had asked them.

Reporter 1   The problem is, probably an Asian youth group asked them here before the community leaders could get hold of them and tell them to put a stop to it, it'll cause too much trouble.

This exchange between journalists keen to make the story 'stand up', illustrates a number of key features impacting upon the accessing of inner city voices. First, an almost desperate bid to find someone, anyone, who will say they invited the Guardian Angels is pursued in order that two sides of the issue can be presented and the story thus presented as a balanced piece of journalism. Second, reference to vox pops is made indicating that perhaps the sought viewpoint could be found, even suggesting the actual form of comments that could be elicited by vox popping local residents. Third, though vox pops are countenanced as permissible and of some use in this instance, a suspicion of 'community representatives' is voiced which implies that grass-roots comment and reaction is likely to be at odds with the representatives of the 'community view'. None the less, the programme editor is determined to find a group who will admit to inviting the Angels over as claimed. A reporter assigned to this particular task recounts his involvement in the following terms.

What we desperately needed, and didn't have at the end of the day, was any group saying that we need them. And we really tried to get hold of a group because otherwise it could seem incredibly unbalanced. But we really tried to get hold of one of those residential groups, or one of those community groups and I tried umpteen times phoning various organizations that wanted the Guardian Angels, but just couldn't. But they just weren't there to be had.

More intent upon balancing the story in order to safeguard the credibility of news impartiality than to reflect the evident uniformity of grass-roots feeling and community opposition to the idea of vigilante groups patrolling inner city streets, tremendous efforts were applied to finding someone who would voice support for the vigilantes. In such cases, the possibility that the strength of community opinion and feeling can be artificially re-presented, and misrepresented, as divided into two opposed camps of equal weight is plain to see.

Vox pops, then, offer the journalist the possibility of providing a quick means of balancing a story, as the reporter so graphically indicated above, by getting 'out on the street with a microphone up peoples' noses'. The pursuit of organizational voices, particularly in the context of major news stories, none the less remains. This is not simply accountable by newsroom procedures and the pursuit of guaranteed, easily accessed views and opinions. The noticeable silence of the voices of black youth across the entirety of the Handsworth riots coverage, for example, is explained by an involved newsroom reporter in the following way.

Yes I have to admit, as you know, it's standard procedure. One of the problems is that it's one of the tenets of the media, unless you can describe someone as something then somehow they don't carry any weight. And therefore simply, 'Winston Smith, black youth', as a caption doesn't carry any weight. But

'Winston Smith, community leader' does carry weight. And that in itself is a reason for talking to him, if you can put that as a caption.

Though ordinary people and their reactions are taken to be the stuff of vox pops, and the regional news programme as a whole places great store upon accessing ordinary people, when it comes to a contentious issue, an issue going to the heart of the inner city debate, the voices and views of ordinary black youth are not considered representative. Their viewpoints failed to find public expression and were also exempt from close public scrutiny and discussion. The search for community leaders and representative figures, therefore, is more than an organizational requirement reflecting the pressures of time and limited resources involved in finding appropriate 'sound bites'; it reflects the pursuit of representative figures, spokespeople, who can speak with a degree of authority for others and is based within the journalists' pursuit of news credibility and programme authority. If the Clinton McCurbin story demonstrated the extent to which issues of access are dependent upon the professional conceptualization of the story and routine source dependency, the practical difficulties of finding representative voices in a situation characterized by diverse viewpoints can also be recognized.

The Handsworth riots was a classical case of, immediately after it happened, who do you get to talk about it? This television station staged through the day special half hour programmes and they included representatives of the black community. Each time virtually one of these programmes went out the phones started to ring with other members of the black community saying, 'why weren't we offered the opportunity, they don't represent us', and that's the problem. Bit by bit they were on, they did get on but you wouldn't find one lot that would say the other lot was representative. We had some on, of what the younger generation would call 'Uncle Toms', who were virtually apologising for what had happened there, and that upset others. It wasn't easy at all. There isn't an agency that you can go to who says, 'black community Handsworth, he's the one, you've got to speak to him'. (reporter)

Faced with such apparent pluralism it might be assumed that the professionals would seek to chart the contending positions in play, indicating lines of difference as well as commonality. The pursuit of representative, that is, organizationally based and authoritative voices permits little opportunity for genuine representation of community differences to be publicly aired and known. Once again, issues of simple balance and the programme's bid for credibility and authority have reduced the question of genuine representation to a secondary concern. In the context of the Handsworth riots, where ordinary members of the community including many black youths took to the streets and engaged the forces of law and order in confrontation, it is all the more important that such voices be found, and provided with an opportunity to put their case. The very fact that some sections of the community could refer to accessed spokespeople in terms interpreted by the reporter as 'Uncle Toms', indicates that alternative and opposing views did exist which were not receiving public expression, and that the news programme was seen by sections of the community as an important vehicle for these.

Case study 3: reporting the Rushdie affair – ethnic voices

Journalists can also actively orchestrate different voices, including vox pops, into a form of polarized opinion which tells us more about the professional conceptualization of the story and its requirements than any genuine attempt to represent the diversity and differentiated nature of public views and opinions.[1] This study also provides a number of insights of more general relevance to the examination of regional inner city news production as a whole.

Perhaps one of the most challenging developments in community relations in recent times concerns the public furore surrounding the so called 'Rushdie affair' following the publication of Salman Rushdie's *The Satanic Verses*. This incident indicates that not all ethnic minorities either seek or can be expected to assimilate white British customs and ways of life, preferring to maintain and defend established cultural identities and practices. As such, the Rushdie incident throws into sharp relief something of the divergences and differences of opinion that can be found within and across ethnic relations, including those of the dominant ethnic group. How such differences of opinion are publicly communicated, and whose voices are permitted to represent the issues, proves of vital importance to wider public understanding of the issues and complexities involved.

The news story examined, though originally pursued by journalists as an ordinary news report, in fact developed throughout the course of the day to become the programme's lead story. Initially informed by phone, the forward planning team alerted the newsdesk of a major rally and march by members of Birmingham's Muslim population against the continuing publication of *The Satanic Verses*. Though previous demonstrations had taken place, a reporter was assigned to this one, since it appeared likely to involve considerable numbers of Birmingham's Muslim population in an unusual weekday protest. The exact form this story might assume, however, was as yet unknown. The reporter attended the rally with a brief containing technical and logistical details only. Having directed the camera crew over the shots sought at this mid-morning rally, the reporter later met up with the crew at the march destination point, the public square outside Birmingham Council House and Central Public Library. Here a further demonstration was held and a petition delivered to a council meeting. An interview with the march organizer in the park was followed by one with a Muslim councillor outside the Council House, and this report was then dovetailed with a piece from a second reporter, involving an interview with the city's librarian and a number of impromptu vox pops. The following is the full transcript of the actual words broadcast in this leading news item, including the introductory 'tease' statement.

Tease	Council set to ban *Satanic Verses* after thousands march in protest.
News presenter	Good evening, Central News this Tuesday. Salman Rushdie's controversial book *The Satanic Verses* looks set to be banned from schools and public libraries in Birmingham. The Council's ruling Labour group has voted to consider the ban after thousands of Muslims marched through the city to hand in a petition. The National Union of Teachers has deplored the move, calling it a form of censorship.
Reporter	The vote is the first step on the way to a ban on Rushdie's book. It followed a march through the city by thousands of Muslims. Scuffles broke out between pro- and anti-Khomeini groups but march marshals quickly dispersed the rival gangs before the police were needed. Organizers said they wanted the book banned and were against the death sentence issued by the ayatollah.
Interviewee [march organizer]	I cannot agree at all. That may be an excuse for the British government to come out and not accept their responsibility. What we are asking for is the British government is, first it owes allegiance to the British citizens. We are all Muslims living in this country for the last 20 years and we have a right over the government to ask them to protect our rights.
Reporter	The Rushdie affair had disappeared from the headlines recently but an action committee has been formed to keep pressure on politicians.
Interviewee	In our minds the book has to be banned. The book must be stopped from circulation.
Reporter	In order to do that a change in the law would be required; a change in the defamation laws. Do you think that is a realistic objective?
Interviewee	That is the only realistic objective. We are asking the government to change the law to include Islam as one of the religions to be protected from such vilifying attempts which are made against any religion.
Reporter	The march gathered more support as it was shepherded through Small Heath and Balsall Heath. Eventually an estimated four thousand converged on the Council House, police flanking the demonstrators throughout. Inside the city council meeting a petition was handed in and a motion carried to consider banning the book from schools and public libraries.

	Muslim councillors deny the ban would be an infringement of civil liberties.
Interviewee [councillor]	The community at large need to understand, I think, that under the banner of the freedom of the press the freedom does not give anybody licence to abuse or insult any religion. The situation here is that the author as well as the printer have misused the freedom of the press. And what we are asking is that this book should be withdrawn. That is the only solution if we want race relations and we want to live peacefully and in harmony.
Reporter	The city council encourages links between all ethnic groups. Some Labour councillors say the decision to consider a ban is simply meeting the demands of the city's 70,000 Muslims.
Reporter 2	Birmingham Central Library has 36 copies of *The Satanic Verses*, between 50 and 80 people are waiting to borrow the book although it is not on public display. The senior librarian says popularity of the book has come with publicity. But he believes in people's right to choose what they read.
Librarian	I personally have an opinion that freedom of expression is important for everyone. I don't know what the circumstances, as I say, at this time I don't even know what the city council decision is.
Reporter 2	Today it seemed anybody prepared to comment strongly opposed a ban in libraries or schools.
Vox pop 1	Well, I think the consequences will be with the Muslims in this country being totally alienated in our society and years of work of integrating Muslims into our society will be destroyed.
Vox pop 2	I think people should be able to read what they want. Given a choice of opinion about what they want to read, I don't think it should be banned at all.
Vox pop 3	If people want to read it they should be allowed to. I don't think there is any harm in it. It's allowed to be published so I don't think people shouldn't be allowed to read the book.
Vox pop 4	Unless we can express our mind it's the end of democracy.
Reporter 2	Have you read the book?
Vox pop 4	Parts of it, I've been told the relevant parts.
Reporter 2	And what do you think about it?
Vox pop 4	It doesn't seem that important to me that anyone reads it.

Reporter 2	Meanwhile copies of Salman Rushdie's book are in short supply at city centre shops. Hudson's had sold out and W.H. Smith had only a couple of copies under the counter. A spokesman said, sale of the book had provoked some threats which are being investigated by West Midlands police.

The first general observation that can be made about this story is, contrary to the impression promoted by the news item, the basis for asserting 'Council set to ban *Satanic Verses*' was very slight. Already aware of the public interest around the Rushdie affair, the reporter assigned to the march believed he was in possession of something of a news scoop, that is, a story which would both regionalize and augment the undoubted interest over the Rushdie affair with a development which would prove both controversial and conflict laden.

A reporter having attended the morning rally, an ordinary news report was filed and duly broadcast in the lunch-time bulletin. This was presented in the following 'trouble' terms: 'Thousands of Muslims are in Birmingham for a rally over the Salman Rushdie book *The Satanic Verses*. Minor scuffles broke out between pro- and anti-Khomeini supporters but were brought under control by rally organisers'. This particular trouble frame, discussed further below, though a particular construction of the event, was later superseded by the notion that Birmingham City Council appeared set to ban the book from public libraries and schools. At this point, both the reporter's and the newsdesk's interest increased considerably, and the story was promoted to a contender for the programme's lead news item of the day.

But the fact of the matter was that a petition had simply been delivered to a council meeting and a decision had been taken to refer the matter to the meeting of the leisure services committee. At no point had the council appeared set to ban *The Satanic Verses*, much less decided to ban the book, as the second reporter informed her numerous interviewees before eliciting their reactions. The lead story, in other words, was the result of a collective journalistic pursuit of the latest Rushdie development and news scoop which failed to attend to the actual details of the developments. As the chief librarian's office later confirmed, the decision to refer the matter to the leisure services committee for discussion could not conceivably be interpreted, contrary to the opening 'tease' statement, as 'Council set to ban *Satanic Verses*'. This, however, was exactly the story as presented by the news account. If the general propositional thrust of the story can therefore be challenged, so too can the journalistic tendency to emphasize conflict and trouble, which becomes clear when the production process is observed close up. This involves both the collection and the subsequent editing of visual footage and verbal statements, as well as the imposition of a journalistic commentary or voice-over.

In the main, the visual component of this item involved two aspects. First, the close-up shots (head and shoulders) of interviewees when interviewed by one of the two assigned reporters and, second, selected shots of the assembled crowds at both the initial rally and the march destination point. As to the former, no general observations are especially revealing other than their highly reduced visual involvement given the selected sound bites (snippets of interviews) included in the final news presentation. However, concerning the scenes of the rally and demonstration itself (witnessed both in person and through reviewing all the ENG rushes shot by the camera crews), an obvious contrast emerges between the generality of such scenes and the scenes finally selected and broadcast. While the rally was generally peaceful and characterized by assembled groups of Muslim men and male youths occasionally breaking into led chants and shouts; march organizers and speakers addressing the crowd; reporters mingling with the crowd and each other; and small groups of police officers standing or on horseback at a distance, the scenes noticeably dominating this aspect of the news item are close-ups of an evident dispute between two demonstrators surrounded by onlookers and juxtaposed with shots of the police.

The close-up on the faces and shoulders of the disputants conveys the impression that the wider crowd was itself similarly locked in dispute, despite the fact that this was an isolated, and highly insignificant incident at the fringe of the loosely assembled demonstrators. It is all the more interesting, therefore, that this visual image should dominate the opening scenes. And, when this scene is compared with another – the isolated burning of a flag by a demonstrator at the march destination point – it is apparent that such shots have been selected according to their perceived contribution to the news story as conceived by the reporter. Only one flag was seen to have been burnt on that day, as was only one disagreement witnessed within the crowd. Both incidents, however, dominate the imagery juxtaposed alongside the sights and sounds of chanting youths holding aloft Khomeini posters, and police marshalling the crowds on their way to the Council House.

Arriving at the rally separately from the ENG crew and witnessing the internal disagreement within the crowd, the reporter asked, 'where's the crew we need some pictures of this'. When the crew were asked later what pictures they were after, they candidly stated, 'we're after shots of the march, the banners, any trouble that there might be'. Relying on the 'news sense' of the film crew, both in terms of visuals and sound recording of Islamic chants and choruses of shouts, the pursuit of conflict finds a visual and vocal reference, notwithstanding its marginal nature during the events of the day. But this is enough to enable the reporter to frame his initial report in terms of a scuffle which supposedly broke out between rival gangs. The fact that a march steward was involved in the scuffle did not deter the reporter from describing rival groups, later changed to rival gangs, because, as he suggested in the editing room later that afternoon, 'it sounds better'.

Remaining for the moment with the visual dimension, it is also interesting to note that a conscious editing decision was taken which increased visually the sense of urgency and possible threat conveyed in the images selected. A selected front-view shot showing the first arrivals, in small groups, of demonstrators ambling into the city square was abandoned and replaced by a side-shot of groups entering the square, thereby introducing a considerable sense of movement and pace. When combined with the voice-over commentary of, 'an estimated four thousand converged on the Council House, police flanking the demonstrators throughout', the impression given is that the march constitued a massive presence purposefully taking up position outside the Council House. While the march may have, according to police estimates, approximated 4,000 at its height, on arrival the assembled number could not reasonably be said to be more than a few hundred and these included lunch-time shoppers and curious passersby.

The constant pursuit of conflict and trouble, which arguably informed the initial interest in the Rushdie demonstration and is found to be followed through in the selective construction of the morning's events between so-called pro- and anti-Khomeini support-ers, is later superseded by the considerably expanded conflict supposedly ready to be unleashed between the Muslim community, who we are told seek to ban the book, and the wider public, who would resent any such imposition. The head librarian of Birmingham Central Library is introduced as believing in 'people's right to choose', while we are told that 'anybody prepared to comment, strongly opposed a ban in libraries and schools'. These comments, including the initial response sought and gained from the National Union of Teachers which 'deplored the move' by the city council, are all marshalled effectively into an aggregate public which is assumed to be opposed to the ban, while balancing the item's earlier focus upon the demonstration and its declared aims as represented by the two spokesmen interviewed.

If the interview statements elicited by news reporters are scrutin-ized more closely and contrasted to the edited sound bites reassem-bled into the final news package, it is apparent that much of the informing bases and differential nature of such opinions has been purposely edited away to leave a simplistic and unrepresentative opposition between the Muslim community, on the one hand, and public opinion, on the other. This is not to suggest, of course, that a genuine and widely held antipathy to the proposed banning of The Satanic Verses does not characterize much public opinion. What is suggested, and can be established below, is that such public expressions are invoked artificially and re-presented in terms which, by and large, are undifferentiated, simplistically positioned, and

presented and packaged according to the journalists' own conceptualization of the story and its requirements.

Editing voices: observations from the cutting room floor

To establish that public opinion has indeed been selectively re-presented, the edited interview bites woven into the final story package
can now be considered individually. In addition to illustrating
something of the selection choices informing the editing process, the
transcripts also indicate lines of journalist inquiry and interest,
sometimes dropped or abandoned, which none the less furnish
further insight into the journalist's craft and practice of story
construction. The full transcript of each interview conducted is given
below. The passages emphasized in bold indicate the actual words
edited into the final item, the rest being consigned to the cutting room
floor.

March organizer   I am member of the Muslim Action Committee of
Birmingham.

Reporter   OK. Why on this Tuesday morning are we faced with another
demonstration regarding Salman Rushdie?

Organizer   So far in Birmingham all the demonstrations have taken place
on a weekend and we just wanted to show to the people that on a working day
all the Muslims will shut their shops down, they will take their days off from
their work, they'll close their offices and they'll still come to the park and
participate in the march.

Reporter   What good will this march do for the community?

Organizer   This march is the first of its kind because all the Muslims of
Birmingham have joined into the Muslim Action Committee, an umbrella
organization representing all the Muslim organizations of Birmingham. This
I hope will make it clear to the British government that we are determined to
fight until the end.

Reporter   You say you're going to fight until the end, what end do you have
in mind at the moment?

Organizer   Well, the end **in our minds the book has to be banned. The
book must be stopped from circulation.**

Reporter   **In order to do that a change in the law would be required; a
change in the defamation laws. Do you think that is a realistic objective?**

Organizer   **That is the only realistic objective. We are asking the government to change the law to include Islam as one of the religions to be
protected from such vilifying attempts which are made against any religion.**

Reporter   You have been arguing your case for many weeks even months.
Do you think you're getting anywhere?

Organizer   Well we've achieved at least one objective so far, that is Muslims after every day that's passing are more determined to come out and express their disgust at the publication of the book and demand from the British government and ask for more support from our Members of Parliament and our representatives.

Reporter   It could be said that you've lost the broad sympathy of the British people because of the death threat which still lies over Mr Rushdie. Do you agree with that death threat?

Organizer   I cannot agree at all. That may be an excuse for the British government to come out and not accept their responsibility. What we are asking for is the British government is, first it owes allegiance to the British Citizens. We are all Muslims living in this country for the last twenty years and we have a right over the government to ask them to protect our rights.

Reporter   And do you think you will get any support from the Lord Mayor to whom you are handing in your petition today?

Organizer   Of course, this is why we are doing so.

The interview above illustrates something of the generally compressed nature of typical news report interviews and, even more, the severity of the editing process. The final transcript reveals that the response to the journalist's concern with the death threat over Rushdie, though elicited towards the end of the interview, forms the initial frame of reference in the broadcast item and is introduced accordingly by the reporters link statement. This aspect, as opposed to the organizer's attempts to claim citizen rights for the established British Muslim community, is introduced as the main issue. The interview also illustrates the way in which interviewee statements can be clipped from their surrounding context, with the consequent loss of the reporter's questions and even parts of the interviewee's opening, and as documented below, concluding parts of sentences. The severity of the editing process can also lead to ambiguities and confusions when interview statements are juxtaposed crudely against inserted voice-overs, as is apparent at the beginning of this particular interview when the clipped statement appears to disagree with the reporter's proposition in his linking statement. The near total dependence of the interviewee upon the reporter's line of questioning and subsequent editing decisions is further illustrated in the second interview with a Muslim Labour councillor.

Reporter   You've managed to hand in your petition and indeed the council has agreed to discuss withdrawing the book from public libraries. Do you think you will succeed?

Councillor   Well I hope so because I think the situation is, **the community at large need to understand, I think, that under the banner of the freedom of the press the freedom does not give anybody licence to abuse or insult any religion. The situation here is that the author as well as the printer have misused the freedom of the press. And what we are asking is that this book should be withdrawn. That is the only solution if we want race relations and we want to live peacefully and in harmony.**

Reporter   Do you think that withdrawing the book from schools and public libraries would not actually add to the discord between the races and ethnic minorities?

Councillor   Well I don't see, I think the message is, I think the host community should try to understand that this book is not a literary work; its just a filthy book, a fictional book and the author as well as the printers have sought to publicize this book simply for financial reasons. This is not an authentic book and therefore I can't see the need why this book should be available in schools and libraries.

Reporter   According to British law it's a legal book, do your, does your community not follow British law?

Councillor   Well for example this government only a couple of months ago had banned a certain political party in Northern Ireland that their interviews cannot be broadcast on television and radio. Where is the freedom of the press in that instance? Why are we two million Muslims being lectured about the freedom of the press – we are in favour of the freedom of the press, but what we are asking is that the freedom of the press should not give anyone a licence to print money by insulting other religions.

Reporter   Final question. There have been calls recently from the community in Small Heath and Balsall Heath for Roy Hattersley to change, if you like, his colours and come out in favour of banning the book. Do you think he will lose votes if he doesn't?

Councillor   Well that depends upon the residents and voters of Sparkbrook. What we are saying is, that there is a need for people to understand our stance, our logic. And our logic is that the book is a very filthy and insulting book, not only to our religion but to Christianity as well because it abuses prophet Abraham and so many other prophets. So therefore there is a need for the host community—

Reporter   Do you believe that—

Councillor   —to understand this. It's a fictional and filthy book.

Reporter   Do you believe that, do you believe that the Muslim community should stop voting for Roy Hattersley?

Councillor   Well, I think that when the general election comes along it is up to the Muslim community how they feel they have been supported in this—

Reporter   Would you vote for him, as it stands?

Councillor   —hour of need by their Members of Parliament.

Reporter   Would you vote for him, as it stands?

Councillor   Well, I'm a Labour Party member.

Reporter   So you'd vote for him?

Councillor   Being a Labour Party member I'll still fight with other Labour Party members to get this book withdrawn.

Reporter   Thank you, (to crew) I'll need a two shot very quickly.

Here the reporter selects and edits an initial statement introducing and qualifying the idea of the freedom of the press advanced by the councillor in support of his claim to have the book banned, though the subsequent reference to the government restrictions placed on the reporting of Northern Ireland is not also selected. The three principal questions posed to the councillor concern the degree of discord possibly unleashed if the protestors' demands are implemented, a direct invitation to the councillor to respond to the challenge 'does your community not follow British law' and, finally, a sustained and persistent attempt to elicit a statement concerning a possible Muslim–Labour Party rift involving Sparkbrook's MP, Roy Hattersley. This last line of questioning, pursued with some vigour, seeks to draw the councillor on this particular issue and, if successful, would have been instrumental in raising the political stakes involved while adding a further dimension of discord, between the region's 'races and ethnic minorities (sic)'. The persistence of this line of questioning did not, on this occasion, furnish the results sought and was dropped in the editing room by the reporter, who claimed: 'I can't use it; it won't hold up, he didn't go far enough'. The attempt actively to help an interviewee 'to go far enough', in providing a statement guaranteed to cause further controversy and division – all key ingredients to a good story – is further illustrated in the second reporter's interview with the city's central librarian.

Reporter   Brian Caldan what has demand been like for Salman Rushdie's *The Satanic Verses*?

Librarian   We have 36 copies of the book, and to my information in excess of 50 reservations for it at the present time.

Reporter   What has demand been like since you took the book in?

Librarian   Well the demand has accelerated since the publicity. When we first had it, it was just bought as any ordinary book. But since this of course, we've had a considerable increase in publicity.

Reporter   Has this caused you to take on extra copies of the book.

Librarian   We haven't bought any extra but in the normal course of events it follows an increase in demand, we would do that. Yes.

Reporter   How unusual is it to have 50 to 80 people on a waiting list for a book?

Librarian   Not necessarily so unusual, but for a book by a modern novelist perhaps that is unusual, yes.

Reporter   What is your reaction to the decision of Birmingham City Council to ban the book from this library?

Librarian   I don't know of that decision. I can't comment on it I'm afraid.

Reporter   On the basis that the decision has been made what is your reaction?

Librarian   My reaction is that this City Council will do, what they believe is the best thing to be done and I presume this is what they have done on this occasion.

Reporter   Do you support that decision?

Librarian   I'm not here to have an opinion on that matter. I'm here to support the City Council in their decision.

Reporter   So whatever you think you are sticking by the City Council ruling?

Librarian   That is the case, yes.

Reporter   How do you feel about the fact that Birmingham City Council has become one of the first authorities to ban the book from the library?

Librarian   I'm not in possession of that information that they are amongst the first at this time.

Reporter   A lot of people feel they have the right to choose what books they borrow from a library. What do you think about that ?

Librarian   I personally have an opinion that freedom of expression is important for everyone. I don't know what the circumstances, as I say, at this time I don't even know what the city council decision is. But I believe they act in the, what they believe to be the best interest of the city is.

Reporter   On the basis that you believe in freedom then, do you umm—

Librarian   Sorry, you told me you weren't going to ask me this sort of question. I'm sorry I shan't answer any more.

The second reporter – having been assigned early in the afternoon, following the animation of the newsdesk concerning the erroneously perceived imminent ban – interviewed the principal librarian and all subsequent vox pops under the illusion that *The Satanic Verses* had, in fact, already been banned by the city council. This was information that the city's librarian was, wisely enough, not prepared to comment on until confirmed, though the subsequent vox pops were in no position to challenge the reporter's assertion of fact. The interview, having established a few 'facts' concerning the public's apparent interest in *The Satanic Verses* in terms of the library's waiting lists and so on, proceeds to elicit a response concerning the council's 'ban' and clearly seeks to secure a statement of opposition to the ban. With the librarian firmly maintaining a position which is not prepared to challenge the council's right to decide upon such matters, the best that the reporter can achieve is a 'personal' statement yielded after many attempts to get the librarian to commit himself to disagreeing formally with the council.

Interestingly, this personal statement is the only statement finally used and is clipped from its subsequent qualifying statement and numerous preceding statements concerning the city council's efforts to work for the interests of the city as a whole. The librarian's edited statement, in other words, has been produced and appropriated to suit the reporter's own conception of public opinion assumed to be opposed uniformly to 'the ban', notwithstanding the librarian's evident dismay at this persistent line of questioning. The interview abruptly ended; with the transparent efforts of the reporter to elicit a statement of condemnation towards the ban 'On the basis that you believe in freedom then', the interviewee refused to answer any more questions and walked off.

If the librarian managed to maintain a degree of formal control over the interview and refused to be drawn on the matter, thereby only providing partial support to this construction of public opinion, the use of ordinary people via a series of vox pops provided the reporter's conception of the sought balance to the demonstrator's aims. Of the eight individuals approached outside the city library, four refused to comment. All those approached, with one exception, were white, and none were asked if, or declared that, they were Muslim. Public opinion at the level of the vox pop was not considered to include the ordinary voices of Muslims, much less the differences of opinion found within the Muslim community, but was actively sought in terms consonant with the reporter's preconceptions concerning public opposition to the ban. It needs to be remembered that all the street interviewees were approached under the opening question, 'Could I ask you for your reaction to Birmingham City Council's decision to ban Salman Rushdie's *Satanic Verses* from public libraries and schools?'. The fact that no such occurrence had taken place, and that the item was broadcast under the still exaggerated claim 'Council set to ban *Satanic Verses*', did not temper the use of such interviews.

Vox pop as: selecting verbal 'bites'

Reporter   Can I ask you about your reaction to Birmingham City Council's decision to ban *The Satanic Verses* from libraries and schools?

Vox pop   Well, I think the consequences will be with the Muslims in this country being totally alienated in our society and years of work of integrating Muslims into our society will be destroyed because the British people have always been very evolutionary rather than revolutionary and this kind of protest doesn't do anything for the Muslim cause and doesn't do anything for the minorities in this country at all.

This first interview illustrates how the reporter's questions have been edited out, and only the initial part of the interviewee's response has been used. The informing base of ideas to this reaction has also been edited out from the final 'bite' used, although this formed the latter part to, and justification of, the proposition offered in this integral sentence. The ambiguous sounding claims offered in the first part of the sentence – is the interviewee concerned with the Muslims themselves or rather the 'work of integrating Muslims'? – become clearer in the second part of the sentence where an opposition is set in place between British people and Muslims. That is, the opinion offered appears to be dependent upon a wider view of tolerant British people seeking to integrate minorities. While differing interpretations and criticisms currently may challenge or support such an assimilationist viewpoint, the public engagement with such a position is effectively denied by the editing process.

Vox pop as: first-hit success

Reporter   Can I ask you about your reaction to Birmingham City Council's decision to ban *The Satanic Verses* from libraries and schools?

Vox pop   I think people should be able to read what they want. Given a choice of opinion about what they want to read, I don't think it should be banned at all.

With the desired sound bite in the can, this particular vox pop was not pursued, unlike some of the interviews noted above, and the interviewee was permitted to go on his way without further ado.

Vox pop as: constructing an informed confident stance

Reporter   Could I ask you for your reaction to Birmingham City Council's decision to ban *The Satanic Verses* from the libraries and the schools?

Vox pop   I didn't actually know they had. What they're banning it from schools and libraries?

Reporter   Schools and libraries in the city.

Vox pop   Well I think that's very bad.

Reporter   Why?

Vox pop   Well I think it should be allowed. I know a lot of people are against it and so on. But everyone's got a right to read it if they want to, I don't think there should be any sort of banning of it.

Reporter   So what do you think about the fact that the city has given in to pressure from the Muslim Community?

Vox pop   Well I don't really know the whole sort of story of it so it's difficult to comment, but I think if people want to read it they should be allowed to. I don't think there is any harm in it. It's allowed to be published so I don't think people shouldn't be allowed to read the book. That's all I can say really because I don't know a lot about it (laughs nervously). OK?

The woman interviewee, not surprisingly unaware of the ban, is encouraged to react to this situation and declares her opposition to the ban. Her admitted lack of knowledge leads her to make provisional and qualifying statements to her position both preceding and following the final edited sound bite. These have been edited away – in mid-sentence. If a position on the public banning of *The Satanic Verses* is to be publicly aired, it is important that the informing basis of such an opinion is also heard if rational deliberation, debate and public discussion as well as genuine representation are sought. This clearly has not happened here, while the reporter's assumption, stated as fact, that 'the city has given in to pressure from the Muslim community' is unlikely to elicit a more considered viewpoint. It is likely, however, to produce the desired public opinion actively sought by the reporter. The last interviewee edited and used in this part of the report is of particular interest because it clearly illustrates something of the extreme, not to say idiosyncratic, positions characterizing public opinion – and yet even here the reporter's desired viewpoint can be obtained

Vox pop as: 'cranks' and creative editing

Reporter   Can I ask you about your reaction to Birmingham City Council's decision to ban *The Satanic Verses* from libraries and schools in the city?

Vox pop   I feel very sorry for what will happen in the future.

Reporter   What do you think will happen in the future?

Vox pop   We'll have to fight them you know. I think there will be a war.

Reporter   Why?

Vox pop   I study the human race you see, I have all my life. I think there will be a war.

Reporter   As a result of this?

Vox pop   No, not as a result of this. I think it's the inevitable consequence of what's happening. It's the profoundest tragedy that's happened to the English race is the sudden arrival of tens of thousands of people. It's damaged the very heart of what it meant to be an Englishman.

Reporter   So what about the banning of this book from libraries and schools?

Vox pop   It'll be a great mistake.

Reporter   Why?

Vox pop   Freedom of speech. Unless we can express our mind it's the end of democracy.

Reporter   Have you read the book?

Vox pop   Parts of it. I've been told the relevant parts.

Reporter   And what do you think of it?

Vox pop   It doesn't seem that important to me that anyone reads it. Have you read the book?

Reporter   I haven't. There's a huge waiting list for the book inside the library.

Vox pop   But wasn't that bound to have happened; wasn't that the inevitable consequence of the whole charade. You see it's my own opinion that they've got their big stick now. It's what they wanted all along. We've just seen the tip of an iceberg.

Reporter   You think Birmingham City Council has given in to pressure which they shouldn't have given in to?

Vox pop   The whole of the English nation has collapsed. It has for a long time. I've written poetry on this.

Reporter   Thank you very much.

If public discussion, debate and representation is genuinely pursued by the use of vox pops, as occasionally claimed by professional journalists, opinion cannot be divorced from the informing web of rationalisation, justification and general perspective or point of view upon which opinions depend. In this instance, the fact that the interviewee apparently holds just such a matrix of beliefs, values and rationalization informing his opinions is conveniently edited away from the final selected sound bite. Seemingly based within a colourful, indeed racist, invocation of Englishness, the reasonable sounding opinion 'unless we express our minds it's the end of democracy' takes on a different connotation and meaning when presented in the context of its original formulation. Ironically, this same statement, 'unless we express our views its the end of democracy', has itself been subjected to the imposed requirements of another author and placed in the service of the journalist's own conception of the story and its need for the balance of a particular form of public opinion. This public opinion, as documented through-out the above discussion, was manufactured artificially and may have served to further increase the possibilities of racial discord previously laid at the door of the Muslim community by the reporter earlier.

This detailed discussion has served to illustrate something of the dependencies and subordinate role afforded to accessed voices within the editorial process. Initially selected as representative, directed in interview, subsequently clipped and edited into bites, and finally juxtaposed and packaged into an overall verbal and visual narrative, interviewees offer up their words to the journalist's craft and professional practices. This particular story, it has to be remembered, was itself based upon the erroneous foundation of, 'Council set to ban *Satanic Verses*', which acted as the springboard for the selective construction and orchestration of public opinion both within the item and perhaps beyond. As the lead item, the major regional news story of the day, the pre-existing interest and public disquiet surrounding the Rushdie affair were given a further twist which contributed little to the public examination and debate of the complex issues involved. While it would be supposition to claim that this media portrayal resulted in further misunderstanding, not to say antipathy, between the region's communities it certainly provided little or no evidence of an attempt to unravel and explore the informing bases, and differentiated nature of public opinion – including those differ-ences of opinion found within the Muslim community and the different positions characterizing public opinion in general.

In fairness to the journalists involved, it needs to be said that the story was manufactured under conditions of pressure relating to time and item duration involving the necessity to secure and package both visual and verbal elements into a final item ready for broadcasting that evening. Reporters had to work speedily and in a highly selective manner to achieve this end. However, observing the development of the Rushdie story throughout the day, it was also apparent that the story developed in the manner of a rumour within the newsroom reaching its height with the dispatch of a reporter under the impression that *The Satanic Verses* had in fact been banned. Here the journalists involved showed themselves keen to capitalize upon pre-existing news interest already generated around the Rushdie affair, while developing possible new lines of conflict and controversy: anti- versus pro-Khomeini supporters; Muslim Labour supporters versus Sparkbrook Labour Party; Muslim voters versus MP Roy Hattersley; city librarian versus city council; freedom of the press versus censorship; public opinion versus Muslim demands.

The final story transmitted though serving many of the requirements of a good story embodying such perennial news values as conflict, controversy, unexpectedness, deviance and drama offered little in the way of explanation or clarification of the complexities involved. More specifically, in relation to the discussion and examination of the accessing of outside voices, it demonstrates the subordinate and precarious position of interviewee statements. These, as demonstrated above, are liable to be selected, edited and juxtaposed in line with the journalists' own conceptualization of the story and its need for balance, even if re-presenting such positions into a simple and exclusionary opposition between Muslim demands, on the one hand, and public opinion, on the other.

These case studies have indicated that professional routines and journalistic judgements appear to have impacted upon the accessing of inner city voices in identifiable ways. Noting how the institutional voice of the police appears to find privileged and routine entry to the news programme, it has also been observed, notwithstanding the programme's more general popular ambitions, how ordinary inner city voices are likely to find, at best, highly limited and positioned forms of news entry, placed at the service of the programme's bid for popular appeal. In addition, the journalistic pursuit of balance, as a means of securing the semblance of professional independence and news credibility, has also been seen to inform the public re-presentation of community views which, in consequence, have failed to find genuine representation. On all these counts, issues of access and representation have been found to be ill-served by existing programme ambitions and journalist practices.

Deciding on news formats: arenas for public contest?

The accessing of inner city voices has been found to be an important consideration in the public mediation of inner city contests and points of view. A further and important consideration here concerns the exact opportunities permitted to such voices by the available array of programme news formats. If, for example, an inner city related news item is delivered by a news presenter within the restricted context of a news studio with no involvement of outside voices or visual images, little or no opportunity exists for alternative or contending points of view to be made. If, on the other hand, a news format includes interview statements, these may be considered to offer a limited opportunity for discursive engagement though, for reasons already demonstrated, if pre-recorded and subsequently edited such an opening may not be considered to be expansive. However, if a news format permits, say, a live group discussion either within the context of a studio or outside location, the possibilities for engaged inner city debate and dialogue are clearly increased enormously. Such expansive formats may be considered to be of particular relevance when news presentations address politically and socially contested issues.

Clearly, on the basis of a number of verbal and visual elements the array of presentational formats accompanying news items can be further refined from the three possibilities of restricted, limited and expansive opportunities noted above. These can be identified and systematically charted later. Here, it is useful to pursue the professional judgements and other factors involved in the deployment of these different news formats at this general level and which impact on the mediation of contending viewpoints. Is it the case that journalists are also concerned to present to the public the differing and contending points of view informing the inner city scene and select different presentational news formats with such considerations in mind? Or do they, perhaps, work to a different set of priorities, a set of priorities indirectly impacting on the news mediation of inner city contest and struggle?

When reflecting on the decline of live studio based formats and the increasing use of ENG interviews across recent years the controller of factual programmes points to a number of factors informing the choice of news formats.

It was a very popular programme but it had become dated, tired, it had become cosy, it needed someone to give it a shake up. And that was the shake up I gave it, to say 'you will become news oriented and be driven by news, driven by the events out there and you will report what's going on outside, and you won't create atmosphere inside the studio' . . . It meant of course that we could get rid of one sixteen hundred square foot studio in Birmingham, and do it from a little end of the newsroom no bigger than the average living room. It also meant that it was a lot more cheaper to work in this way funnily enough; instead of having a grand studio with all its panoply of people, we were able to cut it right down. We've cut it down so far now that in Central South we have 4 technicians doing what 18 do in Birmingham, 19 in Nottingham and formerly 30 odd used to do. When I first came here it took 30 odd people to put out a news programme. So yes, it's partly driven by a news imperative which is mine, it's partly taking advantage of new technology, but because you're driven by the news imperative you can actually reduce costs very considerably.

Here a complex of factors are all implicated in the choice of news formats accompanying the delivery of news items. If economic factors are at work, so too is an empiricist understanding of news seen as the events and happenings reported 'out there', rather than as the discursive contests waged in a studio setting. According to this account, then, it is the journalistic understanding of news itself which is principally responsible for the decline of studio based discussions and interviews. The development of new technologies are also involved, especially in relation to the development and rapid incorporation of ENG cameras in the early 1980s. The increased portability of these lightweight ENG cameras, using reusable and therefore cheap, video-tape in contrast to film which requires lengthy processing, has undoubtedly led to increased news interviews taken in situ, and permitted the possibility of increased accessing of ordinary voices. Such developments have impacted on the choice of presentational formats.

We've got into the habit of using ENG cameras . . . You can do much more with the ENG camera, and so they're producing more material so you have less of a problem with filling your programme . . . Before you had to be more inventive and to make the programme more entertaining, you had to use the studio. We rarely do that now. (head of news)

While helping to guarantee news material, from the point of view of the old school of newsroom 'entertainers', this development also led to less innovation and a more predictable news programme.

The trouble is it becomes so repetitive with ENG stories constantly going back to the buffer of the studio for another link to the next ENG piece, with nothing to break it up. A few years ago we used to have some live studio events, they were good, they lifted the programme. Once we got some opening shots of the new Mini Metro driving down the main road before it drove into the studio which then formed the basis of an important local story which was important for the region; it broke it up. (reporter)

Interestingly, though the perspective of the newsroom entertainers laments the decline of studio based items, this has more to do with the fact that ENG has contributed to a repetitive and boring programme with less scope for studio-based human interest items, than with the increasingly limited opportunities for programme participants to discuss and debate contentious issues.

My biggest criticism of our own programme is that we are inflexible. We go link ENG link ENG and although the end pieces are different in feel and so on, it's monotonous. It's a sort of machine gun approach, no I'd love to slow it down on occasions and get in Mrs Jones who's 96 who is going to tell us what life was like making needles in Redditch in 1903, it would be rather nice. We can't do that anymore; we can do it on film, we can't do it in the studio. (acting news editor)

Though Mrs Jones, in this instance, would be permitted to relay her memories of working class life at the turn of the century in the more relaxed and expansive arrangements of a studio interview, the principal use of such a facility appears to be envisaged as a means of celebrating a romanticized past, rather than as a means of engaging viewpoints actively involved in the contests of the present. However, according to one long-serving reporter, at least, the studio need not be confined to such soft human interest items alone.

But it wasn't just the studio we also did more discussion and live interviews which I think brighten the programme considerably, and the journalists think it keeps them on their toes. You know, you don't always know what's coming next, and I think the audience feel that as well. If you get two politicians fighting it out it certainly gives the programme a bit of an edge, and a discussion also breaks up the programme a bit, it lifts it. (reporter)

Even here, however, it is apparent that live interviews and the accessing of politicians is seen to be of principal interest only to the extent that the programme is thereby given 'a bit of an edge', and the value of a discussion is seen to lie in its breaking up of a monotonous programme sequence. A similar point of view informs the professional judgements of the head of news who recognizes the value of occasional, main story, studio interviews – still an occasional feature of the current programme.

I think it gives the programme a particular authority if you've got instead of interviewing a Chief Constable or a Minister at the scene of something, or doing him in his own house, or doing him in his office, if he's actually in your studio. Speaking to your presenter he gives that programme a completely different look, there's a different authority a different emphasis. People think, 'oh blimey, they've actually got him in the studio', that increases the significance of the stories in itself; the very fact that he's there shows that there is something fairly big that's being talked about. Whereas, if you've just nipped down the road to talk to him, it's not the same at all. It doesn't have the same weight.

Once again, though pointing to the use of a more expansive or open type of news format, the value of this is couched in terms less to do with the furtherance of public understanding and debate, than with the credibility and authority which such occasions lend to the programme itself. Far from presentational formats being deployed on the basis of their contribution to the public communication and representation of contending social and political viewpoints, they are viewed in terms of their programme contribution. In any event the same effect of live studio discussion can be achieved by other means.

We've got a very small studio set here, that does constrain us from having set tos, with two opposing points of view facing each other. But you can do that on ENG anyway, you can intercut, you can juxtapose them right next to each other. You can get that same effect, with perhaps less of the wind you normally get with a set to in the studio. But I think the key interview of the day can carry live very well in the studio.

Apparently attracted to the conflict and drama of a 'set to', the loss of a studio facility is not, on this account, of great importance given that the same effect can be generated through careful editing and juxtaposition of ENG clips. The fact that ENG editing denies the wider public an opportunity to witness and decide upon the strengths and weaknesses of engaged debate and rhetorical contest is apparently not recognized as of importance. In its place the viewer is provided with the artifice of the editor, cutting, juxtaposing and packaging clips of interview statements; these, of course, unlike the positions engaged in live interview remain immune from sustained challenge.

In short, the benefits of such formats in the public communication of important social and political contests do not appear to figure prominently in the professional judgements relating to live interview and studio based formats. With studio discussions and group interviews generally considered of little importance in terms of their contribution to the public debate of key issues ENG interviews, in contrast, are regarded as of increasing importance, reflected in their growing presence within the regional news programme. The choices determining which formats are eventually to be employed, however, remain an editorial decision informed by production resources and the professional understanding of the story and its requirements.

Sometimes it's about resources, sometimes it's about a cake and dividing it up in the morning or as the day goes on. There are some stories that stand out as in need of explanation, as needing an interview, as needing a bit of stretching, a bit of time to tell. There are other stories that are very simple, and can very easily be explained to people and which might have a bit of passing significance. There are other stories which benefit enormously from having interviews in them, by people having a chance to hear the issues and see the people for themselves who are involved. Interviews are much shorter in length than they used to be; in the olden days television interviews used to be in the studio and people talked endlessly because resources were limited, and that was all very well but that was radio not television. Interviews tend to be trimmed down so that the viewers can still see the person who is talking and still hear what they are saying and how they say it. But a lot of it can be paraphrased, and worked into explanation used with pictures around it. The packaging of news is the trend of the last 10 or 20 years where you hope this packaging is a more understandable and more acceptable means of explaining to the viewer what's going on. (programme editor)

Interestingly, though it is recognized that it is important for people to hear and see the news protagonists involved, the conceptualization of the story entertained by the news producers produces and paraphrases viewpoints into a package which is entirely dependent upon the judgements of the journalists themselves. Accessed voices, as noted above, are likely to be clipped and trimmed in such terms. This interpretative effort may, or may not, be accepted by the protagonists involved, but unlike the live interview and studio based formats, the opportunity to effectively realign the story, or shift the agenda of issues, engage with alternative positions and develop counter-arguments are all unavailable from the cutting room floor. Such discursive limitations of the ENG interview are not generally recognised within the newsroom however. Here the ENG interview is often taken to be *the* news interview format.

It's one of the basic ways of getting information and opinions across, it's also to provide the viewer with the means to gauge whether or not they find what is being said acceptable from that person. In other words whether that person is convincing or not, you can look at politicians and say 'I don't believe a word of that', and it's very useful for people to do that. It's an essential part of democracy I think for people to see what's happening for themselves. And you can also look at other people and think, 'he's a great bloke' or whatever. But it brings the thing to life much more; it personalises the news much more and helps the viewer to relate to the information that is coming out. If you get a flood of graphics or a flood of pictures with a narrative over all the time, it's very monotonous, it becomes tedious and the amount of information can flow too thick and too fast for the viewer to take in. In technical terms as well, it's an important way of breaking up and making more digestible and making more acceptable the information that's being put across. A sort of human punctuation in the programme. (programme editor)

Professionally, news interviews are thought to perform a number of functions, not all of which can be seen as supportive of the editor's liberal democratic concern with 'getting information and opinions across'. The ENG interview, in particular, is especially prone to the editorial process in which interviewee statements are severely edited, with clipped statements frequently juxtaposed in a mock contest of selected verbal bites all arranged in accordance with the overall story conceptualization of the news producers. The search for short interviewee statements and bites of information, easily packaged into the overall item, is readily recognized by news journalists and endorsed as a matter of professional pride in terms of journalistic technique.

A skilful television journalist ought to be able to get a self-contained answer from virtually anybody as to what their point of view is. There's a very easy way of doing it; when I used to be a reporter I used to say 'will you tell me why you are doing this?'. Then the answer always begins 'we're doing this because we're furious about the way the council have treated us'. That's your edit you see, 'we are furious at this because'. Now you come back and you can cut that and say, 'that's it !' (acting news editor)

This is not to suggest that such techniques are inherently manipulative, but rather that the seeming integrity of verbal and visual inputs is in fact a highly manufactured outcome dependent upon the news producers' overview of the story shape and purpose.

Clearly, while considerations of presentational formats are of obvious and direct importance for the mediation of public contests, such are not at the forefront of professional journalists' concerns. Working to a different set of expediencies and professional judgements, considerations of presentational format have been found to reflect a combination of commercial, organizational and technological factors as well as competing regional news orientations. If, on the one hand, the old school of newsroom entertainers lament the passing of studio based discussions and frequent live interviews, this is so in terms of past heightened programme appeals to human interest. If, on the other hand, the new breed of newsroom informers welcome the replacement of such formats by ENG video inputs, this is in line with a professional news imperative wedded to an empiricist notion of 'reflecting what's out there'. On both accounts, of course, the idea that important social issues and political concerns are, by definition, constituted by the discursive engagement of contending positions is apt to be under-represented within such professional viewpoints.

Summary

This examination of the production of inner city voices and questions of access has found that such remain firmly wedded to the journalist's prior conceptions of the story, routine source dependencies and general programme ambitions seeking both public credibility and popular appeal. In such terms issues of access are intimately involved in existing programme forms and professional aims. The range of presentational news formats as important arenas for the representation of public contest have also been found to be dependent on professional judgements and programme aims. The professionals involved have indicated how the deployment of news formats do not, principally, either set out to, or in fact provide expansive openings for the public communication of social and political contests in which contending viewpoints can publicly engage with each other and debate the issues. Rather, an array of professional considerations have been implicated in their use, including factors of cost, new technologies, the pursuit of programme authority, varied programme presentation, conflict 'effect', economical use of time, and an informing professional 'news imperative'.

This last consideration is couched within an empiricist claim to report 'what's out there'. However, professional claims to 'reflect the social ills of the region' do not, on the basis of findings above, appear likely to be fulfilled. This is not simply because such objectivist claims to reflect or represent reality are based within an illusory empiricism, though this is also true. Rather, the failing to represent the social ills of the region, as refracted through the region's inner cities, is based within a programme form and professional practice in which the contending perspectives in play find differential openings for public deliberation and discussion. These relate, principally, to the way in which established news priorities and popular appeals mediate such concerns according to a conventionalized programme form. To what extent and with what characteristic impact such a shared programme visualization has, in fact, impacted on the representation of the region's inner cities across a considerable period of time, can now be explored.

Part II

TV news portrayal

5
Mediating the inner city:
TV news portrayal

From the study of regional news production above, it appears that professional practices and newsroom routines look set to selectively appropriate and inflect inner city issues and concerns in line with established programme interests and appeals. To what extent and in what manner such programme forms have, in fact, impacted upon the news portrayals of the inner city can now be considered in detail. In order to gain an overview, a sample of inner city news items was culled from a seven year period involving 288 programmes and comprising 4,608 separate news items. Of these, 357 or nearly 8 per cent were found to be inner city related.[1] In the light of our earlier discussion, in which three competing perspectives on 'the inner city problem' were identified, it is first interesting to inquire to what extent those key inner city issues identified at the centre of each have found news representation. In Table 5. 1 the broad categories of crime and law and order, urban deprivation and social disadvantage, and issues of 'race' and racial discrimination are applied to the sample. Clearly, even from this admittedly blunt overview, it is apparent that

Table 5.1 *Regional news reports on major inner city issues*

Issue	Frequency	%
Law and order	172	52.1
Social deprivation	108	32.7
'Race'/racism	50*	15.2
	Total 330	*100.0*

*For the purpose of this analysis, 'incidental' inner city items or items which reference inner city localities but which do not address identified inner city issues and concerns have been excluded from the sample. Hence total equals 330 and not 357.

issues of crime and law and order routinely inform inner city reports. Moreover, notwithstanding the numerous facets of social deprivation, whether environmental dereliction, poor housing and under-resourced schools, lack of local amenities, high unemployment or general effects of poverty for example, such a wide range of issues are found to inform only a third of all inner city stories, with issues of 'race' and racism finding the least representation of all. On this finding alone, it is apparent that those wider public understandings of the inner city problem discussed earlier, find uneven representation within the routine contours of regional inner city news. The relative saliences and silences of inner city news portrayal can further be identified in relation to an expanded array of inner city themes.

Table 5.2 *Regional news and inner city themes*

Theme	Frequency	%
Crime	114	31.9
'Race'	50	14.0
Policing	47	13.2
Spatial	27	7.6
Housing	24	6.7
Education	15	4.2
Poverty	11	3.1
Environment	11	3.1
Riot	11	3.1
Local economy	10	2.8
Health	9	2.5
Unemployment	7	2.0
Social Services	6	1.7
Employment	6	1.7
Leisure/recreation	6	1.7
Politics/administration	3	0.8
Total 357		*100.1*

It is clear from Table 5.2 that crime news in relation to other forms of inner city news is 'big' news. Generally found to comprise a quarter of all regional news items[2] when focused in relation to inner city areas specifically, this considerable density of crime reporting is further increased to almost a third. Moreover, when combined with issues of policing and riot coverage, two further areas of related inner city law and order interest, this aspect of inner city portrayal predominates over all others. The second and third most prevalent inner city news themes, with over a quarter of all inner city items, are 'Race' and Policing respectively. Interestingly, it is these and their surrounding concerns which have frequently been heard to inform debates on the causes of the inner city 'riots'. To this extent they appear to have an established, if relatively uneven, representation within regional news. In relation to those multiple concerns taken to be part of the general problem of urban and social deprivation it is noticeable that no single inner city issue, whether poor housing, unemployment or environmental squalor and so on, finds prominent news coverage. Moreover, if considering those political concerns often addressed in relation to the inner city, whether to do with strained community–local administration relationships, the impacts of central government's statutory requirements placed on local authorities, or the fragmentary nature of inner city political organization and alliances, it is clear that such receive, at best, minimal representation.

What also becomes plain from the findings above is that incidental or 'spatial' inner city news reports, that is, reports that make incidental reference to inner city areas but which do not address substantive inner city concerns, find routine news involvement. Though not strictly concerned with the inner city at all, this aspect of news presentation deserves brief mention, and indicates how established regional news interests often fail, as a matter of routine, to look behind individual instances of urban distress. Here the two general regional news orientations, referred to above, are in evidence. These concern, first, the journalistic mission to report, in relatively direct and compressed terms, the latest newsworthy events and happenings; and second, the regional news pursuit of stories with pronounced popular appeal. In terms of the first orientation, numerous reports of individual tragedies and accidents are reported with minimal information, but which none the less reference inner city localities and areas. These comprise nearly three-quarters of all incidental inner city reports (70 per cent). Consider the following two news reports, for example.

'A three year old girl has died at her home in a fire at Handsworth. The body of Ravinda Bugwan was found inside a cupboard in her bedroom. The rest of the family escaped from the fire in a flat above a shop in South Road'.

'A twenty-four year old man has leapt to his death from a tower block in Birmingham. The man, believed to be from Erdington, fell from the top floor of Martineau Tower in Newtown this afternoon. There were no suspicious circumstances. Police, who were notified after the tragedy, were contacting the man's relatives.'

Though both reference inner city localities, neither seeks to make a connection to possible informing inner city contexts and conditions. From the minimal information presented it is, of course, impossible to say whether each of these, and numerous other reports, are in fact implicated in wider patterns of inner city distress. A suggestive case can be made however. The emergency services, for example, are fully aware of how accidents are informed by the prevailing conditions of property, including states of disrepair, occupancy figures, and the absence of fire prevention equipment and inadequate escape facilities and how such relate to wider patterns of spatially concentrated deprivation. Similarly, the inner city has long been noted as a site of mental stress and incidence of mental illness. Though the police may conclude, in line with their statutory duties, that no suspicious circumstances attended the man's leap to his death, we, the viewers, may consider that such an action is decidedly suspicious to the extent that it calls for some kind of explanation. The compressed nature of such news reports, simply 'reporting the facts of the matter', serve to disguise and individuate the possible informing parameters and patterns of inner city accidents and tragedies.

The second orientation of regional news, concerned to seek out or inscribe human interest appeal, also indirectly references inner city areas and concerns, though once again prevailing inner city conditions and issues are likely to find, at best, passing reference. Here mention can be made of the seemingly endless royal tours and visits around the regions, always attracting regional news coverage, and occasionally referring to an inner city project or opening of a Prince's Trust Scheme, and so on. The popularity and populist appeal of royalty is well known, of course, and continues to call forth strong feelings and a sense of emotional attachment centred around the symbols of nation and family especially. Such sentiments are not lost on regional news producers. Neither are the family sentiments that surround children and babies.

An item about an abandoned new-born baby in Handsworth makes the point. This was introduced as follows: 'Baby abandoned on a freezing doorstep – he was only three hours old and wrapped in newspaper', and proceeded to interview the woman who found him, as well as the nurses who cared for him and provided him with a name. Stories such as these, then, as well as a number of features on unusual individuals and eccentrics who happen to live in inner city localities, do not work principally at the level of information conveyance, but rather appeal directly to sentiment and affective response. It is perfectly conceivable, for instance, that the story of the abandoned baby was in some way related to the backdrop of urban distress, but impossible to conclude from the individual focus and emotive appeal of its news treatment.

These incidental inner city news stories reflect the general news orientations of the regional news programme and its characteristic news interests and modes of reporting but do not, as such, highlight inner city issues and concerns. They will not detain us here, but it is noteworthy that they routinely figure within the regional news programme while failing to situate such individual stories within the wider contexts of urban distress.

To return to the remaining inner city news themes above, it is also noteworthy that inner city riot coverage, when contextualized in routine inner city news coverage, is not pronounced. This is not to say, as detailed later, that such does not command massive news exposure on those occasions when reported, but simply points to a more extensive and preceding state of inner city news portrayal which serves to contextualize these dramatic events when reported. With these general findings in place, it is now useful to inquire a little more deeply into those forms of news portrayal and types of journalist treatment that typically accompany law and order, social disadvantage and urban deprivation, and 'race' related forms of regional inner city news portrayal.

Inner city news: law and disorder (i) crime news

If the broad concern of inner city crime news is examined, which comprises nearly a third of all inner city related items (31.9 per cent), it is also noticeable that the vast majority of such stories, or nine tenths (89.5 per cent), concern individual crime reports or court reports. These innumerable news reports simply refer to court appearances, proceedings and convictions or to the immediate reports of instances of crime, with both referencing inner city areas. Taken together such types of news reporting confirm the general finding which suggests that news is typically framed as an isolated, and invariably decontextualized event influenced neither by historical process nor social structure. However, to say that the generality of crime news appears to be focused as an isolated event, is not necessarily to suggest that such is incapable of sustaining meaning. Here, given those silences concerning the wider contexts, background and social patterning of crime, the meaning 'preferred' within such an event framework is likely to be that of an 'individual/rational man' understanding (most reported crimes do in fact refer to men and not women) where deviant individuals are seen to be held responsible for their actions and misdeeds.

Such a preferred meaning finds support when we consider how such news stories report and rehearse day after day essentially similar news accounts while imparting little background information. In such terms these incessant crime reports can be approached as part of a ritual display, affirming societal disapproval towards particular forms of crime while implicitly policing the boundaries of acceptable behaviour and norms. This daily ritual is sustained by those restricted newsdesk presentational formats which generally deliver crime news reports, and which therefore involve little or no accessing of outside voices other than those reported comments of the police and judiciary. Consider, for example, the following typical crime news reports.

'A man's been jailed for life for what the judge said was a brutal and wicked murder of a Birmingham pensioner. Albert Harper was found dead in his flat in the Castle Vale estate of Birmingham. He'd been beaten with his own walking stick and stabbed three times.'

'A man's appeared in court after amphetamines were seized from a factory at Hockley, Birmingham yesterday. Michael Moore, from Edgbaston, is charged with producing and supplying the drug. He was remanded in custody.'

'An 18 year-old girl was raped by two men in Birmingham. She was pulled into a car after refusing a lift in Handsworth and driven to a wood and raped. She was then dumped back in Birmingham.'

'Three men accused of a £50,000 arson attack on a supermarket during last week's riots have appeared in court. They're charged with causing criminal damage to the Food City Supermarket in Lozells Road at Handsworth. They were remanded in custody for a week.'

It is apparent that such reports, in a sentence or two, convey a minimum of information in highly compressed form. Frequently silent as to questions of informing background and context, as well as issues of motivation and intent, such reports by default prefer an individualized interpretation and condemnation of the crime in question. If such daily news items provide a stream of essentially similar crime reports, reliant for the most part upon the routine operations and occasional reported voices of the courts and the police, more substantial crime treatments occasionally complement the 'machine-gun rattle' of such quick succession items.

Every few weeks or so a news item has tended to select a spate of specific crimes for more extended news treatment. In the review sample these included an alleged rise in violent street crime; the problems of vandalism within tower block estates; attacks and vandalism on specific bus routes; violent attacks perpetrated upon inner city doctors conducting late night calls; the formation of a women's self-defence group following a spate of serious sexual assaults; and a publicity campaign involving Scouts aiming to combat the numbers of burglaries within a particular inner city area. Typically these 'specific' type of crime items (6 per cent) involve a more elaborate, if not expansive, news treatment involving the accessing of outside voices and viewpoints. These might, for example, involve the graphic account of a bruised and hospitalized pensioner relating how she was mugged, or the official police response to the latest spate of 'mindless vandalism'. On occasion, however, the news programme goes further and seeks to address questions of crime in general (3 per cent). Consider the following example.

News presenter	Well, now to more serious matters because Coventry, the post-war boom-town which became a Mecca for as many races as New York, now finds itself in a crisis of violence. Over the weekend busmen protested against the late night assaults on crews. And in a savage attack a 60 year old widow was raped after a burglary at her home. Doug Carnagie reports on the new viciousness that has gripped the city.
Reporter	The headlines in Coventry's papers say it all. Mugging is back on the front pages and behind those headlines the ominous fact that Coventry's violent are increasingly the young, remorselessly pitting their

	boots and fists against the old and frail. Coventry, the city that three years ago bounced from factory closures with the New Wave of pop music is now under threat from a wave of crime. One who has suffered is 80 year-old Charlotte Smith.
Charlotte Smith	At ten to five I came out to see, they'd about ten or five coming down the tunnel as the boy snatched the bag, what would be about 12 years of age. Pushed me against the wall. Yes, you know, all of a sudden like, wasn't expecting it.
Reporter	You came down from Cumberland with your husband 30 years ago. Do you think things in Coventry are getting worse?
Charlotte Smith	Oh I think it's terrible in Coventry, worse than I've ever known it. Yes, very much worse. The violence is terrible. For the old people, well I am, I'm 80 I can't scamper about like I used to, no.
Reporter	Coventry's problems mirror those of Liverpool: both cities shed thousands of car workers' jobs in the late '70s and while both are in the vanguard of revolutions in the pop world those bubbles too have burst. And it burst with a vengence on Coventry singer Lindoln Golding, former guitarist with the Specials when, earlier this month, a gang smashed a spanner into his face in a night club. This is the housing estate in Willenhall where Charlotte Smith was attacked. Nobody wants to live here. Whether it's the fault of those who do, or of bankrupt housing policies the estate is a mess. On almost any index of community well-being its score would be zero. At weekends the police, whose sub-station resembles an outpost in Dodge City, ride shotgun with local buses to halt attacks on local drivers. This estate used to be just open fields when the biggest teenage pastime was probably stealing farmer's apples. But now it's glue sniffing, and according to police in the area children are buying it in economy sizes. Ron Hutchinson, the Coventry writer whose play *Risky City* explored the new violence, believes that parts of Coventry are in danger of becoming no-go areas like those of Belfast, and soon.
Playwright	I was a visiting officer of the National Assistance Board for supplementary benefit here, and many a day I've walked down here with a brown briefcase, chucking stones at the stray Alsatian dogs with the gutters dripping and the main line express thundering by down here, by a master stoke of planning.
Reporter	But cities like Wolverhampton and others have all got estates like this. What marks Coventry apart? Why is it becoming so violent?

Playwright	I suspect a lot of kids in Coventry don't know their grandparents. Because there's not that generation of family with them – they're back there in Lanarkshire, Belfast or Cardiff. Therefore when a kid of that age sees somebody in the street with a handbag he doesn't see a person, he just sees two walking sticks and a handbag and he wants that handbag and 'bang', he goes in and gets it. I think one of the problems about Coventry is the lack of regional identity. Like, you've got a West Midlands Gas Board, and an East Midlands Electricity Board, there isn't even an accent or a cliche to play up to like there is in Liverpool or Newcastle or London. Maybe the identity of the Coventry kid is someone who is always in trouble, whose down the precincts for a 'rumble'. There's always been a strain of violence in the town centre. Now every one of us might be at risk, and the age rate of the kids who might be after us is likely to be dropping.
Reporter	Are there any rules left?
Playwright	I know that there is a trade in Coventry in the lunch hours in the factories in turning out knuckle dusters, coshes and sapps, things to look after yourself with. And that to me is a sign that this town has got something seriously wrong at heart with it. I think the main attraction of Coventry is the fact that it's got fast motorways out, and there's a very efficient intercity service twice a day, and I'm sure there's people going to be heading out faster than they arrived here in the '50s and '60s.
Reporter	On the optimistic front there's no doubt that an upturn in the economy, a jobs boom even a good run for Coventry in the Cup would deflate those rising crime figures. After all the city does know a thing or two about rising from the ashes (sound of World War II air raid alarms/scenes of blitz).

News items such as these, then, seek to make sense of a number of crimes and forms of socially deviant behaviour, whether rape of the elderly, burglary, street attacks, glue sniffing or vandalism, by reference to a form of spatial pathology. The item, with the help of graphic visuals, including close-up shots of a battered and bruised pensioner's face, newspaper headlines proclaiming 'Subway terror at Gunpoint', 'Thugs Rule of Violence', and scenes of derelict houses and windswept precincts, effectively reduces and simplifies a number of social issues under the catch-all concept of 'violence', which in turn is apparently explained by reference to the generational dislocation encouraged with the development of a new post-war city.

Such arguments may be considered specious at best, what is perhaps more interesting, however, is the news treatment which enables such simplicities to be made. Making rich use of visual and verbal metaphors, whether the scenes of graffitied walls, hanging windows and roaming dogs, or the ironic close-up on the pensioner's wall hanging proclaiming 'Home Sweet Home', or references to Dodge City and the police riding shotgun, or even the mythic invocation of a rural and crime-free past and scenes of the Blitz, the journalistic treatment trades in a succession of emotive and popular images. Accessing the voices of an elderly pensioner and permitting a local author to develop his particular, if idiosyncratic, interpretation of this 'city of violence', the news item orchestrates a number of emotional and affective appeals, notwithstanding its lack of conceptual or analytical clarity. Clearly, this is a very different form of crime treatment, deliberately proclaiming its subjectivist stance in contrast to the more objectivist tones of the newsdesk presenter, and yet it is apparent that its preferred view of crime is not that different. Informing both, it can be suggested, and notwithstanding the occasional allusion to wider contexts, is a preferred view of crime as located within the deviant, typically violent behaviour of the individual offender demanding a punitive response.

Even when seeking to entertain in more self-conscious terms, the regional news programme appeals to the same common sense view of crime and criminality. Consider this opening programme tease statement in which the presenter, adopting a populist identity with his presumed audience, accepts uncritically the informing assumptions found within a MP's proposals.

News presenter   And welcome to Central News. Now, you'd think they'd thought of everything to deal with vandals, hooligans and muggers. But nobody's thought of this until today. How about shaving their heads into a Mohican hair-style and painting what's left bright red ? Well that's the idea seriously put forward by a Midland MP. Jim Lester the Tory MP for Beeston in Nottingham says we've got to shame them into behaving like normal human beings. Tonight we're going to serve up one of those haircuts to a willing volunteer – later in the programme we're going to see what it looks like and talk to the MP involved.

In summary, regional inner city crime news can be taken as a curious species of news. In the main content to rely upon the recurrent and ceaseless news reports supplied by either the courts or the police, crime news can perhaps best be seen as a form of daily ritual, policing the boundaries of deviance and normality, while furnishing little insight into either the wider patterns and social circumstances of crime or the individual motivations of those involved. The predilection of news for violence is, if course, well known and reflects the operation of those deep-seated professional news values concerned with conflict, deviance and drama. In the context of inner city reports, however, this underpinning news sense finds exaggerated expression, with crimes involving violence routinely selected for news treatment.

While the majority of crime reports can be summarized as above, the extent to which reports such as these provide a backdrop to an occasional and more elaborate news treatment of either specific types of crime usually referenced as a 'crime wave' or even societal upturn in criminal, and usually associated violent, behaviour in general alerts us to the possibility that though a repetitive ritual, crime reports may well furnish a key interpretative resource sustaining a wider perspective upon crime, criminality and the identified problems of the inner city. Moreover, to the extent that regional news has been found to invoke popular myths, potent images and deliberately inscribe emotive appeals into their news treatments, so these may 'bring home' issues of crime and criminality with particular expressive force. The inner city in such accounts is likely to be identified with, and defined by, such incessant reports of crime, implying that the inner city and those individuals living in its midst are the source of the problem, rather than the symptom of a wider set of social processes and problems condensed within its confines.

Inner city news: law and disorder (ii) police and policing

Issues of policing have found prominent news coverage in relation to the inner city and, when combined with crime stories, comprise over half of all inner city items, producing a pronounced law and order skew to inner city portrayal in general. Exactly what issues and concerns of inner city policing have gained news attention can now be reviewed. Looking at Table 5.3 it is apparent that police powers, equipment and manning comprise over a third of all inner city police reports.

Table 5.3 *Regional news: police and policing (13.2%)*

Issue	%
Powers/equipment/manning	38.3
Malpractice	14.9
Harassment	12.8
Operations	12.8
Community policing	8.5
General policing	8.5
Other	4.2
Accountability	0.0
	100.0

The following report, representative of many such items, simply relays the public statements of a senior police officer without reference to any of the social implications of such a proposal, or contending social viewpoints.

'The Chief Constable of Gloucester, Mr Alfred Passey, says his officers may have to be issued with guns if the safety of the public and the police is to be maintained. Mr Passey's comments come in his annual report, the latest figures show that crime in the county went up more than 5% above the national average last year. Mr Passey's comments follow an incident in June last year when a police officer was held hostage at gunpoint at Gloucester's main police station. Mr Passey says he now sees no alternative to training his force in the use of firearms.'

This thirty-five second news item, typical of its kind, effectively delivers a public pronouncement by a chief constable and repays close scrutiny. It is apparent that this public call for the issuing of firearms to police officers is underpinned by three supporting statements. First, the need to protect the safety of the public and the police; second, the increase in the county's crime rate; and third, the 'incident in June'. While not stating that each is in fact a reason for the call for police firearms, the news report positions them in such a way that the inference is made. In this sense both the call for firearms, and the rationale for such a course of action goes without challenge. The fact that public 'safety', as has been the demonstrated on a number of occasions, can thereby be put in jeopardy, and the types of crime indicated as 'increasing' remains undisclosed, and that 'no alternatives' are said to exist, effectively seals the chief constable's call from public challenge and scrutiny. Once again, the restricted presentational format of newsdesk delivery can be seen to have contributed to this outcome. If calls for increased police powers escape public scrutiny in such reports, such is also found to be the case in relation to the introduction of new police technology – another favourite regional news police story.

The introduction of surveillance helicopters have proved to be a perennial interest within regional news. Typically attracted to good pictures and a display of high technology, such items also implicitly endorse the rationale for their introduction. Possible objections within the regional polity around questions of finance and associated opportunity costs as well as questions of unwarranted intrusion and infringement of citizenship rights, all fail to find expression in such celebratory news treatments. Thus, when a lead statement declares: 'Four police forces in the West Midlands have unveiled a new flying squad. They're literally taking to the air as part of a new experiment in the fight against crime', such journalistic imagery does little to explore the wider issues and opposing viewpoints. While Batman and Robin can be said to be involved in a 'fight against crime' the complexities and differentiated nature of policing as much as those of 'crime' cannot adequately be encapsulated in such terms. The regional news treatment provides an excuse for a celebration of police hi-tech and good visuals, but fails to situate policing activities within the wider field of contending views that inevitably surround policing practices and aims.

Though calls for increased police powers and the introduction of new technology appear, however, to find uncritical news treatment this cannot be taken as simply reflecting pronounced journalist police sympathies. With over a quarter of all policing items dealing in some measure with instances of police malpractice, including operational blunders and cases of harassment, the regional news interest in 'deviance' does not exempt the region's constabularies. That said, items dealing with instances of police harassment have typically focused upon individual cases, and focused these in terms of individual transgression. To what extent, in other words, such individual cases may be part of a wider and institutional pattern remains unexplored. Once again the individual focus of such reports has tended to conceal, rather than reveal, those possible institutional anomalies and systematic practices that others have repeatedly argued have informed inner city policing for a considerable period of time.

In addition to the above, the opportunity for 'good pictures' and dramatic action occasionally offered by the police also finds an opening in regional news. With a camera crew and news reporter assigned to a police unit, 'fly on the wall' news treatments have periodically featured in the programme. When covering the activities of the drug squad and a number of inner city 'busts', such items have lent support to a particular understanding of inner city crime. Interestingly, it was just such an understanding, as is documented later, that quickly came to inform explanations of the Handsworth/Lozells riots, which were seen in some quarters as having been orchestrated by drug barons.

One of the most prominent concerns informing public debate about inner city policing is that of community policing. This has often been addressed in relation to questions of police accountability and community involvement in decision making processes. From the review of inner city policing news however, it is clear that those items referring to community policing have tended to interpret it as simply more 'bobbies on the beat' in a bid to tackle rising crime.

'Earlier in the news we heard about the police in Nottinghamshire being concerned about the increase in street violence. Well, in a week when throughout Britain the soaring crime rate has brought forth mounting pressure for tougher law and order, police are watching an experiment in Derby which could cut crime by turning back the clock. John McLoud reports from the city where the bobby is back on the beat.'

Other community policing news items have simply provided the backdrop to stories about exceptional individual bobbies.

'Police Constable Brian Dobson is a special breed of bobby. He's patrolled his village beat with such dedication that they've decided to name a new road after him. Debi Davies took a trip down Brian Dobson Way to meet him . . .'

Here the long-serving and mythic quality of local bobbies is celebrated, while another news treatment demonstrates a policeman's talent for break-dancing 'all in the name of community policing'. Such items have arguably been included for their individual human interest value, and have clearly not sought to tackle the important issues surrounding community policing. They serve, none the less, to reinforce and sustain a particular and mythical conception of the police and police practices – an image which has been found to have little support in the realities of contemporary inner city policing.

Finally, a number of general police stories have also been found to ignore the wider contexts and issues of inner city policing. These have typically positioned policing questions as a response to, rather than as a contributing factor involved in, recent inner city riots. Whether concerning 'A top award for the hero of the Handsworth riots', 'The police women who say they're ready for riot duty too', or the publication of a chief constable's annual report in which the riots are seen as a major police exercise, each fails to raise those wider questions and public concerns centred around inner city policing. In the main, therefore, regional news has tended to report in uncritical, often celebratory, terms increased police powers and the introduction of new equipment. When reporting instances of police misconduct and harassment, these have typically been focused in terms of individual transgression. In line with the programme's ambition to entertain and, to quote, the news producer 'humanize the news', police stories have also been used as a vehicle to celebrate individual police successes and unusual talents.

In more general terms, however, as with crime news, so inner city policing news has tended to lend support to an understanding of the inner city problem as one essentially centred on law and disorder. Those wider issues of police powers and accountability, and systematic practices of inner city policing which have caused so much public debate and disquiet for a considerable number of years, have failed to find regional news representation.

Reporting social deprivation: reflecting social ills?

With nearly a third (32.7 per cent) of all inner city news stories dealing in some way with the multiple problems of concentrated social deprivation (see Table 5.1), this second aspect of inner city news portrayal finds relatively prominent news attention when compared to issues of 'race' and racism, though noticeably less than issues of law and disorder. The discussion reviews this portrayal and identifies something of the characteristic way in which such concerns have been mediated to a wider public. Issues of housing, though a minority of all inner city news reports (6.7 per cent), is the most prevalent of all news stories dealing with issues of social deprivation (see Table 5.2). As such it usefully introduces a number of characteristic forms of reporting which appear to inform the news treatment of social deprivation generally. These include the related news features of 'problem' definition, relational appeal and individualized news inflexion.

In general terms the problems of housing have tended to concentrate on housing conditions with a strict minority addressing issues of homelessness, debt and eviction. Local authority announcements and/or local protests and demonstrations routinely enhance their regional news value and help secure news visibility. However, it is also interesting to note how the housing problem can, in fact, be subjected to processes of problem redefinition and transformation. Rather than referring to the housing problem in terms of the squalid conditions daily endured by tenants and householders, the news programme can on occasion redefine the problem as one 'for all of us', as encapsulated in the following lead statement: 'Now an issue that affects all of us: the state of our houses'. This particular news story then proceeds to identify the poor condition of local authority housing as a problem for each individual rate-payer. While maximizing its sought relevance to the widest number of people, the item also distances the problem of those directly experiencing poor housing conditions. This is a form of news treatment which is not confined to issues of housing however. Consider, for instance, the lead statement from the following news story addressing issues of inner city pollution.

'If you're concerned about your health and worried about eating the right things you might think the answer's growing your own vegetables. But it seems not. Half the vegetables grown on inner city allotments may have been polluted with lead from traffic. That's the conclusion of a disturbing report published today, as John Mitchell explains.'

This story also seeks to maximize its potential audience appeal by directly addressing all those individuals who are 'concerned about their health, and eating the right things' – how many people, if asked, would admit to not being interested about their health? The news treatment appeals to each individual viewer, personalizing its address both in relation to the private habits of food consumption and directly in terms of its mode of address: 'If *you're* concerned . . .'. In this professional bid for viewer interest and engagement the story also transposes or shifts the nature of the problem of inner city pollution. While the research report's findings point to yet another aspect of inner city deprivation – lead pollution – impacting on questions of inner city health, the story transforms this to the more generalized interest of healthy eating. This is achieved by invoking, then challenging, the popular assumption that 'healthy home-grown vegetables' are better for us. The context of inner city disadvantage is thereby displaced only to be replaced by a generalized appeal to consumer interests. This news treatment, just as the housing example discussed above, appeals to its audience as individual consumers, whether taxpayers or vegetable eaters, and not therefore as citizens with a wider concern for the collective plight of others.

The failure to examine the complexity of conditions informing problems of social disadvantage and deprivation is apparent across a number of news stories.

'One in four children in the region is at risk according to a new survey out today. The National Children's Home warns that more young girls and boys face homelessness, poverty, abuse and bad health. But in Birmingham, a pilot scheme is trying to put things right by teaching young mothers how to care better for their children.'

Introducing an item concerned with homelessness, poverty, abuse and bad health, this news story once again uses the publication of a research report to set the story up. However, before the complex conditions and causes of the problem are even addressed the news treatment proceeds to report on a scheme 'trying to put things right'. In the process, those complex structural conditions and social processes generally acknowledged to inform issues of homelessness, poverty, poor health and even abuse, and generally recognized to involve questions of insufficient income, are all displaced with the inferred solution of 'education'. The inescapable inference is that the problems of homelessness, poverty, abuse and bad health are all simply a matter of young mothers unable to look after their children properly.

Occasionally, however, a more adequate form of regional news treatment can be found. Here two inner city related stories about health can usefully be compared.

'Health workers in Staffordshire were told today that thousands of poorer people were dying needlessly. The claim came in a report published today linking wealth and health. Len Tingle reports.'

Once again making use of a published report to authorize or 'set up' its news treatment, the item then proceeds to access statements from the pressure group Age Concern, challenging the government provisions for the elderly, especially those on low income. The news report does in fact manage to grapple with some of the complexities involved, and accesses informed points of view. This can be contrasted to another news report concerned with hypothermia illustrating how a superficial news treatment can effectively dissimulate the problem of poverty and health. In this instance a couple found dead from hypothermia, simply stated in the programme tease as 'Couple die from the cold', proceeds to suggest, having reported the 'facts', that elderly people should take the official advice of eating regular hot meals, keeping the heating on throughout the day, and wrapping up in warm clothes. Hypothermia is thus explained as the outcome of inadequate behaviours of the elderly themselves, and not wider pressing concerns relating to ability to pay, individual resources and the availability of adequate care and support services.

Clearly, these two reports indicate that news treatments of these issues are of varying adequacy and therefore tendencies to generalize need to be treated with a degree of caution. That said, it is striking how many of the reports focusing on social deprivation issues have failed to communicate anything of the lived realities informing such conditions, much less begun to indicate the wider contexts, inter-relationships and general complexities of concentrated social deprivation.

If issues of problem redefinition and relational appeals have so far been found to be implicated in a number of social deprivation news treatments, so too have stories tended to individualize what may on occasion be better seen as collective and/or structural problems. For example, an item introduced by the tease: 'A cancer patient who needs constant medical care is living in a hostel for down and outs because there's nowhere else for him to go' effectively distances both the increasing numbers of (semantically marginalized) 'down and outs', as well as those institutional processes and lack of resources which have led to his particular plight.

The tendency to individualize wider social problems, not so much as a means of providing an example of wider collective experiences, but simply because certain individuals are newsworthy in their own right, has perhaps found its most prominent expression in relation to numerous news treatments of the unemployed. Throughout the review period a number of news items were found to report on unemployed individuals not because they were representative of the growing problem of unemployment frequently found to be most concentrated in inner city areas, but because they were unusual: the young unemployed mother who became a knife-thrower's assistant for example, or the young girl who decided to train as a trapeze artist, or the young unemployed man who taught himself to become a talented snooker player, or the young man who wrote over three hundred job applications in a week. Such items, though referencing unemployment, are in fact attracted to the unusual, if sometimes quirky, personalities and activities of individuals who happen to be unemployed. Moreover, to the extent that such individuals are deemed of news interest this appears to be informed by their exceptional qualities of individual tenacity and resourcefulness, qualities which, by implication, appear to place them outside the pool of the ordinary unemployed.

The individualism inscribed into many regional news treatments thus effectively dissimulates the collective realities of inner city conditions and circumstances. The manner in which serious issues of collective social deprivation find only incidental or tangential reference is also found in news items attracted to novel or unusual developments. Take for example the news item which reported on the success of a bread shop in a 'poorer district of Birmingham' which sold day-old bread to 'the old, the poor, and the bargain hunter'. Notwithstanding the fact that such bread had previously been sold for pig-fodder, it is the business success of the shop in question and the length of the queues not seen for a generation which appear to be the focal point of news interest. Why so many should once again be forced to accept day-old bread in a modern welfare-state society and with what impact on those concerned, is a question not entertained within the news presentation.

Finally, as was demonstrated above in relation to news treatments of crime, so too can regional news make light of a number of social deprivation related concerns in its bid to entertain, trivializing what for many may be considered less than amusing. Here such examples include the publication of a European Community study which found Birmingham to be one of the 'worst places to work and live in', and another finding areas of Birmingham's inner cities to be the dirtiest in the country. Rather than prompting an examination of the reasons why this should be so and with what impact on the people concerned, both items indulge the antics of a humorous presenter who makes light of such findings. In another, also delivered in a humorous refrain, a local authority video aimed at promoting Birmingham to potential 'yuppie' house buyers from London, is subjected to a degree of merriment and concludes: 'Of course, sooner or later the incoming yuppies will find out about – well the bits the video doesn't show – the Handsworths, the Balsall Heaths, and Sparkbrooks.' Once again, the problems associated with such localities are only invoked to poke fun at the claims of the video, rather than presented as the means by which a more serious look at the problems of the inner city could be subjected to public examination. What is interesting about these 'humorous' stories is the manner in which even the most serious of inner city issues can be co-opted and inflected according to pro-gramme ambitions, bringing them back into line with the conven-tional appeals of an established programme form.

In summary, problems of social deprivation are likely to be mediated according to the characteristic forms and audience appeals routinely built into the regional news programme. Though some reports have managed to report on some of the deep-seated complexities that surround discussions of social deprivation, typically buttressed with expert opinions and the publication of an authorita-tive report, numerous instances of reporting have pursued other forms of news treatment. Here reference can be made to the manner in which, in a bid to appeal to the widest possible audience, issues of problem redefinition, relational appeals and individualizing news inflexion, as well as the use of humour, have all coloured the news treatment of serious social concerns. In such instances, it has been noticed how news treatments can frequently posit superficial under-standings of complex problems, rendering invisible their deep-seated and multiple determinations, while preferring simplistic solutions. In short, the characteristic forms and appeals of the regional news programme have contributed to the failure to convey a sense of the extensiveness of urban misery and thwarted hopes found across the region's numerous inner cities. Such have simply been displaced from public view.

Reporting 'Race', racial discrimination and social injustice

Comprising only 14 per cent (see Table 5.2) of all inner city related news items, issues of 'race' and racism find relatively little representation within the routine programme portrayals of regional news. Given the earlier discussion in which such concerns have been identified by some at least to be at the centre of inner city rebellions, such omissions are clearly of interest. Table 5.4 breaks down the broad category of 'race', racism and racial disadvantage further into a number of recurring news interests. At a cursory level it can be

Table 5.4 *Regional news: 'race'/racism/discrimination (14%)*

	%
Racism/discrimination	40.0
Ethnicity/culture	32.0
Immigration/emigration	14.0
Community struggle	8.0
Other	6.0
	100.0

noted that the bulk of such news items have concerned the topic of racism and discrimination, while the second most prevalent topic has related to various aspects of minority culture and ethnic identity, with the third specifically dealing with the issues of immigration/emigration. The remaining items have featured news stories reporting community projects and initiatives while three items were deemed to be outside the main categories of news interest above.

By far the most prevalent topic of inner city story relating specifically to the problems and issues of racial and ethnic minority groups is that of racism, racial disadvantage and discrimination. If these various items are subjected to further consideration it is found that the majority of items, in this instance three-quarters, refer to individual cases of discrimination brought before the courts and tribunals. The majority of all such items principally involve individual cases of racial discrimination, while the remaining have focused upon wider implications of court rulings, and those published reports documenting widespread practices of discrimination.

News stories reporting individual cases of discrimination and racial harassment are thus by far within the majority of all items and tend, in a manner similar to the majority of crime reports discussed above, to report in similarly compressed and individuated terms.

'A Sikh has been awarded damages against a golf club for racial discrimination. The Wrekin Golf Club in Shropshire must pay one hundred and fifty pounds to Mr Pranjit Singh. He'd been refused membership and today a court ruled that it was because of his colour. They've ordered the club to think again.'

In such reports as these, then, the collective realities of racial discrimination and disadvantage find little if any point of reference, seemingly implying that where individual cases of discrimination occur they will inevitably be brought before the courts and compensatory awards made. Treated in such individual and individuated terms, racial discrimination is apt to be seen as an individual aberration, perhaps a matter of individual attitudes or prejudice, but susceptible to court rulings. The collective realities of discrimination, harassment and attack are thereby rendered invisible as is the historical genesis of the dominant culture that continues to inform widespread practices of racism. Moreover, to the extent that the complexities of racial disadvantage cannot simply be reduced to discriminatory behaviour and attitudes, so too is this more complex reality rendered invisible.

Regional news items focusing upon aspects of ethnic identity and culture form the second most prominent group of 'race' related items. If the first group can be viewed as largely reactive reports to the negative practices of discrimination and racism, albeit within a mainly individuated form and dependent upon the processes of the courts, this second group can be seen in more proactive and positive terms, celebrating notions of cultural difference. Here the regional news programme's predisposition for positive and affirming news is much in evidence. Attracted to spectacle and popular notions of the exotic, ethnic minorities find increased positive representation within the regional news programme when compared to other news forms (for a general review of this literature see Van Dijk 1991; Cottle 1992). The general absence of news concerned with the region's sizeable Chinese community, for example, finds an exception in annual features on Chinese New Year celebrations or the publication of the latest AA Good Food Guide and its recommendation of a Birmingham Chinese restaurant – 'bringing', to quote the news presenter, a 'touch of the Orient to Birmingham'.

Such celebrations of cultural customs and traditions, however, may be thought to work with a particularly restricted understanding of culture, in which minority ethnic customs and rituals become reduced to a colourful display. This was previously in evidence in the forward planning meetings discussed earlier. If culture here tends to be severed from its historical and social underpinnings, so too are those minority cultures which are best approached as 'a way of life' frequently trivialized. Minority ethnic culture appears to be treated as an exotic extra, the top coat of an identity unpacked and worn with pride after the main business of the day has been done. Compartmentalized into a traditional leisure interest, culture does not so much display an organizing basis for social identity, difference and even social opposition, but serves as a journalistic presumption to a shared and universal human interest in all things exotic and entertaining. Occasional features celebrating the cultural achievements and ethnic artefacts of talented minority individuals, whether photographers, cooks, artists or poets, fails to engage with the idea of culture as a negotiated way of life. In this sense, such news features appear to be informed by a liberal humanism, keen to taste cultural difference yet disinclined to recognize those underpinning forces of exclusion and inclusion informing cultural production and creativity.

A possible exception to this marginalized news construction of culture is when the world of work and the world of culture conjoin, with the skills and crafts born of cultural traditions being employed within artisan business and enterprise. Whether news stories feature the business successes of Asian goldsmiths found in the Belgrave area of Leicester, the Chinese restaurateurs of Birmingham or Afro-Caribbean traders selling Caribbean foodstuffs in Handsworth, each is treated in terms which emphasize popular notions of the exotic, while celebrating commonalities of business enterprise and success. Consider the following opening statements of just two such representative news stories.

News presenter	Now for a story of survival in these times of recession, for showing true initiative two Birmingham brothers have cornered the market for making commercial radio advertisements aimed particularly at the Asian community. Using local talent they've built up a highly profitable business as Wendy Nelson has been discovering.
Reporter	The piping voice delivering the message is simple Hindustani: 'vitamin D is what you need to avoid rickets' – an advert aimed at the Asian parent and brainchild of the Joshi brothers, Shierish and Ashrok. From this backstreet studio they produce a hundred jingles a week and hold a monopoly on advert slots on Asian programmes broadcast through the commercial radio network. The demand is so great that JK promotions have a six month waiting list . . .

A similar news treatment begins as follows:

News presenter	Thank you for joining us again, and we move straight into the world of glamour. Leicester is fast becoming something of a centre for the production of handmade jewellery. The prosperous jewellery quarter is growing as Asian goldsmiths bring their ancient skills to the city. Here's Malcolm Moore:
Reporter	There are no less than 26 Asian jewellers in just one

> stretch of road in Leicester. Asian goldsmiths with skills
> handed down for generations have turned the Belgrave
> area of the city into a jewellery centre. Their main
> trade is the elaborate Asian wedding jewellery. A
> traditional set of bangles, necklace and earrings starts
> at around one thousand pounds . . .

Such forays into the world of the Other, while celebrating cultural difference, can also affirm the world of the known – the regional TV news world of individual enterprise, success and achievement. Individualism affords an opportunity for positive good news, but conveys much else besides. Not least of which, of course, may be the impression that minority cultural achievements and individual successes give the lie to wider conceptions of collective minority disadvantage and patterns of social inequality. To the extent that this particular news form has not been found to address wider patterns and processes of social disadvantage, so celebratory news features may compound this significant omission and contribute to a distorted image of the region's communities, their conditions of existence and life chances.

An area of 'race' related news, established in past studies as central to 'race' reporting, has been news of immigration (for a review of media research on 'race' reporting see Cottle 1992). In recent years, however, the preoccupation with numbers, always carrying the inherent risk that the problem of immigration was centred on the numbers of immigrants, and not the reactions to such immigration (thereby, 'blaming the victim'), has given way, in regional news terms at least, to items that focus on the individual stories of family members and relatives denied entry, or under threat of deportation by the Home Office. Such items have often adopted a supportive and/or challenging role in defence of the individuals and families under threat. The fact remains, however, that these items are usually about individual cases and rarely is extensive coverage afforded to some of the wider social, political and legal ramifications involved. As was found with news of social deprivation, however, occasional exceptions can be found. In the sample period, for example, one lengthy item of over ten minutes duration was found, which began thus:

'A report just out accuses the Home Office of discriminating against blacks who want to join their families in Britain. The Commission for Racial Equality says immigration officers are so keen to prevent illegal entry into Britain, they're turning away people who have every right to come here. A special report from Richard Barnett.'

The news feature goes on to provide details of a number of individual cases, accessing representative voices and points of view, before providing a platform from which politicians and others could publicly challenge the practices of Home Office officials. As such, this item demonstrates that regional news, with the authoritative support of yet another published report, can occasionally pursue such serious issues in relative depth as well as stepping outside of the predominant individualized forms of news reporting. The story also demonstrates how the programme's underpinning populism can, on occasion, be disposed to challenge social authority and bureaucracy in the name of common sense and the ordinary person.

Clearly, regional news reporting of 'race' is not a unified and closed perspective. That said, such features have been found only rarely, with the generality of 'race' related news coverage tending to selectively highlight some areas of concern and not others, but generally focused in individualized terms. If the populism of regional news can champion the individual against a faceless bureaucracy and inform the programme's presentation of immigration/emigration issues, its noted pursuit of individual success and novelty can, in the context of 'race' related issues, also assume an unfortunate aspect. Consider the following story and introductory link piece, for example, broadcast at the beginning of the 1980s just as the recession began to bite.

Presenter	Of course if the royal couple do move it could worry some householders around Highgrove. Now to more people who are moving but in a very different way. Repatriation for Britain's immigrants has long been an emotive issue. But as the dole queues lengthen so the number of blacks trying to leave the country increases. David Foster has been looking at the latest boom business and how one East Midlands firm is cashing in.
Reporter	Disillusionment is fast setting in amongst Britain's blacks. Whatever the discrimination laws say, they find it harder than most to get jobs with so many whites out of work. And so thousands are just packing up, as they put it 'going home'. Its costing Vincent and Lydia Johnson their life savings to get back to Jamaica. They say they just miss home, but they're only too well aware of the problems in jobless Britain.
Vincent Johnson	The problem towards jobs its very difficult.
Reporter	Do you expect more and more people to go back to the West Indies now?
Vincent Johnson	O yes.
Reporter	But there's one Derbyshire firm laughing all the way to the bank. Transpakship moves families lock-stock-and-barrel back to the Caribbean. They charge around two thousand pounds for removals. Flights per family is extra, the man in charge Steve Oldershaw finding it hard to meet demand.

Manager	Well, business right now is absolutely booming. We couldn't be doing better just at this present time.
Reporter	Just how many jobs are we talking about each year then?
Manager	Well, I was just thumbing through my diary and having a look at what we did. In 1980 we shipped three hundred and twenty people back to the West Indies, in 1981 we had six hundred and seventy, in 1982 I would think we are going to have over a thousand families that have returned particularly to Jamaica and the other West Indian islands.
Reporter	But for the hundreds heading west, was it a mistake to come at all? Did they mistakenly think the grass was going to be greener over here?
Community Relations Officer	It depends on which grass we're talking about. I think if we look at what happened in the early 1950s, people came to this country with high expectation. They'd expect that they would be able to obtain certain benefits from a country they'd regarded as their mother country – milk and honey would be flowing. It hasn't flowed, there's no gold on any particular street. And its come to a point that people want to make a decision that they will go back to their roots.
Reporter	With unemployment showing little sign of dropping, transatlantic removals could be the business of the future. David Foster in Derbyshire for Central News.

Clearly good news very much depends on who you are, and the perspectives that you bring to bear on such news stories. In the context of 'race' related reporting what is particularly lamentable about this type of news treatment is its noticeable failure to address those questions of racial inequality and discrimination which inform this particular business success. Moreover, not only are such informing conditions not examined, in a number of the reporter's comments and questions they appear to be considered as not important, with the reporter preferring to raise issues of immigrant 'false expectations', than issues of racial discrimination and historic- ally informed disadvantage.

The inner city scene has long been recognized to be characterized by organized differences and forms of community involvement and mobilization. With only 8 per cent of all 'race' related news reports and little over 1 per cent of all inner city related items together (1.2 per cent), such concerns have found infrequent portrayal. Further- more these have typically only found incidental news reference. The news story below is representative in this respect.

News presenter	The new Minister who has just been given special responsibility for the problems of the black community in Britain's cities has been visiting Birmingham, first stop on a nationwide tour. Sir George Young went to several community centres in the city including the Handsworth Cultural Centre run by the County Council. It provides a range of activities for young people some of whom are on probation. He also met local councillors, police and businessmen.
Sir George Young	We're spending more money through the Urban Programme next year in Birmingham and what I want to do is make sure the money is well spent backing projects that people in Birmingham feel are relevant. And by spending a bit of time here talking to people, it's that much easier for the Government to make sensible decisions on the future of the Urban Programme.

Here it would appear that the operation of routine news values take precedence over declared intentions of news producers to report the life of the region. The forty-six second news report above only deals with community organization and resources incidentally while also singling out the fact that some of those involved in the cultural centre are on probation. Clearly, the main news value of the story as framed by the news producers resides within the ministerial visit itself. The fact that no other voices other than those of the presenter and the minister gain access also effectively grants the minister an unopposed opportunity to make a political speech. Organized and collective forms of community expression and struggle find little serious news attention. An important resource for the understanding of the inner city as a site of community action and creative response, as much as a site of social problems, is thereby denied public recognition.

In summary, news of 'race', racism and racial discrimination bears many of the hallmarks of the regional news programme in which, and through which, they find wider public representation. Though dealing with issues of racial discrimination and racism, these have been found to be covered generally in individual and individuated terms, placing in abeyance wider questions of systematic discrimination and leaving totally untouched structural patterns of disadvantage. Moreover, the celebratory inclination of the regional news programme has also left its stamp on the array of news features keen to familiarize the wider audience with the exotica, individual talents and business success stories of minority ethnic groups. The informing politics of inner city community organization, struggle and opposition in contrast, has found few if any opportunities for news representation.

Issues of 'race', then, have not been informed by a single, much less a coherent point of view. Rather they have been mediated according to existing news programme interests and audience appeals. These have resulted in, at best, a fractured and fragmentary portrayal of some of the issues and concerns of those minority communities living in and around the region's inner cities, but all carrying the hallmarks of the regional news programme and its characteristic forms. At worst, such portrayal has tended to bury issues of minority exclusion and marginality beneath a preferred celebration of individual success and cultural difference, only occasionally alluding to issues of difficulty and then typically in individual and individuated terms.

Representing inner city voices?

In Chapter 4 a number of detailed case studies illustrated the way in which certain inner city voices, and not others, are permitted routine news access with a consequent impact on the array of inner city perspectives finding wider public expression. In the report of the death of Clinton McCurbin, journalist reliance upon the police as both provider of essential information and involved inner city actor, enabled the police to establish a particular and uncontested interpretation of events. In the case study of the anti-Rushdie demonstration it was observed how journalists managed to effectively orchestrate a number of voices with which to balance Muslim voices of protest. Similarly, discussion of the news report concerned with inner city vigilantes indicated how 'community voices' were desperately sought to balance what was thought to be unrepresentative opposition to vigilante patrols on the streets of Handsworth. These detailed case studies have indicated that questions of access are of vital importance in relation to the public examination and debate which surround contested concerns. They have also revealed, however, that considerations of access are intimately tied to considerations of editorial control and journalist conceptions of the story. This secondary consideration of access will be returned to below.

Here it is useful first to inquire into the array of inner city voices finding, and not finding, forms of involvement across the generality of inner city news portrayal, since it is here that the discursive contest surrounding the inner city comes into play. Table 5.5 indicates, in stark terms, the relative presence of different voices found across a considerable period of inner city news reporting.

With a quarter of all inner city voices accessed as 'individual voices' such a finding may be surprising to those who might have expected more organizational and institutional voices to predominate. By individual voices is meant those individuals who neither formally (or informally) nor professionally represent others, but are simply present in an individual capacity. Witnesses to a crime, crime victims or local residents all supply individual voices as do those occasional voices of talented or exceptional individuals who form a focal point of interest to regional news features. This finding, therefore, needs to be treated with some caution given the dependent, and frequently

Table 5.5 *Regional news accessing inner city voices*

Social group	Frequency	%
Individual voice	143	25.0
Police	105	18.4
Government	95	16.6
Business	53	9.3
Community voice	45	7.9
Education	42	7.4
Court/legal	22	3.9
Medicine	20	3.5
Celebrity/royalty	14	2.5
Professional/expert	12	2.1
Government scheme	7	1.2
Religion	6	1.1
Social Services	6	1.1
Emergency services	1	0.2
	Total 571	*100.0*

subordinate, role afforded to such voices within the informing news treatment. For example, a tearful crime victim's account or eyewitness's emotive description of a dramatic event, though providing a human edge to a story may, in fact, be subordinated to a wider and informing expert or professional view. Given previous discussions of the popular and populist ambitions of the news programme, declared by news producers and demonstrated above, such findings can be seen as totally expected.

If the populist leanings of the programme have been found to enhance those opportunities, albeit editorially controlled, for ordinary voices to gain some news access, the predilection for crime news when combined with an organizational reliance upon the police as a source of continuous stories, helps explain the second major category of accessed voices. Here the voices of the police are quintessentially the voices of law and order, notwithstanding those internal divisions of police opinion rarely finding public exposure. Politicians, both local authority councillors and MPs, find considerable access, despite the finding that inner city politics has found few opportunities for news treatment. This points to the involvement of politicians across the span of inner city news reports in general.

The world of business also finds considerable involvement as do 'community voices', that is individuals and groups who formally or informally represent a particular community group, organization or section of the community, but who remain outside of formal political arrangements. When combined with the 25 per cent of individual voices noted above, such a finding indicates that in effect over a third of all entries are allocated/secured by those outside of formal hierarchies of social power. Such a finding qualifies any presumed hierarchy of access within this particular species of news, indicating that access is not only dependent upon routine sources but also reflects established programme aims. In this respect, issues of access can be seen as reflecting informing news epistemologies or 'ways of knowing'. This brings the discussion to those secondary considerations of access noted above.

Regional news access and news epistemology

News has frequently been said to be informed by an objectivist understanding of knowledge, indicated in the detached presentation and authoritative marshalling of facts, professional opinions and privileged access granted to social and political elites. However, other news forms may also be informed, to varying degrees, by a different or complementary news epistemology. The populist appeal of the regional news programme is a case in point, where a subjectivist epistemology also informs the programme's design and patterns of access. Here consideration of the affective and emotional side of life find increased recognition, with the experiences of ordinary people, in contrast to the professional opinions of elites, gaining some news expression. These differing news epistemologies inform the regional news programme and its consequent hierarchy of access, as outlined above. A news feature, concerned with the closure of a major employer, illustrates how regional news typically seeks out the human experiential aspects of the story, and in consequence accesses a number of ordinary voices.

News presenter   Twenty-five years of industrial history came to an end at noon today. Round Oak Steel Works at Brierley Hill closed down. It started off as an iron works; at one time most of the world's supply was made within twenty miles of here. But no more. Workers have had a few weeks to get over the first shock of closure, now comes the dulling realization that most will be unable to find another job. British Steel runs a variety of courses to help the thousands of steel men made redundant over the last couple of years, the European Community also offers financial help. But nothing can really ease the pain of losing your job two days before Christmas. The men stopped filling in the Report Book in November, the day they heard Round Oak was to close. The furnaces are dead and cold. A couple of hundred people are being kept on to tidy up loose ends, dispatch the remaining orders, collect outstanding payments. Some of the last to go will be the accountants.

Director of Personnel   It's a very sad day. I've been here nearly twenty-seven years, man and boy you might say, throughout the whole plant and it's very sad.

Reporter	So what are your feelings as closure ticks nearer?
Director of Personnel	One has become reconciled to it. One recognizes that the steel industry in the UK is in bad decline and we're sick with it as well, sick unto death in fact.
Reporter	Like many old factories Round Oak has a population of cats. Each department has its own animal, or rather each animal has its own humans trained to feed them. It takes a trained fitter to open a tin of cat food. The men have a rota, someone will come in on Christmas Day and Boxing Day and every other day in the new year to feed the cats. This man retired a year ago – but he still comes in. Somehow while the cats remain and prosper there's a feeling there will be life at Round Oak. As for the cats, well they know something is happening. It's very quiet, there's no machinery, no cranes, no rolling stock. The last shift is over.
Workman 1	I've only been here five years but I like the blokes, you know, good atmosphere here. I've got a job to go to in January, but I'd rather stay here.
Reporter	What's that, a memento of happier times (points to a picture of two steel workers in front of works)?
Workman 2	Most certainly, definitely, definitely.
Reporter	It's a grim time of year to find yourself suddenly out of work, isn't it?
Workman 3	Well this Christmas won't be so bad. It's the Christmas after it.
Workman 4	You know, any time of year, you know.
Workman 5	As regards to the future, it's just nil, it's pathetic really.
Workman 6	We'll try to keep together. We'll try to go on courses together as well, you know.
Reporter	But it's a really sad minute for you?
Workman 6	Yes (lingering close-up on tearful face).
News presenter	A sad day for everyone there.

This regional news treatment provides a behind-the-scenes look at the human consequences of redundancy. Making skilful use of visual and verbal images, the piece seeks to impart and invoke something of the human experience and feelings that surround the simple announcement of closure. Visual images play an important role here. These include the opening scenes of the steel works towering above the surrounding area, a sequence showing a slowly closing furnace door, a shot of a works cat peeping out from behind a discarded workman's boot, and scenes of empty workshops, and, finally, a close-up on the tearful face of an elderly workman. Each works metaphorically, to invoke something of the human side of the closure and its experiential and emotive impact on those directly involved. These selected scenes are professionally chosen and juxtaposed to complement the verbal narrative, which also works, for the most part, at the levels of emotive appeal and affective response and includes the interviewer's pursuit of emotional responses from the men themselves.

Such a subjectivist news epistemology, frequently found to inform regional news features, works at a different level from that of the objectivist news report imparting facts in the detached, if authoritative tones, of a neutral observer. Here a subjective involvement is demanded from the viewer, seeking to bring home something of the human tragedy involved. If the feature trades in sentimentality and cliched images it none the less provides a different way of knowing when compared to other forms of news coverage. It also, of course, permits increased involvement of ordinary voices, though it has to be said such remain within the editorial frame set in place by the news reporter and her particular line of questioning.

The point here is that patterns of inner city access, though reflecting pronounced institutional dependencies and programme predilections for crime news in particular, have none the less accessed increased numbers of ordinary voices in relation to news features such as the above, and in accordance with the programme's popular ambitions. Such voices remain, however, dependent upon initial newsroom story selections and journalists' subsequent story treatments. They also remain dependent upon the range of presentational news formats informing the delivery of inner city stories.

Inner city news and the limitations of news formats

Throughout this chapter a number of news items, whether concerned with crime and policing, social deprivation or issues of 'race', have revealed something of the limitations of those accompanying forms of news presentational formats. In discussing the incessant daily crime reports or a chief constable's latest call for increased police powers, it was observed, for instance, how such reports remained sealed from alternative voices and competing points of view. Typically delivered by a newsreader in the restricted format of a newsdesk presentation, such items remain entirely dependent on the newsreader's account, with the minimum of direct reference to outside voices, viewpoints and visuals. As such they remain sealed from challenge or alternative points of view, while those sometimes dubious inferences informing their construction are allowed to pass freely into the public domain. Such news formats may be considered particularly restrictive when applied to an area, such as the inner city, which is the site of discursive struggle and contest.

A presentational format thought to improve upon the restrictive opportunities of the newsdesk delivery, is that of the limited presentational format in which, typically, both accessed voices and visuals are combined under the editorial control of the newsroom. Examples here have included the story above of the steelworks closure, as well as the booming business trade in black emigration, the increasing violence in Coventry, and the anti-Rushdie demonstration story. As noted already, the use of Electronic News Gathering cameras has helped transform both the style and formats of news programming in recent years and increased the opportunity for ordinary voices to find news access. For the most part, however, accessed voices have been found to be dependent upon the subsequent editing decisions involving cuts, selections and journalist juxtapositions that routinely inform the limited format. This was demonstrated in some detail in the Rushdie case study.

A third presentational format provides expansive opportunities when compared to both the restricted and limited formats. This entails either live or full interview inclusion in which the interviewee is allowed to develop his or her point of view at some length, perhaps in engaged debate with an opposing voice. Such a format enables both the strengths of argument as well as its informing weaknesses to be subjected to close examination in engaged dialogue. Possibilities for agenda shifting as well as agenda setting are also increased, to a degree at least, in the interviewee's favour. In relation to the contested terrain of the inner city such a format may be considered to be particularly necessary. Which presentational formats, then, have typically informed the news portrayal of the inner city?

From Table 5.6 it is clear, in line with the regional news programme in general, that the limited format of reporter and film interview represents the news form par excellence with nearly half of all inner city items delivered in this manner. However, nearly half of all inner city items have also been delivered in the restricted formats noted above, which permit no direct participation by outside inner city voices and are therefore entirely dependent upon the voice of the news account itself, which, in turn, is typically dependent upon institutionalized and routine newsroom source contacts. As for the identified expansive formats occasionally found in the regional news programme, and thought to be particularly suitable to the contest over meaning waged in relation to the inner city, these have featured highly infrequently, with direct presentation formats, and studio discussions finding no involvement across the inner city sample at all.

The presentation of the issues and concerns of the inner city has, despite those surrounding social and political viewpoints vying for wider acceptance, been afforded forms of presentation which remain firmly within the editorial control and packaging process of the news producers. The effects of such formats have been detailed in both this

Table 5.6 *Presentational news formats delivering inner city news*

Format[3]	Frequency	%	
Limited			
Reporter & film interview	173	48.5	
			(48.5)
Restricted			
News presenter & film voice-over	75	21.0	
News presenter & still voice-over	38	10.6	
News presenter & Central logo	36	10.1	
Reporter & film voice-over	14	3.9	
Reporter, film in view	8	2.2	
Reporter direct to camera	3	0.8	
Reporter & still voice-over	1	0.3	
Reporter no inputs Central logo	0	0.0	
			(49.0)
Expansive			
News presenter/reporter studio interview	8	2.2	
Reporter & film group interview	1	0.3	
News presenter/reporter studio discussion	0	0.0	
Direct presentation	0	0.0	
			(2.5)
	Total 357	*99.9*	

chapter and the preceding one, with presented social viewpoints sealed from engaged debate, while others secure no opportunity to contest the journalist's working assumptions and agenda of inner city concerns.

Summary

This chapter has documented in some detail the range and types of inner city story treatments regularly found to inform regional news. These findings confirm earlier expectations derived from detailed observations of newsroom practices and declared programme ambitions by professional news workers. Findings have clearly indicated that of all the associated problems of the inner city it is those concerning law and disorder that have dominated regional news interests. Organizational reliance on both the police and the courts as routine sources of news stories has clearly contributed to this outcome. However, on present findings it would be too simplistic to infer that such either reflects a form of newsroom genuflexion towards the police or simply a bureaucratic expediency to 'tame the news environment'. Given the declared newsroom antipathies towards some of the region's police forces noted earlier, as well as an underpinning pursuit of deviance as an informing news value, the police have not been exempt from critical news coverage. Rather, the explanation for both the predominance of inner city law and disorder news, as well as the prominence of police voices, lies principally in the producers' practices and programme ambitions. Journalists have been found routinely to pursue issues of crime and disorder as an established regional news interest, an ingredient resonating with news values including deviance, conflict and violent transgression. Crime news has also been found to be susceptible to pronounced human interest inflexion, a further programme ambition. In addition journalist understanding of the problems of the inner city as a site of crime and deviance may have served to compound this dominant inner city news representation.

Issues of social deprivation have found less opportunity for regional news exposure, though also subjected to characteristic forms of regional news treatment. Here something of the differentiated nature of the regional news programme is revealed. Unlike most crime or police reports which have been found to be delivered in restricted newsdesk formats and informed by an objectivist news epistemology, social deprivation news has tended to be delivered in limited formats, and informed by a subjectivist news epistemology. Here increased opportunity for outside voices and visuals come into play. Though it would be wrong to imply a strict division between these two news epistemologies, given that both can inform a particular news treatment, it is the case that social deprivation news has typically been inflected according to subjectivist news appeals. Here the pursuit of maximum audience interest appears to account for the manner in which social problems can be redefined in such a way as to address all of us, perhaps as consumers, rather than as a means of focusing on the collective plight of others. Part of the programme's bid for popular appeal has also involved a pronounced individualism in which interest in the region's talented and/or exceptional individuals can often turn a collective backdrop of misfortune into an opportunity to celebrate those individual qualities of enterprise, tenacity and personality seemingly overcoming adversity. In such ways as these, news of social deprivation has tended towards the superficial and slipshod treatment of complex and interrelated social problems concentrated in certain urban spaces.

News reporting of issues of 'race' and racism have also been found to give expression to characteristic programme news interests and aims. As with most crime reports, so instances of racial discrimination have found news representation to the extent that these come before the courts and tribunals. They also, however, tend to be delivered in the decontextualized and individuated forms of newsdesk reports with a consequent displacement of those wider patterns and collective realities informing such individual cases. The characteristic pursuit of 'happy news' also informs the regional news programme's portrayal of the region's minority ethnic communities. Attracted to spectacle and popular notions of the exotic, representations of ethnic culture have tended, however, towards the superficial and the trivial. Cultural difference is too often seen simply as an oppportunity for a colourful display of tradition, and not as a lived way of life in which the realities of the present are experienced, negotiated and confronted. The individualism of regional news has also been found to inform a number of minority success stories, once again distancing the collective patterns and processes of disadvantage *and* collective forms of community organization and action found across the region. Contrary to the declared intentions of regional news workers to reflect the problems as well as successes of the region, programme ambitions have co-opted and accommodated issues of ethnic difference within existing programme interests – leaving those wider collective problems and patterns of structural disadvantage untouched.

Programme routines and journalistic understandings of story requirements have also been found to be deeply implicated in patterns of inner city access and accompanying presentational news formats. Here the characteristic appeals and bid for popular interest has, in part at least, impacted on the specific hierarchy of access found to pattern regional inner city news. Opportunities of news access, however, remain dependent upon the presentational formats on offer if contending views are to find engaged public debate. Professional regional news journalists, contrary to journalist claims that state otherwise, are not principally preoccupied with providing a platform for the public dissemination and debate of contentious issues, all in the name of furthering democratic involvement. Rather, their immediate horizon of professional concerns is centred on the daily production of a popular news programme.

These two aims are not necessarily mutually exclusive, of course, but then neither are they necessarily compatible or coincident. Public debate and engaged studio discussion, it will be remembered, were thought useful for a variety of reasons, including programme variety, projecting a stance of programme authority and manufacturing the effect of interview conflict. Such have not worked in favour of the public contest of meaning surrounding the inner city however. In fact, it was found that few opportunities have existed for outside voices to enter the public domain and challenge in engaged terms the dominant voices of inner city discourse – whether they are the voices of the police, the courts, or leading government politicians. Such opportunities as there have been have remained reliant upon the overall story conceptualization and editing decisions of the journalists involved.

In such ways as these, the programme has rarely managed to represent the range of available voices and contested points of view surrounding the inner city. Certain inner city issues and a limited array of inner city voices have been selected, processed and packaged according to the conventions and appeals of the news form in which they have found wider public expression. These, at best, represent a partial understanding of the nature of the problems of concentrated urban distress. What they have represented, however, are the conventions, routines and appeals of the regional news programme and the way an established cultural form seeks to engage a wide audience. This has less to do with journalist attitudes and assumptions about the problems of the inner city, whether consciously or unconsciously held, and much to do with the way in which the popular appeal and established conventions of the regional news programme are pursued by professional journalists all working to a known result. The implications of such findings for questions of media theory and the study of news will be returned to later. What is clear is that the news programme under examination has done less than justice to the complexities and circumstances of those resident groups and communities across the region who daily endure marginalized existence.

6
Mediating the Handsworth riots: riotous others, silent voices, criminal deeds

Of all the issues and deep-seated problems associated with Britain's inner cities, it is the inner city riots which have grabbed the headlines and attracted the media spotlight. Exactly how such events have been portrayed by regional news and what interpretative resources and accounts have been made publicly available over an extended period of time and by whom, is therefore of central interest to this study. This chapter takes one particular disturbance which, in terms of loss of life, substantial property destruction and damage as well as subsequent political interventions and general media interest, can be considered one of the most serious outbreaks of inner city disorder in recent times. First finding extensive news treatment on the evening following the previous night's and subsequent afternoon's disorders, the news programme was introduced as follows:

News presenter   Good evening. In Central News tonight the full story of the Handsworth riots which erupted again this afternoon. Shops and cars are burnt as the violence continues throughout the day. Bodies are recovered from the wreckage – there may be others. And the local community is left to pick up the pieces. Tonight the city of Birmingham is counting the cost of 24 hours of rioting: two dead, two people unaccounted for, thirty-five injured, and a trail of property damage running into millions of pounds. Fifteen hundred police have been drafted into Handsworth and the Post Office have closed all their offices in the area until further notice. Later in the programme we'll be talking to the Chief Constable of the West Midlands, Geoffrey Dear. But first a look at how the violence erupted . . .

With this initial news programme treatment a protracted news interest in the Handsworth riots began, an interest which, as demonstrated in an earlier discussion, has continued to inform the reporting of Handsworth to this day. In this opening address the news presenter introduces a number of characteristic forms of news reporting informing its programme treatment but which also continued to shape many subsequent news reports broadcast over the following twelve months (the period chosen for detailed review).

The news treatment is focused on the events themselves, misleadingly termed 'the full story of the Handsworth riots'. Piecing together with verbal testimonies and available film footage an account of what happened, the programme catalogues the unfolding drama including its immediate effects on victims and property, as well as initial police and official reactions. Seen as first and foremost a massive outbreak of destructive violence, the Handsworth riots are treated almost as an object, reified into a wave or outpouring of violence which simply 'erupts' without reason. Though an array of voices are permitted to advance their particular interpretation of the riots and their causation during the course of the programme, it is noticeable that the use of lengthy studio interviews is confined to two voices only: those of the Home Secretary and the Chief Constable. In the course of this privileged form of access both interviewees placed unopposed interpretations on the disorder, literally telling people how to view these events and the sorts of response required. It is also noticeable that they alone had the opportunity to dismiss and debunk rival viewpoints.

Home Secretary   We're dealing here with an unstable area of
                      Birmingham which has social problems, in which
                      public money, your money, taxpayers' money has been
                      poured in recent years, twenty million pounds in
                      Handsworth alone. Now, three-quarters of that is
                      Government money, the rest comes from local
                      authorities who have made a great effort there. And
                      therefore that is not the cause of the thing. What
                      happened last night was criminal activity – looting,
                      burning, putting people's lives at risk, and three people
                      so far as we know lost their lives – that is criminal
                      activity. The reaction to it must be a reaction to crime.
                      A criminal investigation following immediately after
                      the restoration of order.

Similarly:

Chief Constable   There's been enormous money, as the Minister's just
                      said, and a tremendous effort by the police and by
                      many, many other people as well, to try and make
                      Handsworth something worth living in. And of course
                      it's gone wrong. But I don't think it's fair to single out

us, or indeed any other group, and say therefore all the
evils of what has just happened in the last 24 hours is
because of them. What has happened is that a group of
three or four hundred hooligan criminals have decided
that they can get a lot of pleasure out of looting, out of
smashing property up, and hell to the consequences as
far as they are concerned.

Such forms of access can be contrasted to all others within the
programme where particpants were granted, at most, a sentence or
two elicited on the streets and subsequently edited into the final news
package.

Now, it could be maintained that such programme characteristics
simply reflect those very real pressures and difficulties confronting
journalists who, faced with the immediate events and surrounding
confusion of inner city disorder, seek to report such happenings as
best they can, accessing those prominent voices who are charged with
the official responsibility of responding to such events. If this can be
challenged in the short term on the basis that official responses are
unlikely to represent 'the full story of the Handsworth riots', it can
most certainly be challenged in the longer term where community
voices and perspectives would be expected, on the basis of declared
regional news aims, to find representation. The question remains,
then, to what extent and in what manner those competing views on
inner city disorder begin to find increased access and representation
across a much wider time frame, perhaps long after the immediate
event and initial journalistic responses? This analysis seeks to
address such questions via a detailed examination of one full year of
riot and follow-up riot news reports. Examining issues of language
use, access, general narrative structures and the range of riot-related
issues finding representation, as well as the important questions of
news visuals, this chapter presents a detailed analysis of the manner
in which the Handsworth riots of 1985 became mediated to a wider
public.

News language: contested terms

The words, or lexical terms, that we use frequently do not simply refer
to something, they are also ways of signalling a particular social
framework of interpretation and understanding – whether consciously held or not (Williams 1988). As such they provide insight into
the informing perspective and often preferred understanding of the
events in question offered by a speaker to his or her audience. In
relation to the contested site of the inner city, therefore, it should
come as no surprise that differing perspectives on the inner city
problem, and instances of inner city disorder particularly, should
produce competing repertoires of preferred terms.

Take the term 'riot' and its semantic challengers first. Whereas the term 'riot' in current usage[1] tends to position the event of disorder as a problem for the forces of law and order, in that it carries connotations of criminal mob behaviour confronting the agencies of order, the terms 'rebellion' or 'uprising' shift the semantic field to that of the purposeful action of a united group, who, reacting against an oppressive social order, collectively react against the problem which is now perceived to be an illegitimate state of social exclusion and oppression. In many respects this radical response can be seen as reversing the semantic field invoked by conservative understandings of riot. Such terms as 'disorder' or 'disturbance', in contrast, can be regarded as signalling a more intermediate discursive position. Though not challenging the illegality of such behaviour, such terms, generally supportive of a liberal perspective on social disorder, imply that such events may be informed by a context or preceding social conditions which help to explain them. This is unlike both the conservative view which is disposed to see the event of a riot as naked criminality, as well as the the radical viewpoint informed by its sense of legitimate collective protest against the illegitimate actions of an oppressive state.

Such terms thus work to mobilize meanings which surround the contested site of the inner city, seeking to place the events of inner city disorder within a wider, if particular, interpretative framework. Such keywords may be regarded as anchor points seeking to attach chains of signification to a wider, and invariably partial, river of social meaning and interpretation. At least three sets of keywords can be identified as of particular importance here, these concern (a) the naming or labelling of the event itself, as discussed above, (b) the labelling of involved social participants, and (c) the labelling of the social space in which the disorders occurred. Before examining each of these sets of keywords, it is first interesting to learn who exactly has been involved in such processes of semantic assigning. Who, in other words, has managed to deploy these three sets of interpretative 'anchor points'?

Table 6.1 *News labelling: social groups placing keywords*

	Participants (%)	Event (%)	Social space (%)	All (%)
Media	53.7	77.5	60.4	68.3
Police	22.8	8.2	14.6	12.5
Community	8.9	4.0	7.8	6.0
Politician	3.2	4.9	7.5	5.5
Others	11.4	5.4	9.7	7.7
	(n)123 *100.0*	(n)427 *100.0*	(n)268 *100.0*	(n)818 *100.0*

Table 6.1 shows that of all the keywords deployed across one full year of 'Handsworth riot' news reports and involving 153 separate news items, it is media presenters and reporters themselves who

place most of these, from half to over three-quarters for each group of keywords. This is interesting in that it may be taken as qualifying any blanket assertion of the news media as simply providing a platform of access for the direct relaying of the accounts of others. The news media, from this initial finding, may be more deeply implicated in those processes of so-called 'primary definition', or the placing in the public domain of preferred frameworks of interpretation, than is sometimes argued. Noticeably, it is the police who thereafter secure the second most opportunities for providing such terms, with over twice as many keywords deployed in comparison to any other accessed social group.

News language: labelling the event

If the array of terms used to refer to the disorders is examined these can be located broadly within five groupings. First, the event may be signified as a criminal event, and here reference to violence and criminal activity is invoked. Second, the event may simply be referred to as a 'riot', or the 'Handsworth riots'. Such terms as these have, over a period of time and with repeated use by the media, become established as the general descriptives used in discussions of such events. While this may be taken as confirming the establishment of a preferred understanding of the 'riots', it could also be argued such terms are now used without necessarily accepting the underlying conservative premises noted above. In other words, such terms have simply become the lingua franca of riot discussions. On this basis it would be misleading to simply interpret the use of such terms, in the absence of attending to their surrounding linguistic, thematic, narrative and visual contexts, as supportive of a criminal interpretation. In terms of this preliminary analysis, then, such terms may be thought to be discursively ambiguous and can therefore be treated, for the moment at least, separately from other event labels. Third, though not necessarily aligned to a strictly criminal association, the riot may be designated by terms which indicate some form of disturbance or trouble, while, fourth, a more neutral terminology may be found which simply refers to the 'events' or 'occurrences' and so on. Fifth, a radical lexicon may be identified which seeks to indicate the event as a form of collective protest and reaction against a perceived state of oppression and injustice.

Descriptive	Examples
Criminal/violence	'violence', 'orgy of looting'
Riot	'riots', 'rioting', 'Handsworth riots',
Trouble/disturbance	'troubles', 'disturbances', 'disorder'
Incident/event	'incident', 'event', 'occurrence'
Rebellion	'rebellion', 'revolt', 'protest', 'uprising'

Table 6.2   *Social groups labelling Handsworth 1985: the event*

	Criminal	Riot	Trouble	Incident	Rebellion	All
Media	13.9	73.4	10.3	2.4	0.0	77.5
Police	17.1	71.4	8.6	2.8	0.0	8.2
Community	17.6	29.4	23.5	17.6	11.8	4.0
Politician	38.1	42.8	4.7	14.3	0.0	4.9
Other	34.8	39.1	26.1	0.0	0.0	5.4
Overall usage	(n)71 *16.6*	(n)291 *68.2*	(n)48 *11.2*	(n)15 *3.5*	(n)2 *0.5*	(n)427 *100.0*

Note: percentages indicate frequencies in usage of event terms in each social group; overall usage indicates each term's occurrence as percentage of all event terms.

Once again, Table 6.2 indicates that by far the vast majority of key event terms are provided by news personnel, followed by the police. The term 'riot' is employed most often, with a criminal reference assuming the second most frequent association. Thereafter, the event is most frequently referred to in terms which emphasize an aspect of 'trouble', while the anodyne terms of 'events', 'occurrences', and so on are rarely employed. With 0.5 percent of all designations invoking radical associations of protest and revolt, clearly the Handsworth riots has found uneven lexical support in relation to those contending positions on inner city disorder.

Moreover, if the terms deployed by the media and police are compared it is noticeable that similar terms are found to be deployed by each, which is not the case if media and community terms are compared. With the community references tending to place the event in terms which involve 'trouble', 'incident' and 'rebellion' the media and the police are more inclined to refer to the riots in terms which stress their status as 'criminal', 'riot' and 'trouble' events.

News language: labelling the participants

If the range of labels used to describe those actively involved in scenes of disorder is examined, the following kinds of descriptive labels are found across the news reports.

Descriptive	Examples
Political extremists	'shadowy figures', 'anarchists', 'extremists'
Organized criminals	'drug barons', 'hardened criminals'
Unorganized criminals	'rampaging mob', 'looters', 'hooligans'
Rioters	'rioters', 'Handsworth rioters'
Participants	'people responsible', 'youngsters', 'those involved'
Disadvantaged/disaffected	'unemployed youth', 'disaffected part of the community', 'alienated youth'

If participants are described as 'rampaging youths' or 'looters', or perhaps 'hardened criminals' or 'hard core criminals' the variants of an essentially conservative discourse, invoking either conspiratorial and organized criminality or ideas of moral degeneration and mob gratification, are implicated. Similarly, the idea of political extremists, orchestrating the mob from afar, can also be seen to be supportive of a conservative understanding to the extent that it distances any notion of real grievance and/or collective purposeful intent. In contrast, if rioters are referred to as 'unemployed youth' or 'that disadvantaged section of the community' then the possibility of mobilizing a liberal or even radical interpretative frame appears to be in the offing.

Table 6:3   *Social groups labelling Handsworth 1985: the participants*

	Extremist	Hard-core	Criminal	Rioter	Participant	Disaffected	All
Media	1.5	9.1	51.5	25.8	10.6	1.5	53.7
Police	10.7	21.4	42.9	21.4	3.6	0.0	22.8
Community	0.0	9.1	0.0	0.0	90.9	0.0	8.9
Politician	0.0	25.0	25.0	0.0	50.0	0.0	3.2
Other	0.0	7.1	42.9	14.3	35.7	0.0	11.4
Overall usage	(n)4 *3.3*	(n)15 *12.2*	(n)53 *43.1*	(n)25 *20.3*	(n)25 *20.3*	(n)1 *0.8*	(n)123 *100.0*

Note: percentages indicate frequencies in usage of participant terms in each social group; overall usage indicates each term's occurrence as percentage of all participant terms.

From Table 6.3 it can be seen that a pronounced tendency to label those involved in acts of inner city disorder as criminals has characterized this media portrayal, with the media and the police, the two major voices in this regard, often deploying similar terms. If 'rioter' is, for the sake of this analysis, taken to be discursively ambiguous, it can also be noted that a further fifth of all labels refer to the participants in terms which do not invoke moral censure, while less than 1 per cent of terms invoke the status of rioters as 'disadvantaged' or 'unemployed' and so on. Once again, it would seem, the interpretative resources placed within the public domain prefer a particular understanding of those involved.

If the key terms applied to participants are examined further it is interesting to note how they can sustain differing meanings. While news personnel references to 'youth' involve such associate terms as 'rampaging youths' 'roaming youths' and 'gangs of youths' in over half of all usages, these can be contrasted to all other references, with one exception, in which 'youth' has tended to be used alongside different associations. Though in a minority, here such associations as 'young lads', 'the kids', 'youth of the area' can be found, and have been predominantly deployed by community representatives. While one set of youth terms appears to set young people apart from society, excluded by their deviant actions (and often implied predatory animal behaviour), the other has tended to position 'youth' as belonging to the wider community.

News language: labelling the social space

Labelled in particular terms, and involving labelled participants, the events under question and their media presentation also involved labelling the social space in which they took place. 'Social space' is here used to refer to the geographical, social, political or other domains which help situate the disorders within a particular framework of understanding. At least seven different social spaces can be identified across the news sample which help, semantically, to locate the preferred meaning of the Handsworth riots.

Descriptive	Examples
Criminal	'centre of drug traffic', 'trouble spot', 'area difficult to police'
Volatile/tense	'volatile area', 'tense area', 'no-go zone', 'explosive area'
Racial/'race'	'little Caribbean', 'multi-racial area'
Riot	'riot hit area', 'riot torn area'
Geographical?	'Handsworth', 'Handsworth-Lozells'
Inner city	'deprived area', 'inner city area'
Positive/celebratory	'thriving centre', 'commercial centre'

It is apparent from Table 6.4 that the majority of all references refer to the geographical space of 'Handsworth'. The use of the question mark, however, reminds us that in so far as Handsworth has received a high news profile in the past it may be considered likely that the term already carries far more associations than merely a geographical reference[2]. The fact that news portrayal of Handsworth has been dominated by crime news reports and features (68 per cent) indicates

Table 6.4 *Social groups labelling Handsworth 1985: the social space*

	Crime	Volatile	Racial	Riot	Geo-graphical?	Inner city	Positive	All
Media	6.8	3.1	1.8	9.2	69.1	6.2	3.7	60.4
Police	2.6	5.1	2.6	0.0	82.0	5.1	2.6	14.6
Community	4.8	0.0	0.0	0.0	85.7	9.5	0.0	7.8
Politician	0.0	0.0	0.0	0.0	80.0	20.0	0.0	7.5
Other	3.8	7.7	3.8	3.8	69.2	11.5	0.0	9.7
Overall	*5.3*	*3.3*	*1.9*	*6.0*	*73.1*	*7.8*	*2.6*	*100.0*
usage	(n)14	(n)9	(n)5	(n)16	(n)196	(n)21	(n)7	(n)268

Note: percentages indicate frequencies in usage of space terms in each social group; overall usage indicates each term's occurrence as percentage of all space terms.

that the label may already signify potent associated meanings. A further point lends some credibility to such an argument.

This concerns the astounding finding that the bulk of serious disorder labelled as 'the Handsworth riots' and repeatedly referenced as such by the news media, actually took place principally in Lozells Birmingham, an adjacent inner city ward. Unlike Lozells, however, Handsworth has received considerable past news coverage, including news coverage of the 1981 Handsworth riots, and as such appears to inform journalist expectancies which readily interpret disorders, even when not strictly in the Handsworth locality, as 'Handsworth riots'.

The remaining terms used to locate the disorders, though in an overall minority, also indicate that contending positions have been involved. With just under 8 per cent of all lexical terms referring to the 'inner city' it appears that at least some involvement of a wider discourse, perhaps relating to social deprivation, has occasionally been in play. With almost twice as many references however, the following three social domains of 'riot', 'crime' and 'volatility' together begin to suggest that Handsworth is a place of potential and actual trouble, a designation clearly lending support to a conservative criminal interpretation. Also within a strict minority are those terms either referencing the site of the disorders as a positive place, or one in which issues of 'race' and/or racism are thought to be of direct relevance. While the former may reflect earlier discussions of the celebratory appeals occasionally informing regional news stories, the latter suggests that the resources for either a radical or extreme racist interpretation have not been present in these explicit terms. Once again it is apparent from Table 6.4 that the majority of all such terms are placed by the news media, followed by the police and that, generally, these invoke either 'Handsworth' or a criminal association, with strictly limited use of other social space terms.

From these preliminary analyses of the keywords found across the representation of the Handsworth disorders, such a portrayal cannot simply be described as a form of consistent 'ideological closure', though a particular interpretation appears to have been preferred. This has been sustained, first, by the terms deployed by the media themselves and, second, by the accessed statements of the police. While the majority of such terms appear to be supportive of a conservative perspective on the events, keywords supportive of alternative viewpoints have also occasionally been found. Clearly, though suggestive at this stage, further analysis is called for.

The Handsworth riots: narrative structures

The fact that regional news has provided considerable follow-up news treatments to the regional/national news event of a major inner city disturbance illustrates the possible importance of regional television news, and perhaps regional and local news media generally, in providing sustained news portrayal of important issues. In approaching the extended portrayal of the Handsworth riots over a twelve month period, it is instructive first to identify and chart some of the principal elements which comprise such a narrative, before identifying in detail the substantive content or topics which gain news attention.

The event of a 'riot' is situated in time with both a pre- and post-history as well as an informing context. It occurred, in other words, in a certain place, in a definite form involving certain groups of people in a particular way, for particular reasons. However, if the event of the riot is of immediate news interest and can be investigated accordingly, it is also possible to identify further elements within a wider narrative of riot news reporting.

If the riot can be attended to as an *event*, so too can the immediate *aftermath* of a riot be examined, while both the riot as event and aftermath can both be noted as eliciting a number of *responses*. These three elements, riot as event, aftermath and response, logically form three initial component parts of the mediated reality of a riot. Moreover, they can each be approached in terms of a number of constituent substantive concerns and media interests that 'fill' such narrative structures.

The element of *consequence* can also usefully be identified as a longer term reaction following upon the riot as event. Moreover, if riot as consequence points to the post-history of a riot, riot as *background* points to its claimed antecedents. Both the narrative elements of consequence and background, as well as establishing the event of a riot within a temporal flow also, of course, provide ingredients which may support or detract from particular interpretative frameworks. It is therefore essential, just as with the elements of event, aftermath and response, to clearly identify the substantive news concerns which fill these two elements.

In addition, the narrative element of *future* provides further opportunities for sustaining or developing a particular interpretation of inner city disorder. While consequence may be taken as the longer term reactions or effects following upon the event of a riot, the element of future extrapolates from the riot as event and posits a future scenario. To this extent the extrapolation is very much dependent upon the initial understanding and interpretation of the event itself, and therefore implicitly involves an act of interpretation. The element of *explanation* is an obvious and explicit indication of the interpretative framework informing the news treatment of a riot. One final element can also usefully be addressed, this concerns the involvement of *metaphor* and *allusion*. Clearly, allusions and metaphors inherently contain a capacity to sustain particular interpretative frameworks through their potential to sustain meaning by association, and which often informs their use in the first place. These narrative structures informing an extended treatment of riot portrayal and implicated in processes of riot interpretation are presented diagrammatically in Figure 6.1.

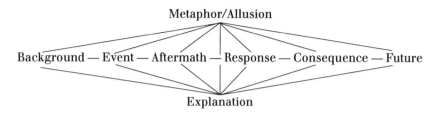

Background — Event — Aftermath — Response — Consequence — Future

Figure 6.1 Riot as narrative: interpretative elements

While the elements considered inherent to the story of a riot obviously point to a narrative unfolding through time, it is clear that such elements can be invoked time and time again with no necessary regard to developments happening within actual time. The narrative element of the Handsworth riot as an event is rehearsed, for example, with every news report returning, for whatever reason, to those initial happenings. So too is it the case with all the other narrative elements. It will be seen that the representation of such riot narrative elements across the extended portrayal of the riot have differing implications for each of the three interpretative frameworks, whether conservative, liberal or radical.

If such narrative properties can be found to differently support or hinder the development of a particular understanding of inner city disorders, the substantive issues and concerns informing news accounts must also be attended to in detail. For the purpose of this analysis then, a wide-ranging list of riot-related references or issues was elicited from the sample of 153 news items across a twelve month period, and a number of principal topics identified. Principal topics refer to what the news item could be said to be about essentially.

If attention is first directed at the overall narrative structures, as elicited by attending to a comprehensive quantitative review of over one hundred riot related references encompassed within these different structures (detailed below), the following is found. From

Table 6.5 *News structures of a riot narrative*

Riot as	Frequency	%
Event	228	19.9
Aftermath	131	11.5
Response	117	10.2
Consequence	266	23.3
Background	246	21.5
Future	55	4.8
Explanation	44	3.8
Metaphor/Allusion	57	5.0
Total references	*1144*	*100.0*

Table 6.5 it is apparent that not all narrative elements across one full year of riot reports are present to the same degree. The event of the riot assumes just under one-fifth of total references, while the immediate aftermath and response each secure little over one-tenth of all references. Over two-fifths of this riot coverage, in other words, is devoted to the 'immediate' riot event, aftermath and initial responses. Clearly, the initial event and related narrative elements, while not dominating the total news coverage, are none the less afforded substantial news attention given the compressed duration of these elements within actual time. It can also be surmised that these initial narrative elements are likely to provide some of the basic resources for interpretation mobilized in subsequent accounts of the riot. While the event can generally be accepted as a serious breach of law and order, if the news coverage continually positions the event as simply that, without involving other considerations perhaps relating to cause, motive or explanation then a powerful interpretative resource has arguably already been established.

The element of consequence assumes the single most prevalent narrative element with nearly a quarter of all references. The riots, though clearly important in and of themselves, are also of news interest in that they have prompted, provoked or elicited further consequences. Such consequences moreover relate back to the initial riot as event and implicitly or explicitly position the event in terms which have necessitated these, as opposed to other, consequences. As such consequences may be regarded as an important resource in the development of a riot interpretation.

The element of background, already noted as a principal contender in the provision of interpretative resources which would help explain the riot as event, secures little over a fifth of all riot references. In combination with the element of consequence, then, it would appear from this initial overview that substantial interpretative resources have been included within the news narrative of this particular riot.

The element of future is present with just under 5 per cent of all references, indicating that the future, though likely to involve an interpretation of the present (and past), is not generally invoked in riot treatments. The element of explanation, an element which explicitly and directly advances an account, including cause, motivation and/or reason for the event of a riot, is firmly at the core of any interpretative framework. Interestingly, however, explanation only figures as 4 per cent of all riot references. While this 4 per cent needs to be attended to carefully, it indicates that in so far as informing interpretative frameworks are concerned they may be sustained by wider features of news portrayal.

One last narrative element, that of metaphor/allusion, which was again thought to be a potentially important resource for sustaining interpretation, has also rarely been deployed in regional news, though these may provide potent images when used.

At this general level of narrative elements, it appears that the immediate events and their aftermath have captured considerable news interest. In so far as such events have been afforded differing explanatory emphases across conservative, liberal and radical interpretative perspectives it can be suggested that such in itself provides a differential resource for the interpretation of inner city disorder. With conservative viewpoints inclined to concentrate upon the violence and destruction of the event itself, given that this is where criminal behaviour and intent is manifest, such prominent news emphases may be found to lend particular support to such an understanding, especially if the event is continually invoked, both verbally and visually, across the extended riot portrayal. Liberal and radical perspectives, though recognizing the centrality of the events in question, require further contextualizing levels of reference with the radical perspective also seeking perhaps an informing historical and structural framework to assist its particular interpretation. Significantly, the element of background has secured considerable presence and it is interesting therefore to inquire below to what extent this may in fact provide either the contextual conditions sought by the liberal perspective or wider historical resources sought by a radical interpretative framework.

The Handsworth riots: news references

At this point, it is necessary to move on from these fairly abstract categories and interrogate the exact references which comprise such riot narrative elements. What interpretative resources, in other words, have been provided in the riot portrayal for each of our contending inner city perspectives? Given the general aim of gaining a detailed and comprehensive overview of this full year of riot coverage each separate news item has been consulted on each of a hundred plus riot references, and then aggregated across the entire sample. Additionally each item was coded according to one of the hundred plus topics if this was deemed to be what the item was principally about. As well as securing an overview of all subsidiary references finding media expression across the 153 items, therefore, those prominent patterns of principal riot news interests have also been gained. The discussion following, then, represents the broad agenda of riot issues and topics gaining news coverage across this extended period of riot portrayal.

With nearly one fifth of all references, the riot as event (Table 6.6) is clearly of importance in establishing a possible riot interpretation. Moreover, to the extent that such an event can be resurrected in its news mediation days and weeks, months and even years after the actual event took place, so such resources can continue to inform media portrayals of the Handsworth riots for a considerable period of time. Given that, as suggested earlier, not all perspectives on the inner city riots are equally preoccupied with the narrative element of

Table 6.6   *Riot as event* (Narrative element: 19.9%)

Topic/reference		Principal Topic	
	%	Frequency	%
Rioting: violence/stoning	28.1	1	0.6
Property destruction/burning	25.0		
Rioting: looting	14.9		
Police operation/amassed	11.0	1	0.6
Emergency service involvement	8.7		
Police under attack	7.0		
Police advance	4.4		
Other/general event	0.9	2	1.4
(n)228	*100.0*	*4*	*2.6*

Note: In this and other riot elements below, percentage figures for topics and references are derived from each particular element which therefore equals 100 per cent; principal topic percentages are based on the total number of news items, thus percentage figures refer to 100 per cent equals 153.

event, such an emphasis may be found to sustain such perspectives differently. This becomes clearer if the constituent references and topics of the event are considered. Here the media is found to be principally focused on acts of violence, the destruction of property, and looting. While unaccounted violence and destruction appear in themselves to be inexplicable, looting may provide a self-evident rationale, though the wider reason for looting within a context of rioting is not necessarily apparent nor, of course, an explanation for the riot itself.

The police operation assumes a further aspect of news interest in relation to the event. In the sense that the police operation is referenced as a reaction against the largely unexplained, or visually inexplicable violence and destruction, the riot is likely to appear as an assault on law and order. This too may appear obvious, since isn't this what defines a riot? The point here however, is that to the extent that the riot as event is portrayed as an uncontrolled and violent assault on the forces of law and order, so the police reaction may be perceived as both necessary and secondary to the event itself. One only need think of those occasional foreign 'riot' reports to realize that such need not always be the case. Here mention can be made of those news crews who have managed to film protests and demonstrations from within the ranks and geographical space of the demonstrators themselves. From this vantage point, riots can be portrayed in a very different light where violence may now be seen as a desperate act of defiance against an oppressive regime and its military and/or police supporters. Violence now becomes explicable, in other words, and the role of the police may be seen as contributing to, rather than as a secondary response to the event.

As it is, the event of a riot is referenced as an inexplicable outpouring of violence, destruction and looting perpetrated by a crowd of rioters whose destructive presence is only known through the evident reactions of a police force confronting acts of disorder. In this sense, the police appear as an external protagonist reacting to the event of a riot, rather than as an agency routinely involved within inner city policing and therefore possibly an internal protagonist implicated in the causation of the event itself.

Table 6.7 *Riot as aftermath* (Narrative element: 11.4%)

Topic/reference		Principal Topic	
	%	Frequency	%
Death of Molidinas	34.3	3	2.0
Devastated property	27.5	1	0.6
Costs of damage	12.1	1	0.6
Injured general	10.7		
Looted property	9.2	1	0.6
Injured police	4.6		
Other/general aftermath	1.4	1	0.6
Injured rioters	0.0		
(n) 131	*99.8*	7	*4.4*

If the event of the riot is firmly situated as an outbreak of disorder and criminality, the immediate aftermath news coverage compounds such an initial portrayal (Table 6.7). As the full extent of the damage began to be recognized, so the bodies of two brothers, the Molidinas, found within the burnt-out shell of a post office gave the criminal placing of the event a further confirming twist. With media references to murder, this tragedy assumed a sinister aspect. Later, it was confirmed, contrary to news anticipation, that the deaths of the two Molidina brothers were not 'murders' preceded by beatings, but deaths by suffocation from fire. Reference to these two deaths assumes the most prominent form of aftermath topic followed by devastated property and costs of damage.

With other aftermath news focused upon injuries and looted property, the event is further reinforced as a criminal outburst and of news interest to the extent of damage and loss of life caused. While such features are of undoubted regional news interest, it is also the case, in combination with event reporting that they have displaced other possible viewpoints on the riots. This becomes clearer when considering that aftermath, as with event, can be rehearsed time and time again throughout the continuing news portrayal which is not confined to reporting in 'actual time'. It is in this sense that the comments above relating to displacement need to be considered. Assuming over one tenth of all riot coverage, and a number of principal news topics, aftermath adds further support to the criminal and violent frame ordering the riot event.

Table 6.8 *Riot as response* (Narrative element: 10.2%)

Topic/reference		Principal Topic	
	%	Frequency	%
Police response	31.5	7	4.6
Police investigations	27.3	7	4.6
Status visit/proclamation	21.4	10	6.5
Local authority response	6.0	2	1.3
Community representatives	5.1	1	0.6
Community others	4.3		
Clearing up/boarding up	4.3		
Other/response	0.0		
(n)117	99.9	27	17.6

Further confirming the initial riot news treatment the narrative element of response (Table 6.8) is heavily skewed towards the police, and the law and disorder perspective seeking to make sense of the riot. Together police responses, that is elicited comments in news interviews, as well as news reports covering ensuing police investigations comprise nearly three-fifths of all riot responses. Moreover, these two topics are afforded over 9 per cent of all principal topics across the entire coverage. Clearly, the criminal frame is further buttressed by such extensive news interest in police responses. Over one-fifth of all other responses are secured by visiting and high-ranking politicians further reflected within over 6 per cent of all principal topics. Local authority responses gain 6 per cent, community representatives just over 5 per cent and 'ordinary' community voices little over 4 per cent of all responses. It would appear on this basis that a hierarchy of response is effectively in operation with the police and senior politicians securing the lion's share of media opportunities to respond to the event and aftermath of a riot while the local authority, community representatives, and ordinary community members share the remainder of responses in descending order of frequency.

With nearly a quarter of all riot references and topics, and over half of all principal topics, the narrative element of consequence (Table 6.9) plays a prominent role in the overall coverage of the Handsworth riots. The various consequences following on from the event of a riot may often provide insight into exactly how the event of the riot and its underlying causes are interpreted and signified within news media coverage. This broad span of consequences can usefully be further subdivided (see Tables 6.10 and 6.11) into forms of policing consequence and other concerns. Initially however it can be seen that, with far in excess of any other single topic, court trials secures over 14 per cent of all consequence items below and one-fifth of all principal news topics (more than three times that of any other single principal topic). Routinely punctuating the year's riot coverage, such reports reaffirm the initial positioning of the

Table 6.9 *Riot as consequence* (Narrative element 23.2%)

Topic/reference	%	Principal topic Frequency	%
Court trial	14.3	31	20.3
Local authority initiative	9.0	1	0.6
Police community relations	8.6		
Effects on traders/trade	8.3	1	0.6
Central government initiative	7.9	5	3.3
Police equipment (offensive)	7.1	10	6.5
Inquiry (Silverman)	6.0	10	6.5
Police riot tactics/training	5.5	3	2.0
Compensation/insurance	5.3	5	3.3
Community organized (traders)	4.9		
Police manning/resources	4.1	4	2.6
Police equipment (protective)	3.4		
Community organized (other)	3.0	1	0.6
Impact on Birmingham's image	3.0	3	2.0
Inquiry (police report)	2.2		
Rebuilding/redevelopment	2.2		
Police cmttee/accountability	1.5		
Inquest	1.1	3	2.0
Funeral	0.7	2	1.4
Inquiry (Ouseley et al)	0.7	1	0.6
Police recruitment (black)	0.7	1	0.6
Media response	0.7		
Police awards	0.0		
Community policing training	0.0		
Other/consequence	0.0		
(n)266 *100.2*		*81*	*52.9*

riot as a criminal event, now further endorsed by the judicial processes of law. In Tables 6.10 and 6.11 policing references are grouped into those which point to an increased police presence and 'tougher' responses, and those referencing the concerns of improved community policing and liaison. Over one-third of all reports dealing with the consequences of the riots involve the police. Of these it is plain that consequences relating to 'tooling up' receive the most prominence with over one-fifth of all reports, and over one-tenth of all principal topics. Together with court trials nearly one-third of all principal topics (48) across the entirety of riot news items are therefore concerned with the enforcement of law and order. In marked contrast, those other features of policing which need not necessarily be regarded as supportive of an authoritarian law and order response, though clearly still very much concerned with inner city policing, receive markedly less news interest. Clearly, in so far as consequence is concerned with policing, it is the issues of 'tooling up', and not community policing or increased police accountability, which has secured the most news representation.

Table 6.10   *Consequence as policing: 'tooling up'*

Topic	%	Principal topic Frequency	%
Police equipment (offensive)	7.1	10	6.5
Police riot training	5.5	3	2.0
Police manning/resources	4.1	4	2.6
Police equipment (protective)	3.4		
Inquiry (police report)	2.2		
(n)70	22.3	17	11.1

Table 6.11   *Consequence as policing: 'community policing'*

Topic	%	Principal topic Frequency	%
Police community relations	8.6		
Police cm'ttee/accountability	1.5		
Police recruitment (black)	0.7	1	0.6
Community policing training	0.0		
(n)29	10.8	1	0.6

Table 6.12   *Riot as consequence: remainder*

Topic/reference	%	Principal topic Frequency	%
Local authority initiative	9.0	1	0.6
Effects on traders/trade	8.3	1	0.6
Central government initiative	7.9	5	3.3
Inquiry (Silverman)	6.0	10	6.5
Compensation/insurance	5.3	5	3.3
Community organized (traders)	4.9		
Community organized (other)	3.0	1	0.6
Impact on Birmingham's image	3.0	3	2.0
Rebuilding/redevelopment	2.2		
Inquest	1.1	3	2.0
Funeral	0.7	2	1.4
Inquiry (Ouseley et al)	0.7	1	0.6
Media response	0.7		
(n)111	41.5	17	11.1

Of those remaining consequences (Table 6.12), local authority and central government initiatives receive noticeable attention. Relatedly, the Birmingham City Council-sponsored Silverman Inquiry (Silverman 1986) received a number of news reports relating to the various aspects of the Handsworth disturbances, and was the principal news topic in over 6 per cent of all riot coverage. Interestingly, the police report written by the Chief Constable of the West Midlands Police (Dear 1985), and the independent report sponsored by the West Midland's County Council (Ousley et al. 1986), both received relatively infrequent news attention, with the 'radical' independent report receiving the least news attention of all. In sum, it can be noted that while riot as consequence assumes the largest proportion of riot coverage, when considered in terms of its constituent and principal topics found across the array of news items, it is the incidents of court trials, policing generally, and policing in terms of the issues surrounding a general 'tooling up' response towards the Handsworth riots particularly that have received most riot news representation. Thereafter, local authority and central government initiatives, and

Table 6.13 *Riot as background* (Narrative element: 21.5%)

Topic/reference		Principal Topic	
	%	Frequency	%
Criminality			
Precipitator/'spark'	6.9		
Villa Cross drugs raid	6.9	7	4.6
Extremists: organized criminals	6.9	1	0.6
Crime/criminality	6.5		
sub-total (n)67 *27.2*		*8*	*5.2*
Policing			
Community police relations	7.7		
Police–black youth relations	3.7		
Model of community policing	2.8	1	0.6
Tension indicators/intelligence	2.8		
Police harassment/racism	2.8		
Insensitive policing	2.4		
Handsworth carnival 1985	1.2		
sub-total (n)58 *23.4*		*1*	*0.6*
Conditions			
Unemployment	11.4		
Social deprivation	9.3		
Economy/recession	2.8		
sub-total (n)58 *23.5*			
'Race' and racism			
Community difference (black–Asian)	8.1		
Racism/discrimination	3.3		
Black disadvantage	2.4		
Black presence/history	2.0	1	0.6
Racial difference (white–black)	1.2		
sub-total (n)42 *17.0*		*1*	*0.6*
Political administration			
Government policy/schemes	2.4		
Local authority policy/schemes	2.4		
Government policy/deleterious cuts	2.0		
Local authority policy/cuts	0.8		
sub-total (n)19 *7.6*			
Political conspirators			
Extremists: political radicals	0.8	2	1.4
Extremists: political right-wing	0.0		
sub-total (n)2 *0.8*		*2*	*1.4*
Total (n)246 *100.0*		*12*	*7.8*

the findings of the Silverman Inquiry assume a secondary news prominence, while concerns relating to trade, commerce and the local economy also receive some news attention.

Once again (Table 6.13) it can be noted how crime and criminality have assumed the largest group of background references. While crime and criminality can generally be seen as providing the most prevalent forms of background reference, in nearly half of all news items this refers to the 'precipitator' and drugs raid on the Villa Cross, both thought by the police to have acted as a riot trigger. An organized coterie of criminals, on occasions referred to as 'drugs barons', has also been frequently invoked in such background terms. Over three-quarters of background crime references, therefore, refer to a particular understanding of crime, generally restricted to the immediate period prior to the riot, an identified place, and an identified group of organized criminals controlling the specific practice of drug dealing. In these terms such news reports include reference to many of those crime ingredients taken by the conservative discourse to be at the heart of its riot interpretation: organized criminals masterminding lawlessness for their own illegal gains.

The general concerns of policing also gain substantial news attention. Here reference is made to community–police relations. Contrary to a long line of academic and other research which has continued to indicate that community–police relations in Handsworth have for a considerable period of time been problematic, this was apparently not shared by either the police or news personnel. A reporter on the night of the riots, for instance, introduces a question to a senior police officer by claiming 'The police have gone out of their way to foster good relations in Handsworth, has tonight destroyed that?' Moreover, the phrase used by Lord Scarman in his 1981 report suggested that Handsworth was a 'model of community policing', while the successful Handsworth carnival at the weekend prior to the initial disturbances was taken by a senior police interviewee as a further indicator of 'good relations'. Nearly half of all references to the police appear to indicate that in so far as policing is of background relevance to the Handsworth riots, community–police relations were considered to be of incidental relevance to the event itself. Indeed, the phrase subsequently employed by the police suggested that the riots came 'as a bolt out of the blue'. Unlike crime and criminality, policing is not the subject of media focus and attention, but is rather referenced in relation to other principal topics.

With nearly a quarter of all background topics referencing social conditions, and unemployment particularly, this broad area of concern has found numerous references though no news item made this its principal focus of news interest. In regard to the array of references to 'race' and racism it is interesting to note that the most prominent topic is that of black–Asian difference and hostility. In so far as questions of 'race' have been raised in relation to the Handsworth riots it is the intra-community concerns of black–Asian difference and/or hostility that is offered by the news portrayal as the central 'racial' concern. Just under 3 per cent of background items have referred to general discrimination and racism, and a few references have occasionally been made to police harassment. While no news items have specifically focused on the concerns of racism and disadvantage, one news item did involve an extended treatment of the history of Handsworth in terms of its black community, though concluding with a focus upon recent police drugs raids and the problems of the Villa Cross.

With a relative absence of references to preceding political background factors, whether central government policies or local authority initiatives and strained community relations, this aspect of the inner city scene, identified in both liberal and radical accounts of the Handsworth riots, has found little news representation.

Finally, it can be seen that the idea of political conspirators, an idea found previously to be advanced from within the conservative viewpoint, has also found marginal media involvement. Here a supposed anarchist group was reported as having secretly fermented the disorders. When considered in the light of the prevalent news interest in issues of organized criminals, drug barons, the drugs raids on the Villa Cross pub and general crime it is apparent that background resources are at hand for a conservative understanding of the riot.

It can be noted, then, how the narrative element of background assumes a major prominence within the overall riot narrative while also containing over half of all principal news topics. These however have tended to be focused in regard to criminal activities and policing concerns. Though issues of unemployment and social deprivation, as well as of 'race' and racism have found limited involvement, these have been considerably overshadowed by the presence of criminal references and principal news topics. Political considerations also receive subsidiary prominence confirmed with no principal news interest topics. To a marked degree the resources found within this important narrative element of background have been found to be supportive of a conservative understanding of the riots. To the extent that both liberal and radical interpretative viewpoints depend on this

Table 6.14 *Riot as future* (Narrative element: 4.8%)

Topic/reference		Principal topic	
	%	Frequency	%
Happy prospects	27.3	11	7.2
Dire predictions	21.9	3	2.0
Calendar landmark	18.2	4	2.6
Future as generalized violence	10.9	1	0.7
Local authority – failed promises	9.0		
Central government – failed promises	7.3		
Other/future	5.4	3	2.0
(n)55	*100.0*	*22*	*14.4*

particular narrative element, more so than the conservative with its central focus upon the event, so both have failed to find a vital interpretative resource.

Though not involving a wide number of general references and related topics, the narrative element of future (Table 6.14) does none the less receive prominent principal topic news attention. While a riot may be regarded as offering little in the way of positive or celebratory news, previous findings have indicated that the programme does seek to appeal to its audience by involving forms of positive news. Whether reporting on a jazz band and its efforts to provide musical relief in Handsworth at the end of the first week's riot coverage, a news item following the Handsworth and police sponsored cricket team to the West Indies, or the portrait of 'Ernie, the unsung hero of Handsworth' carrying out charitable work, or indeed the involvement of the police in school schemes designed to break down possible antipathies held by youth towards the local police, so such stories offer a positive news response to the Handsworth riots and make reference to future 'happy prospects'.

However, this programme disposition for happy prospects does not overrule those established news interests sensitized to the possibility of future riots. Dire predictions or warnings that such a disturbance could happen again also figure prominently here, invariably returning to the violence and effects of the earlier event. In other words the riot begins to assume a new significance not as a past event, but rather as a sign pointing to future things to come. If the Handsworth riots have thus assumed both the possibility for celebratory news coverage as well as dire predictions, it can also assume the form of regular calender landmarks. Thus, whether the first or second anniversary, Chief Constable's annual report, or end of year review of major news stories, the Handsworth riots can be repeatedly resurrected and put to work within differing news items.

In line with previous findings concerning the forms of regional news treatment of crime, the Handsworth riots have also occasionally been put to work in more generalized statements about crime and increased social violence. Most notably the riots have been linked, on occasion, to increased street violence, football riots and general violence. In other words, the criminal and violent aspects of the riots have been pressed into the service of an overview which seeks to maintain that society is itself becoming increasingly violent and the riots therefore simply express such wider changes. The informing contexts and unique nature of the Handsworth riots thus becomes lost from view, submerged within the generalized view of a 'violent society'.

A future scenario has also occasionally been painted which extrapolates from failed government policies and practices to a projected continuation of the problems and prospects already experienced by members of the Handsworth community. In relative terms these are not very prominent, and with no principal topic focus they once again tend, if anything, to point to the lack of considered treatment relating to the politics of the inner city. The narrative element of future, though not prominent at the level of general references, has informed a number of principal news topics and once again demonstrates that regional news can appropriate and inflect even the most serious of social concerns in terms of established programme ambitions and popular appeals.

Table 6.15 *Riot as explanation* (Narrative element: 3.7%)

Topic/reference	%	Principal topic Frequency	%
Crime/criminality	36.4		
Social deprivation/unemployment	20.5		
Racial rivalry (soft)	13.6		
Social injustice	9.1		
Moral decline	6.8		
Police insensitivity/harassment	6.8		
Other/explanation	6.8		
Racial hostility (hard)	0.0		
(n)44 *100.0*		*0*	*0.0*

In Table 6.15, what is striking about the narrative element of explanation is its relative absence when considered against some of the other elements already discussed. Journalist claims to objectivity and impartiality, though countered by media researchers and others on grounds of philosophical naivety and examined news portrayals, may none the less be found to be implicated in journalist practices in which explicit statements as to 'cause' are largely eschewed. Though acts of interpretation inevitably enter into the journalist's treatment of a news story, as demonstrated throughout this discussion, when it comes to a major social contest over meaning journalists are unlikely to advance an explicit explanation of the type 'this is what caused the Handsworth riots'. This is not to say, however, that the viewpoints of others who will advance an explicit explanation will not be sought and presented within news items. Once again, questions of access and editorial control are found to be of critical influence.

Of the forty-four explicit explanations advanced, over one-third have firmly pointed to the riot as a criminal act perpetrated by criminals. Such accounts have invariably posited 'crime' as an explanation in and of itself apparently requiring no further explanation or underpinning justification. Crime is crime is crime, and from within such a viewpoint any attempt to contextualize it within wider social processes is likely to be seen as tantamount to excusing the criminal activity, or worse, challenging the very definition of what is regarded as a criminal event requiring a law and order response. Within a minority of cases some wider underpinning has been advanced, however, also supportive of a criminal explanation but which refers to a perceived collapse of social morality regarded, or so it seems, as the last line of defence against the Hobbesian nightmare of 'all against all'. Together, then, these two criminal explanations assume the vast majority (43.2 per cent) of all explanations.

Explanations which point to widespread social deprivation and acute levels of inner city unemployment have found more limited expression while explanations invoking issues of 'race' and racism have only been explicitly raised in terms of a perceived intra-community or black–Asian schism thought, in some quarters, to have informed the Handsworth riots. Once again, issues of systemic racial disadvantage and institutionalized discrimination thought, in one perspective at least, to be at the centre of the disturbances have not found representation. What is worse, viewed from this perspective, when issues of racism have been raised these have centred on the minority ethnic communities themselves – once again localizing the problem to a question of intra-community rivalry. A further explanation, though finding strictly marginal involvement, has raised the question of police harassment and insensitive policing.

If issues of 'race' and racism have been advanced only within a minority of all explanations, it is also noticeable that 'hard' racialist accounts which have sought to place the origin of such social disturbances within a racist understanding of racial difference, inferiority and failure of an assumed immigrant population to assimilate to traditional British culture and way of life, have also been absent. In summary then, though within an overall minority of all narrative elements, explicit explanations have occasionally been advanced. The majority of these have sought to account for the riots as a criminal event requiring a law and order response. Nearly one-fifth of the remainder of explanations have invoked issues of high unemployment and social deprivation as the principal cause, while issues of 'race' have tended to be posited as an intra-community difference existing between black and Asian communities within the Handsworth area. Issues of social injustice, in part referencing minority communities, and problems of insensitive policing have found the barest of programme involvement as explicit explanations – notwithstanding their centrality in a contending social discourse.

Table 6.16 *Riot as metaphor* (Narrative element 5.0%)

Topic/reference	%	Principal topic	
		Frequency	%
World of nature/instinct	33.3		
Other inner city riots	24.6		
Handsworth riots 1981	17.5		
Northern Ireland	10.5		
American race riots	5.3		
War-time Britain	3.5		
Historical mainland riots	3.5		
Contemporary acts of disorder	1.8		
(n)57	*100.0*	*0*	*0.0*

One last element deemed to be particularly instructive in terms of the analysis of riot coverage is the use of metaphor and allusion (Table 6.16). With a third of all uses of metaphor and allusion the 'world of nature and instinct' secure the majority of all such instances. Whether the rioters are said to be engaged in an 'orgy of destruction' or 'descended like a plague of locusts on vulnerable shops' or 'roamed the streets in packs' such phrases invoke the forces of nature and instinct. As such the associations are set in place in which the riot is seen as an uncontrolled violent force, without purpose, design or rationality. Reference to instinct may also be regarded as particularly revealing in that it accords with conservative responses already discussed earlier where, either through the sinister design of others, or the libidinal forces which are seen to generally inhere within us all (though some more than others) such finally overrun forms of social and moral control. In this sense such use of metaphor can be regarded as a further endorsement of a particular way of making sense of the riot.

Nearly 44 per cent of all use of metaphor and allusions have referred to other inner city riots and contemporary acts of disorder, including the Handsworth disturbances of 1981. While such allusions may begin to situate the latest riots within a more generalized phenomenon, they do not in themselves of course necessarily provide any further degree of explanation. Frequently posited as similar to, or a further example of, this now generalized phenomenon of crime or violence, questions of interpretation remain undeveloped and leave the way open for a conservative understanding of such events.

Allusion to Northern Ireland, particularly in connection with the ensuing debate over the introduction of baton rounds (plastic bullets), has provided an occasional parallel in so far as the differences pertaining to these two situations have been distanced under the surface similarity of a particular form of state response to 'trouble-makers' – once again preferring a conservative interpretation of inner city disorders.

American race riots have also been referred to on occasion, as has war-time Britain, indicating that though riots may not be entirely without precedent, in the former a geographical distance is indicated and in the latter similarity is forged on the basis of scenes of conflagration and destruction. The long history of mainland riots found both in the last century and the present have largely been ignored. The use of metaphor and allusion therefore, has tended to support an interpretation which sees the Handsworth riots as essentially an irrational and instinctual eruption of purposeless destruction and mob violence. To this extent the deployment of metaphor and allusion may be regarded as particularly supportive of a criminal understanding of the events in question.

Summary findings

It has been noted across the discussion that the story of the Handsworth riots has unravelled over an extended period of actual time. Indeed, with references to Handsworth riots continuing to inform news reports to this day, it would appear that the story can run indefinitely. The riots appear therefore to be in distinct danger of assuming the status of a contemporary myth, that is, an established and condensed set of images, concerns and issues whose force and vitality lies not in the depiction of a past event, but rather in its potency as an organizing set of ideas and images capable of providing 'insight' into the affairs of the present.

Attending to some of the fundamental narrative elements deployed across this mediated account, the riot story has been found to exhibit a structure which involves different elements in different degrees. These, it has been suggested, provide potentially differing degrees of explanatory and interpretative support for the three interpretative frameworks discussed, as well as encompassing the substantive news agenda of riot issues and concerns broadcast across a considerable period of time. It has been demonstrated that while explicit explanations are relatively rare, the remaining narrative elements can be regarded as providing the necessary infrastructure which, taken together, represent the resources supportive of particular interpretative frameworks.

A conservative understanding of the riots has been effectively supported and sustained across the riot narrative, though a liberal concern with issues of social deprivation, disadvantage and unemployment has also found some sustenance within and across the elements discussed. If the radical interpretation is considered, which has clearly posited a central concern with issues of racism, disadvantage and police brutality at the heart of its interpretation, then few resources are found which could help sustain such a viewpoint. The main finding here, then, is that contending perspectives on the inner city, as focused through a major incident of inner city disorder, have found differing degrees of interpretative support, while significant silences have effectively denied the infrastructure for at least one perspective, and undermined the possibility of forging a coherent and adequate interpretative position of another. Such has not been found to be the case with the conservative criminal understanding of the Handsworth riots which has consistently been privileged across the various elements discussed above.

The Handsworth riots visualized

Commonly, it is said that part of the power of TV news, when compared to the press or radio, is the medium's capacity to deliver authenticating visuals – 'seeing is believing'. While this popular idea ignores the extent to which preconceived ideas, beliefs and values can filter and influence what is seen – 'believing is seeing' – it is undoubtedly the case that TV news visuals do provide an important resource for the accomplishment of meaning. This analysis cannot remain at the level of narrative and verbal characteristics alone, therefore, but must also seek to address the role of news pictures. What has the visual dimension consisted of? Is it the case, perhaps, that visual resources can also prefer a particular interpretation of the Handsworth riots, and not others? If so, how can we chart this, given the special difficulties associated with film and visual analysis?

For the purposes of this analysis, a complementary approach has been adopted to the analysis above. Consulting each of the 153 riot news items broadcast over a twelve month period in terms of the presence or absence of over one hundred references and their visual counterparts, an aggregate picture of those repetitive patterns of visual presences and silences can be obtained. This method, seeking an aggregate overview, avoids the problem of moving pictures given that only visual presences and absences are sought within each item, and not their repetition.

First a word or two of clarification is called for. Visual news images can be said to be of two fundamental types: iconic and indexical (Monaco 1981: 130–40). An iconic image represents an object by its similarity to it. In the case of a photograph or film image it is a direct representation of that to which it refers. Roland Barthes has observed, for instance, that 'no doubt the photograph involves a certain arrangement of the scene (framing, reduction, flattening) but this transition is not a transformation (in the way a coding can be); we have here a loss of equivalence characteristic of true sign systems and a statement of quasi-identity' (Barthes 1987: 36). Thus a news film sequence, scene, shot or accompanying still concerned with the Handsworth riots, and depicting say, a burning street, looted property, or injured police denote these very things. In such cases, while not necessarily indicating how such visual imagery is to be interpreted they directly indicate at a denotative level the visual resources which are available. This is not to say, however, that certain visual images are not, at a denotative level, more likely to be supportive of certain interpretations than others, given their reference to certain key happenings, and not others. To the extent that visual images appear to authenticate particular verbal statements and points of view, they may also be thought to provide a particularly potent interpretative resource.

An indexical image, which indicates by its relationship to, rather than direct likeness of an object, can be further broken down into two forms: synecdoche and metonymy. Synecdoche is here taken to refer to the visual practice of referring to an object by visually naming a part, or vice versa, while metonymy indicates an idea by its associated detail. Clearly, these may at times all exist together within the same visual image. A picture of a police car, for example, may indicate visually the actual presence of attending police while also metonym-ically indicating the presence of the police understood as a social institution and agency of law and order. These two forms of visual image are thus more likely to work in Barthes' terms at a connotative level, and in so far as this is found to be the case, the verbal track may well provide an increased directing role. 'When it comes to the "symbolic message", the linguistic message no longer guides identi-fication but interpretation, constituting a kind of vice which holds the connotated meanings from proliferating' (Barthes, 1987: 39).

Even here, however, it may be ventured that when synecdochic or metonymic images are deployed within a news context they are of a highly conventionalized, and therefore immediately accessible kind which may appear almost iconic, such is their immediate recognition. The visual scenes of the removal of bodies or burnt-out ruins of the post office, for instance, in association with the verbal commentary 'the death of the two brothers' is immedi-ately recognizable. Scenes of police officers searching through the debris of the post office is readily understood as depicting 'police investigations' and so on. While certainly working above a strictly iconic level such scenes do not serve to visually relay a higher message, though they do clearly involve a degree of indexicality (or, in Barthes' sense 'symbolization'). On the infrequent occasions when such imagery has been employed, unlike iconic images noted above which may be identified without attending to the verbal track, such images have been captured in combination with the accompanying voice-over.

In the context of news visuals, a third visual image finds repeated involvement and this concerns the journalists' dependence upon 'talking heads'. A further visual distinction can thus be introduced here, and this concerns 'personification'. Personification is taken to be a further sub-species of either, or both, synecdoche and meton-ymy. Thus, if a community is represented by a community spokesper-son, for instance, both the community as a whole and the idea of the community is arguably signified by the visual presence of a spokes-person. Similarly with other institutions whether the government, local authority, police and so on.

The first interesting finding, following a visual analysis involving the above distinctions, is that contrary to many discussions of film and even studies of news visuals (Glasgow University Media Group 1980; Davis and Walton 1984: 45), the visual images deployed in relation to the extended Handsworth riots portrayal exhibit a high degree of iconicity (see Table 6.17). That is, the visual images found across the riot portrayal tend to represent directly what they depict and rarely seek to work at a more symbolic or indexical level.

Images tend to work at an essentially denotative level, while con-notative associations and relatively sophisticated visual interventions

Table 6.17 *Riot news visuals*

Images	Frequency	%
Iconic	377	65.3
Personified	107	18.5
Metonymic	87	15.0
Synecdochic	6	1.0
	Total 577	*100.0*

which relay the overall narrative are not generally found within the bulk of all riot visuals. News imagery, it is maintained here, has few exceptions to a general prevalence of iconic and personified images. Table 6.18 looks at the involvement of visuals across the narrative structures of the Handsworth riots.

Table 6.18 *Narrative elements and riot visuals*

Riot As	Verbal narrative %	Visual narrative %
Event	19.9	31.9
Aftermath	11.5	12.7
Response	10.2	16.1
Consequence	23.3	24.3
Background	21.5	8.1
Future	4.8	4.3
Explanation	3.8	0.9
Metaphor/allusion	5.0	1.7
	(n)1144 *100.0*	(n)577 *100.0*

With two major exceptions it is apparent that the visual references approximately follow the pattern already found across the narrative elements. However it is noticeable that the event of a riot secures much increased visual reference, while aftermath and response also secure increased visual reference relative to the other narrative elements, with background, explanation and metaphor and allusion securing less. If riot visuals appear to have emphasized, in relative terms, the riot as event, aftermath, response and consequence, what images are found across these different narrative elements?

In terms of the visual dimension the event of the riot assumes a much increased presence across the riot narrative (Table 6.19). This, as discussed earlier, is not confined to the mediated coverage following closely upon the initial events in actual time, but is found distributed across the entirety of riot news coverage. In so far as these visual references tend to depict the initial event in terms of violence and destruction, with the police posited as apparently an external protagonist ill equipped and under assault by an unidentified mob, such scenes tend to continually reaffirm the riot as a problem of law and order, no matter the media time of news delivery within the unfolding narrative.

Table 6.19 *Riot as event* (Narrative 19.9% Visuals 31.9%)

Topic/reference	Narrative %	Visuals %
Rioting: violence/stoning	28.1	10.9
Property destruction/burning	25.0	43.5
Rioting: looting	14.9	0.5
Police operation/amassed	11.0	15.8
Emergency service involvement	8.7	12.5
Police under attack	7.0	7.6
Police advance	4.4	9.2
Other/general event	0.9	0.0
	(n)228 *100.0*	(n)184 *100.0*

Clearly the event of the riot is visually referenced in such terms in nearly a third of all riot news items. As such, a consistent stream of riot items across the twelve month period resurrect, and in part at least, re-run the event of the riot with all the drama, violence and destruction that this entailed without necessarily advancing the overall understanding of such an event. Indeed, it could be maintained that in so far as such imagery is constantly invoked, with many of the limitations attendant upon a visual focus on the immediate violence and devastation, the advancement of a wider frame of understanding, contextualization and even interpretation is repeatedly narrowed for all, except one, particular interpretative account which happens to place the riot as event at the heart of its particular discourse.

The aftermath visual dimension (Table 6.20) is seen to increase slightly upon the relative presence of aftermath references and topics,

Table 6.20 *Riot as aftermath* (Narrative 11.4% Visuals 12.6%)

Topic/reference	Narrative %	Visuals %
Death of Molidinas	34.3	30.1
Devastated property	27.5	47.9
Costs of damage	12.1	0.0
Injured general	10.7	5.5
Looted property	9.2	11.0
Injured police	4.6	5.5
Other/general aftermath	1.4	0.0
Injured rioters	0.0	0.0
	(n)131 *100.0*	(n)73 *100.0*

which may already be regarded, given their compressed occurrence within actual time, to have assumed a remarkable longevity across the riot coverage as a whole. A longevity moreover which continually places the Handsworth riots as the scene of two deaths, in addition to an outpouring of violence, criminal destruction and looting. It is notable that though the death of the two brothers found the next day within the burnt-out shell of the post office was clearly not open to iconic representation, the metonymic scenes of the burnt-out post office and subsequent removal of the bodies was repeatedly deployed across the news coverage as evident in the twenty-two separate news items when used. With nearly 30 per cent of all aftermath visuals, it is none the less the effects of devastated property that have secured the most visual reference.

Following the general hierarchy of response already noted, so the visual dimension also appears to broadly reflect this pattern (Table

Table 6.21 *Riot as response* (Narrative 10.2% Visuals 16.1%)

Topic/reference	Narrative %	Visual %
Police response	31.5	30.1
Police investigations	27.3	12.9
Status visit/proclamation	21.4	19.4
Local authority response	6.0	5.4
Community representatives	5.1	6.4
Community others	4.3	6.4
Clearing up/boarding up	4.3	18.3
Other/response	0.0	1.1
	(n)117 *100.0*	(n)93 *100.0*

6.21) with the police, followed by central and local government, community representatives and community leaders all being afforded a visual presence. The clearing-up operations carried out after the riots have also secured an increased visual presence when compared to the verbal narrative. Once again such scenes can be taken as reinforcing the riot as a violent and destructive event. And in so far as such images are constantly replayed the development of a wider understanding may be regarded as inhibited given the constant return to the riot and its immediate destructive effects.

With nearly a quarter of all visual references the element of consequence (Table 6.22) may be deemed to be particularly pronounced in terms of the visual dimension. While the visual reference to court trials is not as pronounced as the verbal line, visual references to policing in relation to concerns of 'tooling up' continue to find twice as many references when compared to issues of 'community policing'.

Overall it can be noted that the visual dimension accompanying the verbal references already considered, tends to visually confirm such an agenda of concerns and its internal prioritization of issues. As such judicial and law and order consequences have tended to take precedence over issues of community policing, while concerns with the local economy in terms of the riot's impact upon local traders appears to also secure, verbally and visually, more news attention than do other community consequences, perhaps relating to the riot's impact on inner city community relations and politics.

Table 6.22 *Riot as consequence* (Narrative 23.2% Visuals 24.3)		
	Narrative	Visuals
Topic/reference	%	%
Policing: 'tooling up'		
Police equipment (offensive)	7.1	6.4
Police riot tactics/training	5.5	2.8
Police manning/resources	4.1	3.6
Police equipment (protective)	3.4	2.8
Inquiry (police report)	2.2	2.8
	sub-total (n)70 *22.3*	(n)26 *18.4*
'Community policing'		
Police community relations	8.6	7.1
Police cm'ttee/accountability	1.5	1.4
Police recruitment (black)	0.7	1.4
Community policing training	0.0	0.0
	sub-total (n)29 *10.8*	(n)14 *9.9*
Remainder		
Court case/trial	14.3	7.8
Local authority initiative	9.0	10.7
Effects on traders/trade	8.3	8.6
Central government initiative	7.9	6.4
Inquiry (Silverman)	6.0	7.1
Compensation/insurance	5.3	5.0
Community organized (traders)	4.9	7.1
Community organized (other)	3.0	5.7
Impact on Birmingham's image	3.0	3.6
Rebuilding/redevelopment	2.2	4.3
Inquest	1.1	0.7
Funeral	0.7	0.7
Inquiry (Ouseley et al.)	0.7	0.7
Media response	0.7	1.4
	sub-total (n)141 *53.0*	(n)89 *63.6*
	Total (n)266 *100.0*	(n)140 *100.0*

Interestingly, though the element of background (Table 6.23) receives relatively little visual reference when compared to the narrative verbal references and topics, which can perhaps be taken as a visual reinforcement of the riot as event and immediate aftermath and impacts, within this coverage nearly two-thirds of all visual references indicate riot background to be concerned with issues of criminality and, in over 40 per cent of all background references, the drugs raid on the Villa Cross pub in particular. Visually, then, it can be suggested that the Villa Cross raid has indeed, in combination with verbal references, tended to situate the Villa Cross at the heart of the Handsworth riots, clearly positioning a criminal activity and associated group (drug dealers) as the most 'relevant' background consideration.

Issues concerned with policing and urban deprivation and unemployment receive approximately the same relative proportion of

Table 6.23 *Riot as background* (Narrative 21.5% Visuals 8.1%)

Topic/reference	Narrative %	Visuals %
Criminality		
Precipitator/'spark'	6.9	10.6
Villa Cross drugs raid	6.9	42.5
Extremists: organized criminals	6.9	6.4
Crime/criminality	6.5	4.2
sub-total (n)67 *27.2*		(n)20 *63.7*
Policing		
Community police relations	7.7	6.4
Police black youth relations	3.7	4.2
Tension indicators/intelligence	2.8	0.0
Model of community policing	2.8	6.4
Police harassment/racism	2.8	2.1
Insensitive policing	2.4	4.2
Handsworth carnival 1985	1.2	0.0
sub-total (n)58 *23.4*		(n)11 *23.3*
Conditions		
Unemployment	11.4	8.5
Social deprivation	9.3	8.5
Economy/recession	2.8	2.1
sub-total (n)58 *23.5*		(n)9 *19.1*
'Race' and racism		
Community difference (black–Asian)	8.1	0.0
Racism/discrimination	3.3	4.2
Black disenfranchisement	2.4	4.2
Black presence/history	2.0	2.1
Racial difference (white–black)	1.2	0.0
sub-total (n)42 *17.0*		(n)5 *10.5*
Political administration		
Government policy/schemes	2.4	0.0
Local authority policy/schemes	2.4	2.1
Government policy/deleterious cuts	2.0	0.0
Local authority policy/cuts	0.8	0.0
sub-total (n)19 *7.6*		(n)1 *2.1*
Political conspirators		
Extremists: political radicals	0.8	2.1
Extremists: political right-wing	0.0	0.0
sub-total (n)2 *0.8*		(n)2 *2.1*
Total (n)246 *100.0*		(n)47 *8.1*

visual involvement as do their verbal counterparts, though much reduced in absolute terms, indicating that visual references whether iconic, indexical or personified, are not entirely outside the realm of visual representation and possibility. So too is it the case when considering the visual representation of issues of 'race' and racism and formal political background considerations. As such, then, it can be seen that visually, though much reduced in overall terms, the element of background has involved a similar dispersal of riot references and concerns while considerably heightening the mediated relevance of crime and criminality and the Villa Cross drugs raid particularly.

Table 6.24 *Riot as future* (Narrative 4.8% Visuals 4.3%)

Topic/reference	Narrative %	Visuals %
Happy prospects	27.3	44.0
Dire predictions	21.9	20.0
Calendar landmark	18.2	16.0
Future as generalized violence	10.9	8.0
Local authority – failed promises	9.0	0.0
Central government – failed promises	7.3	0.0
Other/future	5.4	12.0
	(n)55 *100.0*	(n)25 *100.0*

Future visuals are found to broadly reflect their verbal counterparts with 'happy news' finding increased visual emphasis (Table 6.24). This can be taken as further indication of the programme predilection for positive news. The pursuit of 'good pictures', though generally not felt to be as important as some news studies have suggested, can be made in more qualified terms in relation to particular types of news subject matter. In relation to stories underpinned by a subjectivist appeal to empathy and emotion, visuals may well be permitted to subsist at a relatively 'unanchored' level. That is, the directing role of verbal commentary can be more relaxed on such occasions.

Table 6.25 *Riot as explanation* (Narrative 3.7% Visuals 0.9%)

Topic/reference	Narrative %	Visuals %
Crime/criminality	36.4	40.0
Social deprivation/unemployment	20.5	20.0
Racial rivalry (soft)	13.6	20.0
Social injustice	9.1	20.0
Moral decline	6.8	0.0
Police insensitivity/harassment	6.8	0.0
Other/explanation	6.8	0.0
Racial hostility (hard)	0.0	0.0
	(n)44 *100.0*	(n)5 *100.0*

With a much reduced visual dimension, the element of explanation (Table 6.25) has tended to confirm the prevalence of a criminal placing of the Handsworth riots while also making some indexical visual reference to concerns of deprivation, social injustice and racial rivalry (black–Asian). However, given the absolute infrequency of such visual expressions, the main finding must be considered as the relative under representation of the narrative element of explanation in both its verbal and visual dimensions.

Table 6.26 *Riot as metaphor/allusion* (Narrative 5.0% Visuals 1.7%)

Topic/reference	Narrative %	Visuals %
World of nature/instinct	33.3	0.0
Other inner city riots	24.6	30.0
Handsworth riots 1981	17.5	10.0
Northern Ireland	10.5	20.0
American race riots	5.3	20.0
War-time Britain	3.5	0.0
Historical mainland riots	3.5	0.0
Contemporary acts of disorder	1.8	20.0
	(n)57 *100.0*	(n)10 *100.0*

Given both the mainly non-filmic quality of news visuals as well as their salient iconicity discussed earlier, it is perhaps unsurprising that metaphor does not readily find visual expression, though allusion to other associated events does (Table 6.26). Of these it is other inner city riots which receive the most visual presence, with Northern Ireland, American race riots and contemporary acts of disorder finding some limited visual expression. It can generally be noted that this narrative element receives relatively little visual involvement.

In summary, attending to the visual dimension involved across one year's news riot coverage has tended, in broad outline, to confirm the agenda and priorities of riot news coverage already discerned across the riot narrative. The extent to which the event and its immediate aftermath have found pronounced visual reference, denoting destruction and violence, and repeatedly resurrected across the extended portrayal, may be taken as once again preferring the conservative discourse with its disposition to focus upon just such forms within its interpretative framework. The prevalence of iconic images may be thought to be all the more authenticating here, to the extent that they appear to provide an independent source of confirmation of the unfolding events. The way in which the police appear visually to be confronting an anonymous mob of rioters, reacting to the event rather than as an inner city participant of long standing, may also be considered as a potent visual resource supportive of the conservative point of view. It can be concluded that collectively the visual dimension both on its own largely denotative terms, as well as in synchrony with the verbal narrative has considerably privileged the interpretative resources required by an understanding of the Handsworth riots as a problem of law and order.

Situating the Handsworth riots: the case of news stills

In numerous discussions of inner city news stories, a useful way of providing a quick insight into what such stories were principally about as framed by the news producers, was to provide the introductory or 'lead'[3] statement by the news presenter. This typically encapsulates in succinct terms the basic journalistic points of news interest. Not only does such a lead statement provide a synoptic introduction, it also serves to direct the interest of the news viewer in particular ways, and not others. Such verbal anchoring, however, is frequently assisted by a visual reference in the form of a news still electronically placed behind the news presenter. This last visual analysis pays close attention to the use of such stills when introducing riot related stories, since it is here that a further, and possibly directing, visual resource is offered. If the array of introductory stills is considered across the 153 riot items, no less than 104 news stories included this introductory visual reference. To assist this discussion the news stills used have been given descriptive names (Table 6.27).

Table 6.27 *Visual anchoring: the case of riot stills*

Descriptive	Frequency	%
Caravaggio Blitz	36	34.6
In the Eye of the Storm	19	18.3
Post-Office Ruin	14	13.5
After the Storm	12	11.5
Police General	11	10.6
Portrait Gallery	9	8.6
Other	3	2.9
	Total 104	*100.0*

Given the number of separate riot items broadcast across the year's coverage a surprisingly limited number of different stills have been used. The still used repeatedly throughout the year and which became perhaps a visual logo of 'the Handsworth riots' was a shot depicting in Caravaggio hues a street silhouetted by flames with a lone jet of water arching over burning roofs. The visual drama of this 'Caravaggio Blitz' still visually positions the Handsworth riots as a major conflagration, perhaps redolent of the destructive force of the Blitz in war-time Britain. The point about this still and the other riot stills used, is that deployed across the majority of all riot related items, many of which are not dealing in any sense with the riot as event, such reports repetitively situate the Handsworth riots as either a violent and/or destructive event.

The second most frequently employed group of stills, 'In the Eye of the Storm', also emphasizes the destruction of the night of the riot, visually referencing street scenes of blazing cars and buildings. This is followed by still depictions of the burnt-out and smouldering ruin of the post office in which the two brothers died. Once again the destructive force of the riot is visually denoted, though this still has been confined in the main to items dealing in some way with the death of the two brothers, including the subsequent court trial and verdicts. 'After the storm' stills depict the glass strewn streets and shopkeepers sweeping up or scenes of bulldozers clearing rubble. Thereafter the police gain still recognition, often via synecdochic and/or metonymic images – a police car's blue light, a lone police constable, and so on. 'Portrait Gallery' contains a number of stills depicting the faces of eminent dignitaries and politicians who have either visited Handsworth or made newsworthy statements about the riots. Thus the Lord Mayor of Birmingham, Independent Inquiry leader, and leading politicians all figure within this select group of individuals privileged with still treatment. Finally, other stills used include the Birmingham City Council logo when referring to items reporting on the council's post-riot initiatives, and the items dealing with the worries attendant upon the city's bid to host the Olympic games.

From these various stills it can be noted that 81 (77.9 per cent) visually reference the immediate events of the riot and its aftermath. That is, scenes of burning buildings, and general devastation and destruction accompany a wide range of riot reports which may or may not explicitly be related to the immediate event of the riot. For the reasons already outlined such visual imagery may be considered as furthering a particular understanding of both the events and their wider interpretation. Though such reports may be broadcast long after the actual events and be only tangentially related, if at all, they are accompanied by this particular visual reference.

In addition to the repetitive use of stills across the year's riot portrayal it was also noticeable how the same moving film sequence also accompanied many items, following the newsdesk introduction. This depicts in chiaroscuro terms the scene of a street ablaze with flames pouring from overturned cars and moving police vans and assembled lines of police. The sequence then moves to a memorable image. Here the silhouette of a lone youth strides in front of the blazing cars, apparently a black youth, possibly a Rastafarian, possibly a rioter – it is difficult to determine given his silhouetted form against the flame and shadows. Once again, this particularly dramatic image is used to introduce a number of disparate news items with scenes of destruction while also seemingly identifying an involved participant and, metonymically, an involved social group. In so far as a black youth becomes silhouetted against the flames of a devastated street the inference is set in place which not only labels the riot as event, but also identifies a possible criminal culprit and by extension a responsible social group.

Again the comments above are not intended to deny the evident reality of the riot as event, which involved violence, massive property destruction and loss of life. The point here is that the persistent signification of the riots in such event terms, even long after the events themselves have passed, is to place within the public domain interpretative resources supportive of a particular understanding of the riots and their causation.

Summary

This lengthy and involved analysis of the portrayal of the Handsworth riots has found this extensive news treatment to privilege a conservative understanding of these events. This has occurred not so much through explicit statements of explanation, whether made by journalists or accessed voices, but more through the interpretative resources relating to keywords, narrative structures, agenda of riot issues and concerns, and visual images informing the portrayal across an extensive period of time. Together such resources have been found to prefer a particular interpretation of the riots, their background, causation, involved participants and necessary prescriptions and response. While, on the basis of the findings above, it would be misleading to talk in terms of a complete 'ideological closure' given the limited involvement of other interpretative resources sustaining of a liberal, or in strictly more limited terms a radical viewpoint, there is no doubting the substantial available resources supportive of a conservative law and disorder view. To the extent that news interests appear to have been repeatedly drawn to the violence, drama and destruction of the event itself and its immediate aftermath and response, and have continued to reference such preoccupations even when invoking issues of background and consequence, so the Handsworth riots portrayal has exhibited a pronounced affinity with basic conservative dispositions. Such findings have found the most dramatic and compelling support in relation to the repeatedly rehearsed visualization of the Handsworth riots as an event of extraordinary violence and destruction. Confronted with such scenes time and time again, such is their regional news value, it would perhaps be difficult to imagine the Handsworth riots as anything other than a criminal outbreak of lawlessness requiring a tough law and order response.

Part III

The wider view

7
Widening the lens:
current affairs and documentary

So far this study has focused on the regional news programme. This has been justified on grounds of audience size, routine inner city coverage and the declared journalistic mission to reflect and report the life and problems of the region. It has also enabled a detailed exploration of the way in which professional journalists conceptualize and produce a popular TV news programme and how, in turn, this has been found to impact on the portrayal of the problems of urban marginality. In a context of broadcasting change and upheaval the continuing existence of regional news looks relatively assured. Safeguarded by the latest statutory requirements placed on regional licensees, as well as its special flagship role both for the regional ITV system and corporate ambitions, as discussed in Chapter 2, the regional news programme looks set to remain a permanent fixture in Channel 3 schedules. If regional news, on these grounds, can be seen as something of a special case, protected to a degree at least from the immediate pressures of the marketplace, other forms of programming are not so fortunate.

Already, following the first round of ITC licence awards and changing statutory requirements placed on broadcasters, notable current affairs and other forms of programmes look set to either vanish from the schedules or be revamped and rescheduled outside of prime time. Pressures for change are not confined to networked forms of programming alone, however, but have also begun to affect the range and forms of regional programming. This follows in the wake of statutory deregulation: 'It should be for the operators to decide what to show and when to show it subject to general regulatory requirements' (Home Department 1988: 22). In the context of this study, pressures for change are of interest to the extent to which they are implicated in the changing forms of regional programming and the representation of major social problems and concerns.

This chapter widens its frame of reference, therefore, and considers the array of regional current affairs and documentary programmes broadcast by the company under consideration. It is frequently said that current affairs and documentary programmes offer enhanced opportunities for the portrayal of important social issues. This contention is explored in two parts: first, in relation to regional current affairs and documentary programmes and their treatment of the contending viewpoints surrounding the events of Handsworth/Lozells 1985; second, in relation to the range and forms of regional factual programmes broadcast across the review period and the manner in which each may be considered a vehicle for the representation of regional urban distress. Both these discussions are, necessarily, more general overviews, rather than detailed examinations. They serve, none the less, to indicate that comparisons with regional news are instructive and that processes of change now underway have already begun to impact, often in decisive ways, upon the range, forms and schedule placing of other regional programming. Finally, the changing context of broadcasting and its consequences for regional programmes is briefly focused in relation to the company under examination, its corporate structures and broadcasting mission. In such ways, the future for regional current affairs and documentary programmes is brought into focus as are the prospects for future representation of the region's urban problems.

Current affairs and documentary portraying Handsworth: a different reality?

Other than the news programme, regional programmes have not generally been found to provide extensive or considered programme treatment of the problems of regional urban distress – notwithstanding the fact that the region includes many of the most deprived localities in the country. In the aftermath of the Handsworth/Lozells disorders of 1985, however, two current affairs programmes and one documentary programme were produced which sought to look at this particular event in some detail. In the light of the above, it is interesting to inquire to what extent these may be considered as providing the resources for a complementary or perhaps alternative interpretation of these events when compared to the regional news representation already examined.

The three programmes comprise: a special half hour programme in the ethnic magazine series *Here and Now,* transmitted on a Sunday at 12.30 pm two weeks after the initial disturbances and attracting an audience of 190,000; a ninety minute *Central Weekend* programme broadcast on a Friday at 10.30 pm nearly five months after the initial events and securing an audience of 496,000; and, finally, a *Viewpoint* documentary titled *After the Riots* broadcast eleven months after the riots on a Tuesday at 10.30 pm and attracting a regional audience of 405,000 and, subsequently, nearly two million (1,925,000) when networked. With the *Here and Now* programme providing the first non-news treatment of the Handsworth riots, its schedule slot and audience size none the lèss place it as the least watched programme, while *Central Weekend* and the *Viewpoint* documentary with considerably increased audiences were placed within the public domain some time after the initial events themselves. Issues of audience size, schedule placing and date of transmission all point to the possibly more muted impact of such programmes when compared to the extensive and sustained riot treatment of the regional news programme which, as noted earlier, routinely attracts a million and a half to two million prime time viewers. While these findings help to place the following discussion into some kind of perspective, further comparisons are none the less instructive.

At the relatively abstract level of narrative elements, already outlined in Chapter 6, and when compared to regional news, these programmes appear to provide differing degrees of programme interest in the narrative elements of event, background and explanation especially – three central elements necessary for the formation of an interpretative framework of understanding.

Table 7.1 *Riot portrayal narrative elements: news, current affairs and documentary compared*

Narrative element	News	Here and Now	Central Weekend	Viewpoint
Event	19.9	14.8	4.9	6.0
Aftermath	11.4	3.7	3.0	4.2
Response	10.2	9.2	6.9	6.6
Consequence	23.2	14.8	6.9	23.3
Background	21.5	42.6	47.5	40.1
Future	4.8	5.5	4.9	9.0
Explanation	3.8	7.4	14.8	4.8
Metaphor	5.0	1.8	10.9	6.0
	(n)1144 *99.8*	(n)54 *99.8*	(n)101 *99.8*	(n)167 *100.0*

Even at this formal level of general narrative emphases identified across the different programmes, important differences can be observed (Table 7.1), differences which may well be found to impact on the range and kind of interpretative resources placed within the public domain. With less attention paid to the event of the riot itself and its immediate aftermath and responses, but with significant attention paid to background as well as increased involvement of future and explanation, it is apparent that each of the three programmes has sustained a different set of riot portrayal priorities when compared to the generality of news portrayal. News reports, predisposed to concentrate on the violence, destructive effects and dramatic images of conflagration and confrontation, have been found to return, time and time again, to the initial event of the riot and its immediate aftermath. In such terms, the resources for a conservative understanding of the disorders have routinely informed regional news portrayal. This can be contrasted to other programmes and their different narrative emphases which, in turn, place different interpretative resources within the public domain.

If the array of themes, references and visuals included in each programme treatment is examined this is, in fact, confirmed. However, rather than detail such findings here, in the manner of Chapter 6, for the purpose of this general comparison these differences can be gauged by attending to the introductory statements opening each programme. These clearly signal the main thrust of the programme's treatment. To take the *Here and Now* programme first, this was introduced by the programme host as follows:

'Good afternoon and welcome back to a brand new series of *Here and Now*. Unfortunately we return under rather sad circumstances and all our thoughts have been dominated by the events of last Monday week. So this afternoon's programme is not the advertised one but a special programme devoted to the tragic situation. Handsworth has always been held up as an example of good relations enjoyed between all the races, so what went wrong? Now nearly two weeks after the event in a somewhat calmer atmosphere we shall be looking at the causes of the trouble, but more importantly the future for all the people living in the area.'

This opening programme statement encapsulates a liberal viewpoint which proceeds to inform the programme as a whole. It can be noted, for example, how the introduction locates, semantically, the Handsworth disorders in terms of 'sad circumstances', 'the events of last week', 'the tragic situation' and 'the trouble'. Through such a lexicon a liberal viewpoint on the disorders is offered which supports both the programme's notional pursuit of causes and an apparent acceptance of a 'race relations' framework for understanding inner city problems. More important than the search for causes, however, the programme is concerned with 'the future for all the people living in the area'. In such ways, the programme aligns itself to liberal concerns and preoccupations, distancing itself from both the terminology and focal interests of either a conservative or a radical viewpoint on inner city disorder.

If the introductory statement to *Central Weekend* is considered, the following opening statement also sets the scene for its programme treatment.

'Tonight we intend to find out what caused the riots in Handsworth. Those in authority tried to blame the situation on everyone but themselves. They said the riots in Handsworth, Brixton and in Toxteth were caused by criminals. Douglas Hurd the Home Secretary pronounced them 'not a social phenomenon, but crimes, criminality pure and simple'. They said the riots were caused by outside agitators. Kenneth Newman, Commissioner of Police for London, described them as 'probably Trotskyists or of anarchist outlook'. They said the riots were caused by drug dealers. Geoffrey Dear, Chief Constable of the West

Midlands said 'these people behind the riots were acting in defence of enormous profits'. They said the riots were caused by moral decline. Norman Tebbit, chairman of the Conservative party, blamed the permissive society which generated today's violent society. They claimed the riots were un-British and alien. Sir Peter Emery MP said 'Anglo Saxon standards must be maintained despite what other ethnic minorities want'.

Tonight we say that the riots were not just the work of criminals or roaming anarchists but were the end product of racism. And denying equal opportunities to black people will inevitably lead to disorder. But how do you prove that? One way is to look to similar events in other countries and see if they had similar causes. In America 18 years ago they experienced the same problems that we face today.'

This challenging statement followed a programme promotion in which an American community relations advisor states: 'The oppressed minority will not endure these conditions of racial oppression without striking out, and the extent to which they feel hopeless that is the extent to which violence will be expressed.' In such ways as these the programme positions the riots as, ultimately, informed by racism and also sets out to debunk many of the official conservative ideas current at the time. The programme proceeds to prove its thesis with the help of film reports and interviews concerning the American experience as well as a lengthy studio discussion in which issues of racism and discrimination across different spheres of life are methodically outlined and discussed. This programme has set an agenda in which many of the key concerns and issues of a radical discourse order public discussion of the Handsworth riots. This is not to say that the programme is totally informed by a fully articulated and coherent radical viewpoint, but it does raise issues and concerns identified at the centre of a radical perspective on black discrimination and disadvantage. In other words, the programme provides interpretative resources which have not been found either in the generality of regional news reports and features or the ethnic magazine programme *Here and Now*.

When considering the *Viewpoint* documentary *After The Riots*, here again a different programme treatment informs its opening sequence. The programme begins to the accompaniment of ominous music and scenes of moving armoured police convoys which, following the words 'And now the fuse is lit, is lit', audibly and visually erupts into scenes of burning buildings and riot destruction. This sequence continues with the voiceover of unidentified voices each proclaiming in summary terms their view on the riots before the opening title *After The Riots* comes into view. After this highly dramatic opening a news report of an interview with Douglas Hurd, the Home Secretary, is reproduced, before the absent narrator begins his commentary:

'In Handsworth the events of the 9th and the 10th of September 1985 were known to some as the Uprising, to the Home Office it was criminal activity which resulted in hundreds of arrests. Chief Constable Geoffrey Dear claimed 'the riot happened like a bolt from the blue, with no warning'. But Handsworth has been simmering for many years and like the rest of Britain's inner cities boils over with increasing regularity. Over the years the fifty-six thousand people that live in Handsworth have become increasingly cynical about promises of a better tomorrow . . .'

Not so strident as the position adopted in *Central Weekend* perhaps, this opening sequence and introductory narrative clearly contradicts the official police and Home Office views and provides, over the course of the programme, numerous opportunities for different voices and perspectives to come into play. Unlike both the news and current affairs programmes above, however, *After The Riots* also calls for a different form of engagement from its audience. Whereas both news and current affairs programmes typically structure their delivery through a presenter and link pieces, leading the viewer through the programme sequence and themes, the documentary works differently. Here the montage of assembled film sequences, interviews, and accessed voices are presented often with no narrating voice whatsoever, inviting the viewer to ponder the competing claims and statements appearing in the programme. Now clearly, such accessed voices are ultimately directed by the unseen hand of the film maker, assembling his or her montage in the editing suite. The fact remains, however, that confronted with the parade of juxtaposed voices and images the viewer is constantly encouraged to make sense of these without the directing voice of a narrator or presenter. To use Barthes' terms, meaning is 'relayed' by sequence and juxtaposition as much as verbal 'anchorage', and calls for a different form of viewer engagement (Barthes 1987: 40–41).

If these different programme forms invite different forms of engagement, they have also provided a very different array of interpretative resources when contrasted to the regional news

Table 7.2   *The Handsworth riots and social actor access: news and other programmes compared*

Riot actors	Regional news	Other programmes (combined)
Police	29.1	15.7
Government	20.3	28.8
Community voice	12.4	23.5
Individual voice	10.4	9.8
Business	9.6	8.5
Expert/report author	7.2	4.6
Court	3.2	0.0
Emergency services	2.8	0.0
Education	2.4	7.2
Government scheme	2.0	0.7
Religious	0.4	1.3
Probation	0.4	0.0
	(n)251 *100.0*	(n)153 *100.0*

programme. This is also evident in the different patterns of inner city access. From Table 7.2, it is apparent that inner city voices have found differing opportunities of access across news and other factual programme forms concerned with the Handsworth riots. Most obviously, it is noticeable that police involvement, though still considerable, is reduced almost by half in relative terms across these different programme forms, while community voices have almost doubled their presence. The voices of government, both central and local, have also increased their relative presence while 'individual voices', voices of the organizationally and collectively non-aligned, find slightly less involvement.

Clearly, from the findings above, these other forms of non-news programmes have provided a very different treatment of the Handsworth riots when compared to the news representation previously analysed. Different lexical terms or semantic markers have often been deployed, different narrative emphases found, an expanded array of discursive themes considered, and lastly, a different hierarchy of voices has been permitted access to the TV stage. In short, these examples of regional current affairs and documentary programmes have provided a much enhanced opportunity for competing and alternative discourses to engage the dominant news definitions established elsewhere within the schedules. While these dominant viewpoints also find representation in each of the three programmes discussed, they do not escape criticism nor challenge from alternative perspectives. If the liberal discourse has found increased representation in *Here and Now,* central concerns of the radical discourse have found public expression in the *Central Weekend* programme, while the relatively open format of the the documentary *After the Riots* has representative voices of all three discourses found within and across its assembled montage.

When compared to the news programme, such programmes, though for the most part not enjoying comparable audiences, production resources or schedule placing, have begun to supplement and occasionally to challenge the dominant definitions and news interests found to structure routine news portrayal of the Handsworth riots. This is perhaps a drop in the ocean when compared to the endless tide of regional news daily washing around regional shores, such programmes none the less indicate that other regional programmes can serve wider interests. In summary, these particular programmes suggest that forms of regional programming have, in the past at least, served occasionally to widen the span of public viewpoints and engage the dominant definitions routinely found to structure regional news accounts of the Handsworth riots. These programmes, it has to be said, were concerned with the exceptional events of inner city Handsworth/Lozells. To what extent these and other forms of regional programming offer, on a more routine basis, opportunities for portraying issues of urban marginality and distress can now be considered.

Regional programming: punters, pubs and the erosion of the public sphere

This section briefly reviews the array of regional programmes broadcast across the review period and notes how each may, or may not, be considered a strong candidate for giving voice to problems of concentrated regional distress. The discussion also occasionally observes how these different programmes conform to the programme visualization or concept held by programme makers. Once again, though not possible to pursue in this part of the discussion, it would appear that programme makers are very much working to a professional conceptualization of programme form and content, which indirectly affects the selection and subsequent treatment of substantive issues and concerns – including those of direct interest to this study. The discussion also notes how processes of change have already made their mark in terms of the discontinuation of some programmes, and the rescheduling and/or revamping and transform-ation of others, but all in line with the Channel 3 imperative to produce popular programming for a mass audience. To take regional current affairs programmes first.

Regional current affairs: schedule slots and sexy TV

Two likely programme contenders for giving expression to the region's concentrated social ills have already been introduced above. Both the ethnic magazine series *Here and Now*, and the lively studio audience discussion programme *Central Weekend* might appear, at first glance, to be vehicles for inner city representation and public debate. Central's 'ethnic series' does not enjoy auspicious ratings or schedule position however, broadcast, at the time of research, on Sunday afternoons at 12.30 pm with an average audience of approximately 65,000. The company's in-house publicity describes this particular current affairs magazine programme in the following terms: 'A Jewish American woman who has become one of India's leading classical dancers, a TV presenter who helps AIDS sufferers in her spare time and an adventurer who has travelled through forbidden territories of Asia. These are just some of the people who have recently taken part in Central's *Here and Now*, the 30 minute magazine programme which covers social and political topics affecting the country's ethnic communities. The programme also sets aside time for art, music and dance'.

A review of the subjects covered in the latest completed series confirms the range of subject interests and individual-based items promoted above. Thus, in a recent series of eleven weekly twenty-minute *Here and Now* programmes comprising twenty-six different items, eleven involved performances of dance, theatre and music; twelve involved interviews with artists, writers, film actors and successful individuals, with three remaining items involving a studio discussion about 'same race' fostering and adoption, and film reports on black women in business and a woman photographer from Handsworth.

Here and Now, though occasionally involving consideration of wider social issues, remains content to celebrate minority ethnic culture and individual achievements, whether in the worlds of business, culture or the arts. Such findings are in line with the director/producer's programme visualization and aims.

The philosophy certainly is to deal or to reflect the timeless and the more cultural. And there is so much of that, fortunately there's so much that is happening, not just in the art world, but in drama, in literature, in poetry which I think should get an airing. I think it is important that somehow the achievement angle should be highlighted rather than, it's very easy to highlight or to pinpoint or to even underline the negative, the non-achieving, the naffness of it all. God knows there's enough of that. But it gives a bit of a boost, a moral boost if you like . . .

When considering the relative absence of programme discussion and debate on black issues, particularly in relation to the fragmented nature and contending viewpoints of black inner city politics, these are not thought helpful to the programme's pursuit of positive images.

Strangely enough it's nothing but wrangles, nothing but bickering and I felt that if you want to show or reflect the degree of bickering it's very, very counter productive.

If the representation of black viewpoints, patterns of collective disadvantage and organized forms of action and response find few openings within the producer's programme visualization, practical and technical considerations also undermine its capability to address immediate events. Limited access to studio time and editing facilities leads to a situation where two, three or even four programmes must be planned and pre-recorded well in advance of broadcasting; relatedly, a technical dependence upon 16 mm film as opposed to 'betacam' also involves programme makers in lengthy editing processes compounding the programme's disinclination to deal with the latest or most topical of issues. These, as far as the producer/director is concerned, are in any event best left to mainstream programming.

The other thing is, in order to discuss issues, which I do not think should be discussed on *Here and Now,* they should be discussed on Central News, they should be discussed on mainstream programmes because they are issues that concern the lives of all communities and life generally.

Unfortunately, while the director of *Here and Now* places the onus of responsibility on regional news and other mainstream programme makers to deal with major issues affecting the region's black communities, producers of news are apt to identify regional current affairs, including *Here and Now,* as the means by which such issues can be addressed. News personnel have maintained, for example: 'Current affairs is the area of television where people talk about the issues and look at the issues in great depth', or 'We can't go into the issues as much as a discussion programme or a documentary', and specifically in relation to questions of minority ethnic disadvantage, 'there are other vehicles for that in Central anyway'. Such professional views on their colleagues' programmes usefully enable each to disclaim responsibility for the notable silences found among these different programmes.

The main finding here, however, is that *Here and Now* conforms to a programme visualization in which issues of collective disadvantage and ethnic inequality are displaced from consideration in the pursuit of positive images and the celebratory treatment of culture and the arts. If the programme is of more marginal interest to the concerns of this study than might have been anticipated, so too has it become increasingly marginalized in the schedules. Originally producing twelve programmes a year, this was then increased to thirty-three programmes and more recently reduced to twenty-four, and rescheduled from its original 10.30 Thursday evening slot to 12.30 Sunday afternoon with a reduced running time of twenty minutes.

In contrast, the lively ninety minute programme *Central Weekend* attracts a large audience, is transmitted within a peak viewing slot and also considers topics of controversy and public interest, some of which relate to the problems of regional urban distress. How then, has this programme represented such issues? According to its own in-house publicity: 'It's live, it's controversial, and it keeps over a million viewers entertained and informed. Ninety minutes of live discussion where anything can happen – and usually does.' Broadcast on a seasonal basis, usually on a Friday evening at 10.40 pm, this programme based around controversy probably attracts the largest audience of all regional programmes and takes place in front of a studio audience.

The format has undergone considerable change in recent years however. Unlike the earlier programmes, of which the programme dealing with the Handsworth riots was an example, the programme now deals with three issues each week, not one, cutting to a third the amount of available time for any one issue. If the opportunity for relatively in-depth discussion has thereby been lost, a review of over 300 programme topics included in the programme across a three year period also reveals something of the characteristic programme interests. These appear to be structured around a number of populist themes, not dissimilar to the regional news programme. Thus across the programme contents lists is found: a prominent interest in crime with items on hooligans, lager louts, the Krays; issues of consumption and leisure with items on football, DIY, soap operas, fishing, smoking and drinking, food additives and fat people; British sentiments towards animals appealed to in items on fur trade, RSPCA, dogs or fox-hunting; interest in the paranormal including discussion of UFOs, astrology, hypnotherapy, clairvoyants, mediums, witchcraft and aliens; as well as a pronounced interest in sexuality including prostitution, male strippers, Page Three girls, sugar daddies, toy boys, porn, transvestites, homosexuality, nudism, sex change, and celibate priests. Amongst such programme dispositions, though still attracted to public controversy, are other occasional issues dealing with more recognizably political issues including Salman Rushdie, the poll tax and student loans. Many of the above have reappeared on the contents list for a second, or even a third time across the years.

As with the regional news programme, so this programme also appeals to popular concerns and anxieties around crime and the ordinary preoccupations of consumption, leisure and domestic based living. Unlike regional news, however, broadcast with a paternalist eye to 'family tea time', the programme reaches deeper into the private sanctum, and engages popular interest in issues of sexual behaviour and deviance. It is within this populist mix, conducted in the pursuit of 'lively' controversy, that the exploration of such public issues as racism, the police or vigilantes find public expression.

As with the regional news programme, so the executive producer visualizes his programme's appeal and constituency of interest in decidedly populist terms.

We discuss what people discuss in pubs. We never discuss anything which doesn't affect people, the premise of the programme when it's working is very lively discussion. You only get lively discussion when people care about it, if we don't get lively discussion it's because we were lazy or misguided in our choice of subject. We only do subjects that touch people and we rely very heavily upon their experiences, and the most successful items are when we put the ordinary people, I don't mean this in a demeaning way, against experts, out front. If it isn't punter oriented we've failed. The only reason that people talk about things in pubs is because they actually fascinate you, in which case they are new or because there is a bit of controversy there at some level. We are saying to our audience 'please stay in your seat and watch us to midnight because we believe what you will learn from the debates is worth it'. You can only do that if you present it in a lively manner. I don't think it's entertainment at all, because it does concern us when, you know, it crosses over into fisticuffs as happened on one night, but that's the nature of live television.

Once again the direct appeal to affective response, the involvement of personal and experience based accounts, and the accessing of ordinary people positioned in relation to consumerist interests is seen as essential to the programme's success. Moreover, this championing of ordinary experience is deliberately counterposed to the world of officialdom and the experts with their different epistemologies or ways of knowing. Such routinely informs the programmes design and delivery, and all underpinned by the entertainment value of live controversy – notwithstanding the producer's 'concern' about fisticuffs. *Central Weekend* represents a growing breed of live discussion TV programmes, relatively cheap to produce, and yet regularly gaining and delivering to advertisers large audiences apparently attracted to the spectacle and controversy of live debate. Whether such programmes truly represent forms of public engagement and political response from the grass-roots up, or represent rather a co-opting of ordinary concerns and sentiments channelled into the politically innocuous arena of entertainment and spectacle is a question too broad to address here (see Livingstone and Lunt 1992). What is clear is that amongst the populist mix of themes is an increased array of ordinary voices finding occasional opportunity to challenge issues and debate the viewpoints found elsewhere on the media public agenda.

This populist strategy of programme makers also informs the company's regional political programme *Central Lobby* in which, according to its editor, there is a 'conscious attempt to make it more entertaining to a general audience'.

There's nothing more interesting than people, personalities and people, their excitements and traumas nearly always making compelling television . . . I think the worst crime is not to make it interesting, that's the worst crime of the lot.

The programme brief is indicated in in-house promotional terms as follows: 'The political issues that concern the Central region are tackled by *Central Lobby* when it returns this autumn to follow a new parliamentary session. The half hour programmes look at national issues from a regional point of view and focus on topical items which relate directly to the area – as well as presenting portraits of the politicians in the Central region.' Oriented within a largely institutional idea of politics and the political, where concerns of power are implicitly located within Westminster and the formal expression of political parties and politicians, the programme seeks, none the less, to 'take the stuffiness out of politics and show how it affects everyone at every stage of their lives'. Contrary to such claims, however, when it comes to the concrete realities of inner city politics and the manner in which the politics of Westminster have affected the conditions and life chances of marginalized communities, the programme fails to live up to its promotion. As the programme editor concedes:

We have not done to my recollection a single item about the inner city, despite Margaret Thatcher's pronouncements on the stairs after the election. And every one then said 'ah, Margaret Thatcher, inner cities', but look what happened after that, not a lot. OK I get a few glossy brochures through from various government departments about partnerships schemes, and we're doing this that and the other, but it's pretty dull I have to say. You'd really have to twist my arm to get me to do an item about the inner city as such I must

admit, because I have a feeling that the subject to most of our viewers is dull.
I think they think it's worthy and it's dull just to say the inner city. We've done
items looking at aspects of the inner city. But I would never do a cerebral
analysis of that because I think anybody who lives in the inner city would say,
'oh my God I don't want this, it's like the open university, no thank you very
much' and switch off. And also I notice how small the electorates are in many
inner cities . . .

Once again, in the name of popular interest, this political programme
anticipates that the inner city as a political issue is 'too dull' to be
taken seriously, notwithstanding the fact that demographic move-
ments have altered the traditional political allegiances and voting
influence of many inner city wards. More to the point, perhaps, a bid
to appeal to the widest possible audience is construed in terms of
generalized interests, and appears to assume that viewers will only be
interested if directly affected. The fact that government inner city
schemes can be thought 'pretty dull', rather than as a means of
contrasting government claims and publicity against the continuing
backdrop of inner city deprivation and disadvantage, points to the
failure of political imagination on the part of the programme makers.
Though striving to entertain ever larger audiences, this long-running
programme, as with *Here and Now*, has been reduced from thirty-
three programmes to twenty-four per year. Transmitted on a
Thursday evening slot at 10.40 pm audience figures have averaged
76,000.

The three programmes discussed above, given their general remit
– minority ethnic interests, public debate on issues and controversies
of regional interest, regional politics – may have been thought to be
the principal contenders in which, and by which, issues of concentrated regional distress could have found wider public exposure and
examination. For the most part, this has not been found to be the case.
Informed by particular programme visualizations, each has failed to
address and convey those substantive concerns previously identified
at the heart of contending social viewpoints on the problems of the
region's inner cities. Issues of black disadvantage and discrimination,
as much as collective forms of organization and action have not found
representation in the celebratory horizons of *Here and Now*, with its
pursuit of individual success, achievement and restricted understanding of culture. The pursuit of live controversy and increasingly
populist underpinning to *Central Weekend* has, at best, provided
relatively few opportunities to tackle issues of social marginality and
concentrated urban disadvantage. These, when included, are subject
to a programme form in which spectacle and entertainment, as much
as engaged debate and public representation, inform its presentation.
In relation to *Central Lobby* both the restricted programme vision of
politics and its deliberate inscription of populist appeal has undermined the possibility of representing either the politics of the inner
city or the effects of central politics on inner city communities and

conditions. On all three fronts, the collective patterns of urban disadvantage, concentrated social distress and discriminatory practices found in so many of the region's localities have been, with the exception of the Handsworth riots, largely ignored.

If these three programmes represent the most likely candidates for inner city representation, other factual programmes can also be mentioned. Though not strictly a regional programme, the *Cook Report* is produced by Central and broadcast across the ITV network as a whole. The company's in-house promotion suggests, however, that the issues selected for programme inclusion are likely to be confined to issues of crime and deviance: 'Award winning Roger Cook, scourge of conmen and swindlers, goes after bigger villains in a series of six networked films. He's travelling the world seeking out the "Mr Bigs" behind rackets like drugs, pornography, terrorism, smuggling, robbery and murder. It sounds dangerous – and probably will be – but Roger's already been hit, punched, knocked down and run over more times than he'd care to remember.'

With the entertainment value of filmed conflict, and personal assault on the presenter, not undervalued by Central's promotion department, the orientation to certain subject areas, and not others, is also apparent. The first series included four out of five programmes investigating/exposing criminal activities, for example, while the second series included running to ground violent drugs pushers and loan sharks. If the last two items reference the backdrop of inner city squalor, such remain of strictly peripheral interest to the main focus of investigation as well as the, always present, threat of assault on the presenter. Transmitted at 8 pm on Tuesdays, the *Cook Report* has secured, on average, audiences of over a million viewers; it is not predisposed however to tackle wider inner city issues, other than those refracted through criminal activities focused in relation to the programme pursuit of individual miscreants.

Other programmes have also informed the company's regional programme production but generally positioned within the quiet backwaters of the schedule and addressing particular constituencies of interest: the religious, *Focus* and *Encounter*; the elderly, *Getting On* or the disabled, *Link*. Two public service inserts can also be noted as of marginal interest. *Police Five*, a weekly five minute and independently produced news programme insert, has been run on a seasonal basis for over twenty-five years. In its bid to captivate audience interest and support for the police it has frequently referred to inner city areas but only, of course, in relation to crime. *Job Finder* was first produced and broadcast by Central Television, between 4.40 am and 5 am, alerting the region's unemployed insomniacs to a handful of regional vacancies. This service has subsequently been expanded and taken up by other ITV companies.

From the programme discussions above, it is apparent that informing the production of each programme is a definite programme visualization, often justified in terms of its imagined audience and their assumed preoccupations. Though the imagined audience is based on little, if any, substantial research, it is all too real in terms of its effect on programme visualization. These different programme forms and their professional visualizations could, in the manner of the regional news study above, be subjected to detailed discussion, eliciting the manner in which each contributes, as a matter of routine, to the production and delivery of a recognizable pattern of programme subjects, delivered in a certain inflection and incorporating an identifiable range of voices. Such programme conventions provide a level of insight into the recurring nature of established programme forms and the manner in which each mediates in characteristic fashion wider public concerns and issues.

These programmes and their conventions have recently, however, come under increasing pressure to tailor their appeals to the pursuit of maximized audience ratings. If this has always informed the design, production and delivery of commercial TV programming, such appears to have assumed an overriding aspect in recent years, with established programmes revamping themselves according to this now dominant imperative. Typically this has involved programme producers pursuing a deliberate populist strategy of viewer engagement. Here consumer and leisure interests are sought and the levels of the experiential and affective appealed to. In addition, known popular interest in the world of the supernatural, the private domains of home, family and pets, and the intimate sphere of personal relationships and sexual proclivities are all likely to be invoked as well as the private lives of stars, celebrities and personalities. Such appeals can be inscribed into even the most unlikely of programmes. Consider, for example, the following summary by a religious programme producer of the sorts of issues featuring in his programme. Even the ethereal realm of religion, it would seem, can be inscribed with the decidedly more corporeal, materialistic and earthly preoccupations, pleasures and pains of ordinary existence.

The sorts of subjects that we've looked at over this year: January we looked at the way individuals experience some sort of radical change in their lives, the religious thing would be a conversion, going from one religion to another. February we were looking at astrology, the Chinese New Year we picked up on that. March we looked at child abuse . . . She was able to talk in graphic detail, we almost had to cut her down in what she was saying. April, loosely a suicide programme and the 'compassionate friends'. . . obviously it's something that is very painful and yet has a slightly ghoulish human interest quality in it – there's a little bit of the voyeur in all of us I think. May, the question of religious dating agencies – it's a sort of rising phenomena, there's a new one in Leicester for the Hindu community which is really a bit on the iffy side, there's a Jewish one costing two thousand pounds to just get on their book so we've got Claire Rayner coming and picking up on that question. June we're looking at something lighter, we're looking at food and the way food is used by different religions and the different aspects of it. July, in the West, we're looking at death and the way people approach death, in the East, we're looking at the Kegworth disaster on the M1 and the people who go into action helping these people and the emotional pressures that poses for the people helping. In August we're looking at alcohol, it's in the region that the Catholic organizations have launched alcohol free bars. September we're looking at adoption and particularly where someone is adopted into a family and religion which isn't the one they were born into. Later in the year we'll be looking at evil and the satanic wicked side.

While it is only possible to marvel at the ingenuity with which a religious programme has been fashioned to resonate with populist appeals and interests it is a tendency which, in the face of deregulation and increased competition for ratings and advertising revenue, continues to transform existing programmes. The producer again:

If our rating got indescribably low people would say 'let's axe it anyway'. So at the very least I've got to get a modest rating, the programme's got to have a slightly more glitzy and glamorous appeal, it's got to become more populist.

Such strategies for survival are not confined to regional current affairs programming however.

Regional documentary: the demise of the authored poem

Processes of change have already been found to impact in the most detrimental of ways on the regional documentary and its 'creative treatment of actuality'. While it is perhaps misleading to suggest that documentary can be discussed as if it were a uniform, unchanging and pure form, a strong tradition can none the less be discerned which, informed by mass observational techniques, tenets of social realism or the pursuit of verite, has involved a 'naturalistic' stance towards its subject matter (Corner 1986). Often presented as a personal view or authored statement, documentary has also been exempt from the strictures of balance and impartiality informing the production of news and current affairs. Within the different aesthetic of documentary, then, subjects have frequently been able to present their personal views often at some length, and within the idioms and environments with which they are familiar. As such it has provided a qualitatively different treatment of actuality, when compared to either news or current affairs programmes. In such terms the demise of regional documentary can be regarded as a qualitative erosion of the formal possibilities for representing, and giving expression to, the lived experiences of the region. In corporate terms the demise of regional documentary is not in dispute. The controller of features, concedes as much:

I think they are undoubtedly under threat. I think there will always be room for minority subjects, the only thing then is whether or not the documentary area of that will survive. But that original regional programming is now covered much more by the regional news team and current affairs team than it is by documentary.

Unfortunately, the existing array of regional programmes and processes of change currently underway do not support this optimistic view, a view moreover which appears, surprisingly, to underestimate the qualitative and distinctive contribution of documentary to regional programming. Existing regional documentary programmes have, in the face of rescheduling and the pursuit of maximum ratings or possible discontinuation, been forced to transform themselves into more popular formats and select subjects thought to have wider popular appeal.

Central's environmental documentary programme *Eco,* for example, has been rescheduled from its 10.30 pm slot to 7.30 pm while changing its format to that of a magazine programme. The producer intimates the envisaged change as well as incurred costs as follows:

I think we will make it lighter and more accessible and we'll probably make it more magaziney and we're thinking about taking it to parts of the region. And we'd probably include more natural history because people like that too ... One thing we could do at 10.30 in half an hour was actually analyse quite seriously and responsibly, that can make it quite inaccessible for some people and that makes it quite hard for us to come down to reduce something when we already thought you needed an hour to weigh up the pros and cons of certain issues. To now reduce it to ten minutes and make it meaningful is harder ... It's not going to be easy to do it at all.

Similarly, Central's business documentary programme *Venture* has also been rescheduled to a 7.30 pm slot and forced to rethink its form and audience appeal.

We decided to make the programme a lot more consumer oriented. So although our programme was concerned with business our ordinary audience had to see what its relevance was. They had to be able to make some connection with it. Any subject we did now should have some direct relevance to ordinary people's lives, that's one thing. And secondly, they should be fairly short items, so that people might not feel that just because they're not interested in that item that the whole programme might not be of interest. (assistant producer)

Existing regional documentaries have been rescheduled from the traditional 10.30 pm slot, which is now seen to be within peak time, to 7.30 pm, and placed up against such mass audience programmes as BBC1's *EastEnders*. Here a residual audience for regional programmes is thought still to be found, though the controller of features maintains 'the half hour documentary won't sustain itself at 7.30 pm but the magazine show will'. Hence, existing regional programmes have been forced to adapt, in order to survive at all.

Other programmes have disappeared from the schedules entirely. The long-running documentary series *England Their England,* for example, had occasionally produced programmes of inner city relevance in its bid to reflect the life and customs of different communities around the region. Initially producing twenty-six programmes per year, this was later reduced to eighteen and finally twelve before the programme was discontinued in 1989. As one of the involved producers remarked: 'There's no longer room for that carefully prepared poem.' According to the controller of features this programme had outlived its usefulness anyway; other regional programmes, especially news with its use of portable and fast ENG cameras, are thought to represent the life and times of the region. This, of course, is a view at odds with the findings already detailed in relation to the regional news programme.

In the place of *England Their England,* and in line with the Government's strictures requiring ITV companies to commission at least 25 per cent of original programme material from independent producers by 1992, Central commissioned a series of films entitled *City Watch,* a set of programmes documenting the life and experiences of ordinary, if sometimes unusual, people living and working in an urban landscape. This series is instructive in that it demonstrates how independents do not escape the pressures for change impacting on in-house producers; in fact, if anything, the pressures to produce popular based, high ratings programmes may be even more pronounced (for a wider view of independents and their failure to provide increased programme diversity, see Robins and Cornford 1992).

Given the dependence on commissioning editors and their pursuit of high ratings within fixed and/or reduced programme budgets, independents tailor their programme proposals in terms which are most likely to succeed. Continued independent economic viability both in the short term and in the longer term demands nothing less; a relative lack of production capital further undermines commercial independence. In other words, independents though formally outside of corporate structures, are just as much tied into a competitive system increasingly dependent on reduced costs, mass audience programming and the maximization of advertising revenue. If 'sweetheart deals'– the awarding of commissions to ex-employees – also colours the independent sector, the main constraint on programme diversity has to be seen as the economic dependence of independents on the commissioning organization. The independent producer of *City Watch* – an ex-Central producer – observes, for example, how reduced budgets and the programmes sought by commissioning editors inevitably inform programme proposals and treatments.

There is a certain stringency of budget, which means that you have to film within a certain week on a day, but it has to be a certain week because everything is booked . . . I think we would go into situations inside Central if we wanted to do something about urban community care in the next series, which is a subject we would very much like to do – I can hear them saying just now 'absolutely not', 'boring'.

In order to win commissions, programme treatments must be pitched in terms which accord to the new realism of corporate schedule goals. The producer of *City Watch* reflects on how he deliberately tailored the treatment of a particular programme in line with such constraints.

'The Rat Catcher', you are presenting a very sexy treatment with nice photographs with three pages of words of not more than three syllables, so you find that what you are doing is selling, because it's a foot in the door, without Roger Cook, it's real people doing it. So you find that you are locked into a system, it's a way of making films for the next six months. The hype becomes more important.

In summary, what has been discerned so far is a progressive shift away from regional documentary and an increasing popularization of regional current affairs programming. This has led programme producers to pursue, as a deliberate strategy, populist subject matter, lively styles of presentation and short programme items packaged within magazine formats. In such ways, the already limited openings for the representation of regional issues and concerns have recently been further reduced, with many programmes literally marginalized to the quiet backwaters of the schedules. Furthermore, the increased role of independents, far from helping to promote 'quality, diversity and popularity' in line with the Government's declared objectives has been found, in this context, to conform to in-house programme expectancies and schedule requirements. Clearly, the changing programme visualizations that inform the professional production and delivery of regional factual programmes have been prompted by a wider context of change, including technological developments, market pressures and statutory deregulation.

This last discussion, therefore, briefly situates the changing nature of factual regional programming within the changing structures and corporate strategy of a major commercial TV company. This company, as with all commercial ITV companies, has had to radically rethink its market position and gear itself up to survive in the changed context of commercial broadcasting. If the costs of this strategy have already been evidenced in relation to the demise of regional documentary and increasingly populist nature of current affairs, the corporate response to broadcasting change helps to explain this erosion to the region's TV public sphere.

Corporate restructuring: change in progress

With the development of terrestrial and satellite communications a dramatic expansion of TV channels and services is underway, leading to increased competition for limited advertising revenue and, relatedly, competition for available audiences. A changed statutory framework which requires licensees to pay both an annual levy, based on a percentage of advertising revenue, as well as the highest cash bid subject to a quality threshold in order to secure the licence in the first place, further diminishes available finances for programme production in an increasingly competitive market situation. Deregulation has also opened up the possibility of territorial expansion while relaxing the degree of formal involvement of the regulatory body, the ITC, in the day to day overseeing and approval of programming. On all these broad fronts the pressures for change are considerable, and generally point to an increasingly competitive commercial environment. How one of the biggest ITV contractors has recently responded to this environment can briefly be outlined; the impact of such change upon regional factual programming has, of course, already been noted.

Central Independent Television plc is one of the largest companies and programme producers in the ITV system. It is compelled, like all the other contractors, to maximize its opportunities within the changing broadcasting environment. Galvanized into action by the prospects of imminent change and commercial self-interest, the company has systematically set about reorganizing itself in order to take best advantage of the changing broadcasting climate. 'We have planned for an environment in which efficiency and competitiveness will continue to be of increasing importance, while protecting our ability to produce quality programmes of wide appeal' (Chairman, quoted in Central Independent Television 1989b: 3–4).

In many respects, the company can be seen as an example of the 'flexible firm', seeking financial, functional and workforce flexibility in the face of new commercial imperatives. At the centre of this new corporate strategy is the reorganization of the company into 'profit centres' and a number of subsidiary companies. The company has been reorganized into five divisions. The Broadcast Division is involved in the commissioning and acquiring of programmes to construct, promote and transmit a schedule to fulfil Central's licence promises, and to obtain an audience size and mix which maximize the revenue-earning potential of operating the franchise/licence. The Programme Production Division produces the programmes required by the Broadcast Division, using the resources of the Facilities Division and independent producers. It creates programmes for the network, regional and news programmes, and programmes for world and other markets. Central Television Enterprises markets Central's programmes and film library to other broadcasters (TV, satellite, cable) and to video distribution companies both in the UK and overseas, and arranges co-productions and pre-finances. The Facilities Division maintains studio facilities and promotes them within Central and to programme makers world wide. Finally, the Airtime Sales Division sells airtime to advertisers and carries out supporting research into programme appeal, audience composition and advertising effectiveness. A number of other profit centres have also been set up within Central, each seeking cost-effectiveness and promoting its services both within Central as well as to the external market. The commercial logic behind this restructuring, therefore, is to convert 'Central from a single large organization into a team of lean, fit, competitive and customer oriented profit-centres' (Central Independent Television 1989a: 7).

Central's response to broadcasting changes, as noted above, has been to restructure in a manner which will enable the company to maximize its advantages within the marketplace while safeguarding its various 'profit centres' if the bid for the licence should prove unsuccessful. In the event, Central won its licence bid unopposed. The corporate response to these changed circumstances have, however, impacted differently on the organization and production of regional news, current affairs and documentary programming. Regional news programming looks set to continue to provide a spearhead role in the company's bid for its licence and future plans for territorial expansion.

Our news programmes held their position as among the most-watched of any on the ITV network. These are the best possible indications of our success in fulfilling our primary duty as a franchise-holder, which is to provide a diverse, popular and high-quality service to viewers in the region . . . Central South demonstrates our commitment to the Region and our determination to provide the finest possible broadcasting service to all our nine million viewers. (Central Independent Television 1989b)

Other forms of factual programming do not enjoy the same degree of corporate commitment within this changing commercial environment however. In this respect, it is interesting to observe that with the restructuring of the company into divisions noted above, regional documentary programming now falls under the Deputy Director of Broadcasting within the Broadcasting Division. In other words, in line with the demise of regional documentaries and their discontinuation or transformation to forms of regional current affairs programmes, so these programmes have been aligned to the 'journalistic' led department within the Broadcasting Division and not the 'creative' commissioning department of Features. This organizational realignment is important, given that documentary has frequently enjoyed a degree of licence and editorial freedom not countenanced by senior corporate personnel in terms of current affairs and news programming. Indeed, it was this qualitative difference based on ideas of differing programme aesthetics, which was previously found to influence the distinctive contribution of documentaries to regional programming – a distinction now lost under the journalistic-led commissioning of regional factual programmes.

In short, fewer schedule slots deemed appropriate for documentary audiences and the increasing use of independents, in line with government proposals and corporate flexibility gained from sub-contracting, combine with the latest organizational realignment to further reduce the opportunities for creative and risk-laden pro-grammes. The introduction of the 'profit centres' concept and the exposure of programme makers to a form of 'total costing' budgeting where company facilities are now charged to individual programme costs, rather than absorbed by the company as whole in 'below the line costing', has also undermined the commercial viability of regional documentary. In such terms, regional documentary is apt to be seen as a 'cost' to the company, especially as it holds little, if any, resale value. In the face of such increased commercial pressures the fate of the regional documentary has been sealed.

Regional factual programming, then, has been exposed to the technological, commercial and political winds currently blowing their way through the independent television sector and broadcasting industry in general. If regional news has weathered this storm relatively untouched, regional current affairs and documentary, on the basis of this study, have not escaped unscathed. The way in which such programmes have typically sought to maximize ratings through a deliberate populist strategy of engagement has been observed already. Here it can be noted how such individual programme responses reflect the wider corporate goals to attract mass audiences in order to maximize advertising revenue. While advertisers and programme makers have become increasingly aware of the seg-mented nature of audiences and the possibilities of targeting specific market groups, this does not inform senior thinking across the corporate divisions. Rather, within the context of Channel 3, the commercial imperative remains wedded to finding and securing mass popular-based audiences.

We want a very large share of the audience, if you get that large share of the audience you will get the elusive ABC1s that the advertisers cry out for. But remember advertisers aren't just selling brands to that group, they're selling housewife brands too. The bottom line for all ITV companies is to get the largest share of the available audience at any time, and within that you will be able to sell ABC1s too . . . ITV is a popular channel, it has to be populist to survive. We cannot go down the Channel Four route, we cannot be a movie channel. We have to be a broad based popular entertainment channel . . . The emphasis should always be to maximize the audience, maximize the audience, and I don't see how on ITV anyone could argue much different . . . You can't put constraints on a beast that you throw into the free market and tell it to survive . . . We really do have to be a lean and hungry animal to live. (controller of programme planning and scheduling)

Though programme makers are still inclined to invoke a vocabulary of programming and public service rather than markets and sales, there is no doubt that a new realism pervades the industry where the controllers of features and of factual programmes, the two programme areas of immediate concern to this study, concede to the necessity of appealing to larger audiences, and embracing a more popular form of programming.

The challenge that we've got is to take the range of programmes that we've got and make them more universally acceptable. (controller factual programmes)

ITV audiences, unquestionably you want to get the biggest number of people and make it as popular as possible, which basically means pretty populistic, pretty bland programming. But what we must not do is think too much about ITV. As ITV makes less and less of the personal view type documentaries, so you will find Channel Four saying 'that's a vacuum, that's where an audience is, let's go and do it'. (controller features group)

This last statement by a senior corporate decision-maker is revealing, and points to other sectors of TV broadcasting as a means of addressing the failing of his own company and the regional ITV system in general. If news producers are apt to point to current affairs and documentary programming, and current affairs and documentary programme makers inclined to point to the regional news programme as a way of avoiding responsibility for their respective programme failings, here a senior corporate decision-maker now points to other sectors of the TV system as the means by which the failings of the regional ITV system can be remedied. This is a useful ploy in avoiding criticism, but fails to acknowledge the shortfall in corporate commitment to the region, pledged annually in public statements of company intent. It also takes us beyond the regional TV horizons informing this study however. Whether succour can be taken from the presence of other non-regional channels and their ability or inclination to reflect the problems and concerns of the nation's urban poor and socially dispossessed, the marginalized, the angry and the unemployed, the politically disenfranchized and the economically dependent, or, in short, Britain's growing underclass or the residuum of the 1990s, is a question which can only be addressed within a much expanded discussion of broadcasting. All that can be ventured here is that the processes presently underway and documented above do not hold out much hope for the regional representation of such voices, viewpoints and conditions of existence in the future. And this is so in relation to a part of the TV system which, on the basis of statutory requirements, corporate regional goals, professional statements of intent and geographical proximity, held out the best chances of representing the people, the problems and life of the region.

8
Conclusion: some observations on media theory

This study has sought to chart, critically review and help explain the routine failings and silences of regional television programming in relation to problems of concentrated urban distress. Deliberately adopting a case study approach, a major ITV company and producer of regional programming has been subjected to detailed scrutiny. This has enabled close observations to be made of the routine practices and professional programme visualizations informing the production and portrayal of inner city representations. Wider processes of broadcasting change have also been brought into focus as they have been found to impact, in mainly deleterious fashion, and via processes of corporate restructuring, upon the existing range of factual regional programming. Here the already limited openings for the representation of disadvantaged communities and their conditions of existence have been further narrowed and bent to the requirements and conventions of programme forms. On the basis of these findings, this last discussion raises some general points of wider relevance for current media theory and the study of news in particular.

In Chapter 1, when outlining current approaches to television, a case was made for seeking to integrate and combine some of the research interests and insights typically pursued under the 'popular culture' and 'public knowledge' projects. The necessity to do so is evident when dealing with a news form such as the regional news programme, which deliberately courts popular appeal while simultaneously working within, rather than eschewing, basic canons of journalist professionalism. Here we have a news form which seeks to be seen as a respectable, authoritative news service, while also directing its appeal to the interests, preoccupations and anxieties of the ordinary viewer. If the programme seeks to report, impart and inform as part of its journalistic news mission, so too does it seek to address ordinary people, affirm their preoccupations and concerns and celebrate the privatized world of family, leisure and consumption.

The programme visualization of regional news is not simply a response to the exigencies and contingencies of routine news production, therefore, but is a deliberate and, in its own terms, sophisticated ensemble of programme elements and appeals daily assembled in such a way as to conform to the guiding sense of an established programme form. A programme form in which a pronounced pursuit of popular appeal has been openly conceded by all those involved in its daily production. How this particular programme visualization has impacted on the mediation of the inner city has been explored at some length. From the saliencies of news interest in inner city crime and disorder, to the silences of news interest in issues of racial disadvantage and concentrated urban distress; from the pronounced pursuit of individual human interest stories to the displacement of inner city politics and collective struggle; from the characteristic patterns of news access and the privileging of social and political elites to the range and use of different presentational news formats; from the informing objectivist *and* subjectivist news epistemologies to the positioned use of ordinary voices and experiential accounts; and from the use of emotive imagery and visuals to the modulation of presenter modes of address, in all these, and in other ways, regional news has been found to be a highly mediated product, a product which conforms to professional expectancies and known programme parameters. On the basis of such findings this study departs from two principal, if contending, theoretical positions on the news media.

First, it suggests that culturalist readings of news as giving direct expression to dominant viewpoints and assumptions fails to recognize or interrogate the manner in which different programme forms serve to filter and inflect news according to different programme conventions and ambitions. Though news constitutes an important medium in which, and by which contested and contending discourses can find wider public representation, such discourses are none the less mediated according to prior programme conventions, news interests and styles of delivery. If the interpretative resources for certain discourses and not others are found to routinely inform the programme delivery, this may reflect more upon the elective affinities of the programme itself, attracted to certain news interests and not others, than the individual journalists, their attitudes or even subscription to unspoken newsroom assumptions and values. It is in and through the known conventions and sought appeals of the regional news programme as a whole that questions of ideological alignment or partisanship can best be pursued. In this sense, culturalist readings of news would be well served to inquire not only into the way in which specific issues find news representation, but also into the way in which news issues are likely to find characteristic selection and inflection according to the general conventions of the news form under consideration. If this has been pursued here in relation to the popular news form of regional TV news, it also points to a level of insight which could none the less be developed in relation to other forms of TV news.

Second, studies of news organization and production do not exhaust the field of explanatory insight by pointing to the organizational routines and bureaucratic nature of news production, with reference perhaps to the newsroom division of labour, processes of professional recruitment and socialization, news organization source dependencies, or collective journalistic subscription to a generalized set of news values. What is arguably missing from such accounts is the manner in which despite all these features, news organizations can and do produce immediately recognizable differences of news output. Such differences not only require detailed textual analysis and interpretation, which is only now beginning to be taken seriously in relation to tabloid journalism; they also demand to be pursued into the production domain, since it is here that such characteristic styles, news interests and story treatments are purposively fashioned on a routine basis.

This raises a third, more methodological point. Studies of the news media and news production have generally sought to distance themselves from widely held, if inadequate, explanations of the news media which locate the source of perceived news bias in individualistic and instrumental terms. Such accounts all too often collapse into a simple form of conspiracy theory with journalists and/or their proprietors seen as deliberately furthering their particular political viewpoints. Finding that the pressures, constraints and complexities attending news production are granted insufficient recognition in such accounts, media theorists have tended to look for explanations at wider analytic levels.

News production studies, for example, have tended to perceive constraints and pressures at the level of the organization and newsroom routines, while culturalist theorists have identified principal sources of ideological alignment and contest in relation to the wider play of contending social interests encoded into the final news product. Political economists, for their part, have interrogated the impersonal forces of the marketplace – the prohibitive costs of market entry, the pressures of competition and the pursuit of audiences/readers, advertising revenue and copy sales – as the determining force behind the constricted range of news subjects, voices and viewpoints finding public representation. When the journalists themselves have been the focus of serious inquiry, researchers have tended to inquire into the social composition, political attitudes and processes of professional recruitment and socialization thought to inform their output. With the exception of this last approach, which has the closest affinity to widely held assumptions about the news media, the remainder distance themselves from instrumental views on the mass media.

The wider analytic levels brought into focus through such studies therefore relate, respectively, to organization/bureaucracy, culture/ideology and marketplace/competition, each widening its analytic sights beyond the instrumental view of journalists approached in terms of individual/attitudes or, at a slightly more removed level, professional/socialization (for a review of these different approaches see Cottle forthcoming (a)). On the basis of this study, such analytic levels of inquiry can be seen to either ignore an invaluable level of explanatory insight or, alternatively, privilege the working journalist with too much explanatory weight. Between structure and agency is culture which, in the context of the news media, finds expression in and through established and changing news forms. Journalists, in this study, have been found to be acutely aware of the distinctiveness and differentiated nature of the news form to which they daily contribute – colleague esteem, professional achievement, newsroom promotion and successful career moves depend on nothing less. As such they have provided an invaluable level of explanatory insight into the daily selections of news and forms of news treatment purposively inscribed into the news product.

To forefront the professional conceptualization of the news product informing its daily production does not, of course, reduce news to the individual or collective attitudes held by journalists in instrumental accounts. And neither does it seek to explain news with exclusive reference to the unspoken or unconscious ideological assumptions and views apparently transmitted directly into the news product from the surrounding culture. What it does do is spotlight a level of insight which has been found to throw considerable light on the patterns, forms and appeals that routinely characterize a distinctive form of TV news. Now, having elicited such shared conceptualizations, termed in the context of this study 'programme visualizations', it does not follow that these can or should be accepted at face value and, of course, they most definitely are not beyond critical discussion. Rather, they provide a useful, and in the context of this study at least, a necessary starting point in explaining the characteristic news treatment of issues of urban marginality and collective social distress.

These observations derive from a detailed study of the regional news programme. They suggest however, that the exploration of other news forms, whether TV, press or radio, serious or popular, have yet to be fully interrogated with reference to their informing professional visualizations, and the manner in which these are enacted both at the moment of production and displayed in the textual properties of the news product[1]. In this respect, the general categorization of programmes into a limited taxonomy of genres found elsewhere in the literature is not helpful in explaining the specific and internally differentiated programme forms found within broad programme groupings, whether news, current affairs or documentary. Professional programme visualizations, on the other hand, help to locate the specific and differentiated nature of the programme form under consideration and, in the cases of the programmes subjected to discussion, go a considerable way in helping to account for the way in which wider public issues find characteristic programme mediation. When pursued both in relation to forms of programme output as well as practices of professional production, important explanatory gains can be won. This is an area which has yet to be pursued in relation to the variety of news and non-news programmes, including the proliferation of hybrid forms of programming, and their informing professional conceptualizations.

To return to news specifically, looking to professional journalists and their informing programme visualization is not to suggest, of course, that such a level of analysis dispenses with the need to attend to other levels of explanation and insight. The complex nature of news production and its embedded existence within wider social processes and culture is unlikely to lead to a situation where any one theory suffices. Other theoretical approaches and levels of analysis must also be considered. It is to suggest, however, that in the context of TV production professional programme visualization offers an intermediate level of analysis, between wider corporate and commercial pressures on the one hand, and fine grained textual readings and analyses of news output on the other. It provides, in other words, a way of contextualizing the news treatments of specific issues in relation to the characteristic textual properties, established conventions and appeals of a particular news form; and it also provides a useful starting point in relation to which wider pressures and determinants of change can be charted. These, research access permitting, can be traced back through the production domain and informing professional practices to the wider corporate context which, in turn, can be situated within the still wider context of commercial, political and technological pressures and constraints.

To privilege any one of these levels as a theoretical a priori, seems to me to do less than justice to the shifting balance of forces and constraints that combine, at any moment in time, to influence the conditions of programme production and forms of output. Moreover, given the different strategic locations occupied by different programme forms within existing schedules and corporate aims, so such forces can be found to impact differently on different programmes at the same time. Confronted with such complexity, interdependence and multiple sites of determination and influence, generalized theorizing must give way to further empirically based investigations and analyses. That said, on the basis of the empirical findings of this study, the recent claims of leading exponents of the political economy approach to the mass media have found substantial support. If 'critical political economy is concerned to explain how the economic dynamics of production structure public discourse by promoting certain cultural forms over others' (Golding and Murdock 1991: 27), this study has provided plenty of evidence in support of such a basic contention. The economic dynamics of production in the independent television sector have clearly prompted recent changes via corporate restructuring and visibly impacted on the range and forms of regional current affairs and documentary programming.

Technological developments and government de-regulation have recently intensified the commercial and competitive pressures that have always accompanied the ITV system, prompting the corporate search for reduced programme production costs, mass audiences and the maximization of advertising revenue. These changes, as described earlier, have placed increased pressure on programme producers to transform programme formats, subject interests and styles of presentation in a bid for increased audiences. Programme producers have invariably responded in similar ways, pursuing what has here been termed a 'populist strategy' of viewer engagement. In such ways the guiding framework of the political economy approach find endorsement, with public discourse clearly structured in terms of the wider economic dynamics of production. So much is clear in relation to current affairs and documentary programming. But what about the regional news programme?

Here it was found that this particular programme, because of its privileged position in the regional ITV structure and corporate flagship role, appears to escape some of the intensified pressures for maximized audience ratings in line with the commercial imperative. It enjoys, in short, a form of corporate patronage based on its perceived corporate use-value. Though ultimately dependent upon the overall commercial success of the company concerned, programme forms may not themselves always be exposed to the chill winds of the marketplace; exceptions can still occasionally be found, and here the general framework proposed by the political economy approach may be of less immediate relevance.

A further qualifying remark on the necessary, but less than sufficient, explanatory reach of the political economy approach can also be made. If economic forces and increased commercial pressures have been found, in line with the general thrust of the political economy approach, to have impacted on the horizons of corporate strategy and individual programme producers, the response to such pressures have none the less been culturally informed. It has been noted how, for example, and in sympathy with the intensified ITV pursuit of mass audiences, current affairs and documentary programme producers have invariably interpreted their predicament as requiring a populist revamping and/or transformation of existing programme forms. Based on little, if any, serious audience research beyond ratings, so-called 'audience appreciation' indicators and the occasional letter of complaint or congratulation received by programme producers, the imagined audience of the programme makers and its popular interests is based on the flimsiest of foundations. Programme producers are just as likely to have recourse, as observed in the last chapter, to a stereotypical image of a typical 'punter in the pub'. Here it is the culturally informed image of popular culture and its preoccupations, tastes and interests that informs professional viewpoints, an image which may bear precious little resemblance to the heterogeneous composition, interests and dispositions of a mass TV audience. The effect of this cultural typification on the design and execution of popular programmes, however, are real enough.

The main ingredients to this revitalized pursuit of mass audiences on the part of programme makers have been noted earlier, and typically seek to court, that is, inscribe popular appeal. In the context of regional TV programming this has typically led producers to place an increased emphasis upon general consumer and leisure interests and other preoccupations centred in and around the private sphere; the direct appeal to audience emotions and affective response often focused in relation to the unusual happenings or tragic situations of ordinary, that is, non-elite individuals; as well as increased (inter-textual) reference to other media happenings and personalities and the private lives of politicians and other public figures. These have then been packaged into rescheduled and/or revamped magazine formats composed of relatively short items, delivered by attractive presenters in an entertaining/lively style and presented via familial modes of address.

So much is clear. What is less clear, at least in relation to much cultural studies theorizing, is the exact status of the popular within such programme treatments. Cultural studies has, as part of its project, deliberately sought to interrogate the forms and pleasures of ordinary culture, politically distancing itself from the rarefied delib-erations on elite culture found elsewhere in the academy, while recovering the forms and symbols of popular resistance to dominant social interests. Approached in such terms, popular culture becomes a force-field in which contending social interests seek, at the level of culture, to publicly define and position the popular in relation to the play of social power. On occasion this has led to an uncritical acceptance of popular cultural forms, with theorists recovering the way in which they are thought to express, or at least provide a resource for, popular resistance and negotiated understandings of the dominant order.

It is worth remembering here, however, that the term 'popular' continues to carry different connotations, each pointing to a different status and associated cultural politics. A few years ago a commentator astutely noted, for example, how the term has variously been used in the senses of 'belonging to the people', 'of pertaining to the people', 'constituted or carried by the people', 'intended for or suited to ordinary people', 'adapted to the understanding or taste of ordinary people' and 'finding favour with or approval by the people' (Caughie 1984: 118). Each clearly implies a different sense of popular involvement and cultural representation, ranging from the complete representation and expression of popular interests within cultural forms to the complete imposition and definition of popular interests by others. It is as well to keep such distinctions in mind before accepting uncritically, or even celebrating, those cultural forms produced by others for 'popular' consumption.

The study of the regional news programme has demonstrated, for example, how senior corporate decision makers and professional journalists have deliberately worked to a particular understanding of the popular. This, as above, may say more about the imagined audience of the news producers than the actual audience and its different constituencies of interest, demographics, dispositions, beliefs, preferences and tastes, as well as varied information needs. Far from the regional news programme representing ordinary viewers its particular construction of popular appeal has, if anything, minimized the representation of the conditions of ordinary existence as lived by many of its viewers. It has effectively ignored those conditions endured by many of its regional constituency, displacing collective hardships, social inequalities and discriminatory practices and outcomes from wider public view. In such terms the popular has been found to be a highly produced package which, if engaging with popular interests and aspirations at all, has done so in the generalized terms of appealing to consumer interests.

If approaching regional news, or regional programming more generally in terms of its contribution to public debate and engaged criticism, perhaps in terms of a regional public sphere, it is clear that such is nearer to Habermas's 'culture-consuming' 'pseudo-public sphere' than his envisaged 'rational–critical' sphere of engaged citizens (Habermas 1989: 159–80). It is interesting to recall here, then, a recent bid for making TV news even more popular.

It would be better for TV news if it confidently asserted that its position in the repertoire of news media is one that makes its popularity its defining characteristic. It should, therefore, be evaluated less by informational criteria and more by those of popular appeal. We should demand of our television news that it makes the events of the world popular, that it subject them to popular taste and attempt to make them part of the popular consciousness of society. (Fiske 1989b: 185)

This is a position that would, on the evidence of this study, be welcomed by most regional news journalists keen to recruit increased viewer interest and news engagement. The costs of such a strategy have already been witnessed, however, especially in relation to the impact that such professionally inscribed 'popular appeal' has had upon the silences, selections and treatments of news stories relating to the problems and issues of urban marginalization. Much depends, of course, upon who exactly is defining, producing and packaging popular appeal. While Fiske has increasingly focused upon the popular in relation to the moment of audience consumption, when approached, as in this study, from the contexts of production, it is less easy to feel confident about the gains that could be accrued from increased TV news popular appeal. The reasons for this are simple and relate principally to the institutionalized bases of power and determination that inform and surround the operations of the culture industries.

If the popular has, in broad terms, historically moved away from 'the property of the people', to 'packaging for the people' and 'consumption by the people' (Caughie 1984), cultural theorists cannot afford to ignore the moment of institutional production, since it is here that major explanatory insights into the silences and saliences of cultural forms continue to be found. It is here that the cultural resources for consumption are packaged and produced according to professional and commercial logics which have little regard for enhanced public participation and the public expression of contending viewpoints. And it is here, too, that schedules and programmes, messages and meanings are structured and circulated to a wider public. While critics may take comfort in the 'resistance' thought to inform negotiated audience responses to media texts, this should not be allowed to overshadow the profoundly unequal nature of the communication relationship. The industrial nature of organized cultural production, as much as the terms of engagement set out and defined by those who work there, point to a continuing relationship in which audiences must always respond to, rather than define the agenda of concerns. Routine silence, it hardly needs to be said, is difficult to negotiate.

This study, with its focus upon the TV mediation of the problems and issues of concentrated urban distress, has sought to interrogate part of the organized corporate basis of cultural production, attending to processes and practices of professional programme production and their wider contexts. In such ways, insight has been gained not only into the prominent saliences of programme interests, but also into the characteristic styles of programme treatments and routine programme silences. Pressures for change, already well underway, have also been observed to further reduce and inflect what limited opportunities for regional representation may once have existed. Such is the influence of the intensified commercial imperative now ordering the priorities and schedules of ITV companies.

Contrary to corporate and professional claims to represent the life and problems of the region, on the basis of this study, the regional ITV system has increasingly failed to report, represent or seek to explain the conditions of urban distress and social marginality found across the urban landscape. If the news programme has been found to concentrate on aspects of crime, violence, disorder and deviance these do not represent the general conditions of urban marginality, though they may well be an expression of it. It is in relation to these wider, more enduring and collective realities of the region's many inner cities and outer estates that the TV system has failed to communicate. It has, in short, contributed to those very processes of marginalization that we should all expect to be the focus of considerable media attention. Courtesy of regional television, the 'happier classes' have rarely been invited to ponder the lived realities and voices of those growing numbers of people consigned to live in 'separate territories'.

Notes

Introduction: Approaching television

1 For the purposes of this study, both the inner cities and outer estates are taken to be similar. Both represent places of urban marginality and spatially informed processes of social segregation and polarization. This is not to deny that important differences also characterize these localities, including differences of social composition, ethnicity and the degree of social homogeneity. If the inner cities have been associated with urban unrest in the 1980s, so too have many of Britain's outer estates erupted in serious disorders in the 1990s. When referring to the 'inner city', this study is also addressing the issues and concerns of urban marginality and spatially concentrated social distress in general, and refers therefore to many of the problems and issues found on many of Britain's outer estates. For one of the first insightful discussions of these issues see the report *Faith in the City* with its identification of both the inner cities and the outer estates as 'Urban Priority Areas' (Archbishop of Canterbury 1985).
2 These front page headlines, typical of the way in which successive urban disorders have been reported by much of Britain's press, are taken from the following newspapers: the first three concern disorders in Oxford and on the Meadow Well estate in North Shields reported in September 1991, by the *Daily Express*, *Daily Mail* and the *Daily Star* respectively, followed by reports of the recent disorders on the Hartcliffe Estate in Bristol in July 1992, reported by the *Bristol Evening Post*.

4 Mediating the inner city: producing inner city voices

1 This particular analysis has been published previously as 'Reporting the Rushdie Affair: A Case Study in the Orchestration of Public Opinion' (see Cottle 1991).

5 Mediating the inner city: TV news portrayal

1 The sample of 288 separate news programmes subjected to review was taken across the period 1982 to 1988 on a rolling five day week basis. Starting on 5 January 1982 a programme was selected every twenty-one days thereafter. For the purposes of this analysis, news items were coded as 'inner city' related if (a) referencing inner city/outer areas designated by enumeration districts as deprived but not referencing inner city issues; (b) concerned with inner city related issues as defined across the three contending discourses – spatially located crime/disorder, issues of urban deprivation or issues of 'race'/minority ethnicity and racism; (c) if explicit reference to the 'inner city' or via other lexical terms are made. Only 6 per cent of the sample was 'incidentally' concerned with the inner city (see pp. 127–30), while 14.3 per cent of news items made explicit lexical reference to 'the inner city'. The bulk of all items (79.6 per cent) therefore referenced identified inner city issues (31.1) or inner city issues plus reference to an identified inner city locality (48.5 per cent).
2 This finding emerged from a detailed analysis of regional news programmes and their patterns of news content in general, detailed in my PhD study *Television Coverage of the Inner City* (Cottle 1990).
3 For the purposes of this overview analysis, presentational news formats were coded according to their most expansive elements. Thus, if a news item included a newsdesk report and ENG interview as well as a studio interview it was coded as a studio interview, that is, as an expansive format.

6 Mediating the Handsworth riots: riotous others, silent voices, criminal deeds

1 This is not to say, however, that the term 'riot' cannot sustain different meanings. An historically informed understanding of 'bargaining by riot' for instance, may well sustain more radical associations. Here current associations are discussed only. The extent to which 'riot' may have become discursively ambivalent through varied appropriation is considered in later analyses (see pp. 165–9).
2 This argument is developed in an article currently in preparation: 'Stigmatizing Handsworth: Notes on Spoiled Space' in which news reports of Handsworth are found to repeatedly position Handsworth as a place of crime, criminality and deviance. Though only one inner city ward amongst countless others in the TV region, Handsworth appears to have broken through news thresholds for special treatment – that is, Handsworth has become of news value in and of itself.
3 For a more detailed examination of the 'directing' role of news report lead statements as a news structure see Van Dijk's analyses of news schema categories (Van Dijk 1988, 1991)

8 Conclusion: some observations on media theory

1 Pronounced differences of TV news programme forms have begun to be charted with reference to a comparative study of environmental TV news

coverage. Here differences of programme news interests, styles of news treatment and presenter modes of address have all been found to impact in differentiated terms on the portrayal of the environment. Such differences have yet to be pursued into the different production domains and with regard to professional programme visualizations however (see Cottle forthcoming (b)).

References

Altheide, D. L., (1974) *Creating Reality*, Beverley Hills, London: Sage.

Ang, I. (1985) *Watching Dallas – Soap Opera and the Melodramatic Imagination*, London: Methuen.

Archbishop of Canterbury (1985) Commission Report *Faith in the City*, London: Church House Publishing.

Barthes, R. (1987) *Image-Music-Text*, translated by S. Heath, London: Fontana.

Begg, I., Eversley, D. (1986) 'Deprivation in the Inner City', in V. Hausner (ed.) *Critical Issues in Urban Economic Development*, Oxford: Clarendon Press.

Bennett, T. (1986) 'Hegemony, ideology, pleasure: Blackpool' in T. Bennett, C. Mercer, J. Woollacott (eds) *Popular Culture and Social Relations*, Milton Keynes: Open University Press.

Bennett, T., Mercer, C., Woollacott, J. (eds) (1986) *Popular Culture and Social Relations*, Milton Keynes: Open University Press.

Benyon, J. (ed.) (1984a) *Scarman and After*, Oxford: Pergamon Press.

Benyon, J. (1984b) 'The Riots: Perceptions and Distortions', in J. Benyon (ed.) *Scarman and After*, Oxford: Pergamon Press.

Benyon, J. (1986) *A Tale of Failure: Race and Policing*, Policy Papers in Ethnic Relations No. 3, Centre for Research in Ethnic Relations, University of Warwick.

Benyon, J. (1987) 'Interpretations of Civil Disorder', in J. Benyon, J. Solomos (eds) *The Roots of Urban Unrest*, Oxford: Pergamon Press.

Benyon, J., Solomos, J. (eds) (1987) *The Roots of Urban Unrest*, Oxford: Pergamon Press.

Benyon, J., Solomos, J. (1991) 'Race, Injustice and Disorder', in S. MacGregor, B. Pimlott (eds) *Tackling the Inner Cities*, Oxford: Clarendon Paperbacks.

Birmingham City Council (1986) *Inner Area Studies* 1984/5, Birmingham: Birmingham City Council.

Blumler, J. (1990) 'Elections, the Media and the Modern Publicity Process', in M. Ferguson (ed.) *Public Communication – The New Imperatives*, London: Sage.

Breed, W. (1955) 'Social Control in the Newsroom', *Social Forces*, vol. 33, pp. 326–35.

Brown, J. (1982) *Policing By Multi-Racial Consent – The Handsworth Experience* (Foreword by Lord Scarman) London: Bedford Square Press.

Brunsdon, C., Morley, D. (1978) *Everyday Television: 'Nationwide'*, London: British Film Institute.

Burgess, J.A. (1985) 'News From Nowhere: The Press, the Riots and the Myth of the Inner City', in J. A. Burgess, R. A. Gold (eds) *Geography, the Media and Popular Culture*, London: Croom Helm.

Byrne, D. (1989) *Beyond the Inner City*, Milton Keynes: Open University Press.

Cardiff, D. (1986) 'The Serious and the Popular: Aspects of the Evolution of Style in the Radio Talk, 1928–1939', in R. Collins, J. Curran, N. Garnham, P. Scannell, P. Schlesinger, C. Sparks (eds) *Media, Culture and Society – A Critical Reader,* London: Sage Publications.

Carey, J. (1989) *Communication as Culture – Essays on Media and Society*, London: Unwin Hyman.

Cashmore, E., McLaughlin, E. (eds) (1991) *Out of Order? Policing Black People*, London: Routledge.

Caughie, J. (1984) 'Television Criticism: A Discourse in Search of an Object', *Screen*, vol. 25, no.4, pp. 109–20.

Central Independent Television (1989a) Central 1988 Annual Review *Change in Progress,* Central Independent Television plc.

Central Independent Television (1989b) Central 1988 Annual Reports and Accounts *Progress in Change*, Central Independent Television plc.

Chaney, D. (1986) 'A Symbolic Mirror of Ourselves: Civic Ritual', in R. Collins, J. Curran, N. Garnham, P. Scannell, P. Schlesinger, C. Sparks (eds) *Media, Culture and Society – A Critical Reader*, London: Sage Publications.

Chatterton, M. (1987) 'Front Line Supervision in the British Police Service', in G. Gaskell, R. Benewick (eds) *The Crowd In Contemporary Britain*, London: Sage.

Chibnall, S. (1977) *Law and Order News – An Analysis of Crime Reporting in the British Press*, London: Tavistock.

Clarke, A. (1986) 'This is not the Boy Scouts: Television Police Series and Definitions of Law and Order', in T. Bennett, C. Mercer, J. Woollacott, (eds) (1986) *Popular Culture and Social Relations*, Milton Keynes: Open University Press.

Cohen, P. (1982) 'Race, Reporting and the Riots', in P. Cohen, C. Gardiner (eds) *It Ain't Half Racist Mum: Fighting Racism in the Media*, London: Comedia.

Cohen, S., Young, J. (eds) (1981) *The Manufacture of News*, London: Constable.

Connell, I. (1986) 'Television News and the Social Contract', in S. Hall et al. (eds) *Culture, Media Language*, London: Hutchinson.

Corner, J. (ed.) (1986) *Documentary and the Mass Media*, London: Edward Arnold.

Corner, J. (1991) 'Meaning, Genre and Context: The Problematics of "Public Knowledge" in the New Audience Studies', in J. Curran, M. Gurevitch (eds) *Mass Media and Society*, London: Edward Arnold.

Cottle, S. (1990) *Television Coverage of the Inner City*, Centre for Mass Communication Research, University of Leicester (unpublished PhD thesis).

Cottle, S. (1991) 'Reporting the Rushdie Affair: A Case Study in the Orchestration of Public Opinion', *Race and Class*, vol. 32, no.4, pp. 45–64.

Cottle, S. (1992) ' "Race", Racialization and the Media: A Review and Update of Research', *Sage Race Relations Abstracts*, vol. 17, no. 2, pp. 3–57.

Cottle, S. (forthcoming (a)) 'Behind the Headlines: The Sociology of News', in M. O'Donnell, *New Introductory Readings in Sociology*, London: Nelson.

Cottle, S. (forthcoming (b)) 'Mediating the Environment: Modalities of TV News', in A. Hansen (ed.) *Media and the Environment*, Leicester: Leicester University Press.

Cumberbatch, G., Howitt, D. (1989) *A Measure of Uncertainty: The Effects of the Mass Media*, Broadcasting Standards Council, London: John Libbey.

Cummings, B. (1992) *War and Television*, London: Verso.

Curran, J. (1990) 'The New Revisionism in Mass Communication Research: A Reappraisal', *European Journal of Communication*, vol. 5, pp. 135–64.

Curran, J., Douglas, A., Whannel, G. (1980) 'The Political Economy of the Human Interest Story', in A. Smith (ed.) *Newspapers and Democracy*, Cambridge, Massachusetts and London: MIT Press.

Curtis, L. (1984) *Ireland: The Propaganda War*, London: Pluto Press.

Dahlgren, P., Sparks, C. (eds) (1992) *Journalism and Popular Culture*, London: Sage.

Davis, H., Walton, P. (1984) 'Death of a Premier: Consensus and Closure in International News', in H. Davis, P. Walton (eds) *Language, Image, Media*, Oxford: Blackwell.

Deacon, D., Golding, P. (1991) 'When Ideology Fails: The Flagship of Thatcherism and the British Local and National Media', *European Journal of Communication*, vol. 6, no. 3, pp. 291–313.

Dear, G. (1985) *Report of the Chief Constable West Midlands Police – Handsworth-Lozells September 1985*, West Midlands Police Constabulary.

Department of the Environment (1977a) *Inner Area Studies: Summary of the Consultants' Reports*, London: HMSO.

Department of the Environment (1977b) *Unequal City – Final Report of the Birmingham Inner Area Study*, London: HMSO.

Department of the Environment (1977c) *Inner London: Policies For Dispersal and Balance*, London: HMSO.

Department of the Environment (1977d) *Policies for the Inner Cities*, Cmnd 6845, London: HMSO.

Department of the Environment (1981) *Urban Deprivation: Information Note 2*, London: DOE Inner Cities Directorate.

Downing, J. (1985) ' "Coillons . . . Shryned in an Hogges Toord": British News Media Discourse on Race' in T. Van Dijk (ed.) *Discourse and Communication*, Berlin: Walter de Gruyter.

Dunning, E., Murphy, P., Newburn, T., Waddington, I. (1987) 'Violent Disorders in Twentieth-Century Britain', in G. Gaskell, R. Benewick (eds) *The Crowd in Contemporary Britain*, London: Sage.

Edelman, M. (1988) *Constructing The Political Spectacle*, Chicago: University of Chicago Press.

Elliott, B. (1984) 'Cities in the Eighties: the Growth of Inequality', in P. Abrams, R. Brown (eds) *UK Society*, London: Weidenfeld & Nicolson.

Elliott, P., Murdock, G., Schlesinger, P. (1986) ' "Terrorism" and the State: A Case Study of the Discourses of Television', in R. Collins, J. Curran, N. Garnham, P. Scannell, P. Schlesinger, C. Sparks (eds) *Media, Culture and Society – A Critical Reader*, London: Sage.

Ellis, J. (1988) *Visible Fictions*, London: Routledge.

Engels, F. (1987 [1845]) *The Conditions of the Working Class in England*, Harmondsworth: Penguin Classics.

Epstein, E. J. (1973) *News From Nowhere: Television and the News*, New York: Random House.

Ericson, R. V., Baranek, P. M., Chan, J. B. L. (1987) *Visualizing Deviance: A Study of News Organisation*, Milton Keynes: Open University Press.

Ericson, R. V., Baranek, P. M., Chan, J. B. L. (1989) *Negotiating Control: A Study of News Sources*, Milton Keynes: Open University Press.

Ericson, R. V., Baranek, P. M., Chan, J. B. L.(1991) *Representing Order: Crime, Law, and Justice in the News Media*, Milton Keynes: Open University Press.

Fishman, M. (1980) *Manufacturing the News*, Austin: University of Texas Press.

Fiske, J. (1989a) 'Popular Television and Commercial Culture: Beyond Political Economy', in G. Burns, R. J. Thompson (eds) *Television Studies: Textual Analysis*, London: Praeger.

Fiske, J. (1989b) *Reading the Popular*, London: Unwin Hyman.

Fiske, J. (1990) 'Women and Quiz Shows: Consumerism, Patriarchy and Resisting Pleasures' in M. Brown (ed.) *Television and Women's Culture*, London: Sage.

Fryer, P. (1989) *Staying Power – The History of Black People in Britain*, London: Pluto Press.

Gans, H. (1980) *Deciding What's News*, London: Constable.

Glasgow University Media Group (1976) *Bad News*, London: Routledge & Kegan Paul.

Glasgow University Media Group (1980) *More Bad News*, London: Routledge & Kegan Paul.

Golding, P., Elliott, P. (1979) *Making the News*, London: Longman.

Golding, P., Middleton, S. (1982) *Images of Welfare: Press and Public Attitudes to Poverty*, Oxford: Basil Blackwell.

Golding, P., Murdock, G. (1979) 'Ideology and the Mass Media: The Question of Determination' in M. Barrett et al. (eds) *Ideology and Cultural Production*, London: Croom Helm.

Golding, P., Murdock, G. (1991) 'Culture, Communications, and Political Economy', in J. Curran, M. Gurevitch (eds), *Mass Media and Society*, London: Edward Arnold.

Gunter, B., McAleer, J. L. (1990) *Children and Television*, London: Routledge.

Habermas, J. (1974) 'The Public Sphere', *New German Critique*, no. 3, Autumn, pp. 49—55.

Habermas, J. (1989) *The Structural Transformation of the Public Sphere*, Cambridge: Polity Press.

Hall, P. (ed.) (1981) *The Inner City in Context*, Aldershot: Gower.

Hall, S. (1975) 'The "Structured Communication" of Events', in UNESCO, *Getting The Message Across*, Paris: UNESCO.

Hall, S. (1983) 'The Problem of Ideology – Marxism Without Guarantees', in B. Matthews (ed.) *Marx 100 Years On*, London: Lawrence & Wishart.

Hall, S., Critcher, C., Jefferson, T., Clarke, J., Roberts, B. (1986) *Policing the Crisis*, Basingstoke: Macmillan.

Hall, S., Jacques, M. (eds) (1989) *New Times*, London: Lawrence & Wishart.

Halloran, J. D. (1980) 'Mass Communications: Symptom or Cause of Violence?', in G. C. Wilboit, H. de Bock (eds) *Mass Communication Review Year*, Vol. 1, London: Sage.

Halloran, J. D., Elliott, P., Murdock, G., (1970) *Demonstrations and Communication: A Case Study*, Harmondsworth: Penguin.

Hansen, A., Murdock, G., (1985) 'Constructing the Crowd: Populist Discourse and Press Presentation', in V. Mosco, M. Wasko (eds) *Popular Culture and Media Events*, The Critical Communication Review vol. 3, New Jersey: Ablex.

Harrison, P. (1985) *Inside the Inner City*, Harmondsworth: Penguin.

Hausner, V. (ed.) (1986) *Critical Issues in Urban Economic Development*, Oxford: Clarendon Press.

Hausner, V., Robson, B. (1985) *Changing Cities*, An Introduction to the ESRC Inner Cities Research Programme, London: Economic and Social Research Council.

Hebdige, D. (1979) *Subculture: The Meaning of Style*, London: Methuen.

Herridge, P. (1983) 'Television, the "Riots" and Research – Scarman, Tumber and After', *Screen* vol. 24, pp. 86–91.

Hetherington, A. (1989) *News in the Regions*, Basingstoke: Macmillan.

Holland, P. (1983) 'The Page Three Girl Speaks to Women, Too', *Screen* vol. 24. no.3.

Hollingsworth, M. (1986) *The Press and Political Dissent*, London: Pluto Press.

Home Department (1988) *Broadcasting in the '90s: Competition, Choice, Quality*, Cm 517, London: HMSO.

Home Department (1990) *Broadcasting Act*, London: HMSO.

Independent Television Commission (1990a) *Invitation to Apply for Regional Channel 3 Licences*, London: Independent Television Commission.

Independent Television Commission (1990b) *Mapping Regional Views*, A Report on Viewer's Preferences for Regional Television in the UK, Research Department London: Independent Broadcasting Authority.

Independent Television Commission (1991) *Reports and Accounts*, London: Independent Television Commission.

Institute of Race Relations (1979) *Police against Black People*, London: Institute of Race Relations.

Institute of Race Relations (1987) *Policing against Black People*, London: Institute of Race Relations.

Jensen, K. B. (1987) 'Qualitative Audience Research: Toward An Integrative Approach to Reception', *Critical Studies in Mass Communication*, vol. 4, no. 1, pp. 21–36.

John, A. (1972) *Race in the Inner City*, London: Runnymede Trust.

Johnson, M. (1989) 'The Regional View', *Airwaves*, The Quarterly Journal of the IBA, Spring, p. 13.

Joshua, H., Wallace, T., Booth, H. (1983) *To Ride the Storm: the 1980 Bristol 'Riots' and the State*, London: Heinemann.

Kerner, O. (1968) *Report of the National Advisory Commission on Civil Disorders*, New York: Bantam Books.

Lang, K., Lang, G. E. (1953) 'The Unique Perspective of Television and its Effects. A Pilot Study', *American Sociological Review* vol. 18, pp. 3–12.

Lash, S., Urry, J. (1987) *The End of Organised Capitalism*, London: Polity Press.

Lea, J., Young, J. (1984) *What is to be Done About Law and Order*, Harmondsworth: Penguin.

Le Bon, G. (1960 [1895]) *The Crowd: A Study of the Popular Mind*, Viking Press.

Lewis, J. (1982) 'The Story of a Riot: The Television Coverage of Civil Unrest in 1981', *Screen Education*, no. 40, pp. 15–33.

Lewis, J. (1985) 'Decoding Television News', in P. Drummond, R. Patterson (eds) *Television in Transition*, London: British Film Institute.

Lewis, J. (1991) *The Ideological Octopus*, London: Routledge.

Litton, I., Potter, J. (1985) 'Social Representations in the Ordinary Explanation of a "Riot" ', *European Journal of Social Psychology*, vol. 15, pp. 321–87.

Livingstone, S. M., Lunt, P. K. (1992) 'Expert and Lay Participation in Television Debates: An Analysis of Audience Discussion Programmes', *European Journal of Communication*, vol. 7, no. 1, pp. 9–35.

Lodziak, C. (1986) *The Power of Television: A Critical Appraisal*, London: Frances Pinter.

Lodziak, C. (1988) 'Dull Compulsion of the Economic: The Dominant Ideology and Social Reproduction', *Radical Philosophy*, no. 49, pp. 10–17.

MacGregor, S. (1991) 'The Inner City Battlefield: Politics, Ideology and Social Relations', in S. MacGregor, B. Pimlott (eds) *Tackling the Inner Cities*, Oxford: Clarendon Paperbacks.

Mallen, D. (1991) 'Challenges for Education: The Needs of the Urban Disadvantaged', in S. MacGregor, B. Pimlott (eds) *Tackling the Inner Cities*, Oxford: Clarendon Paperbacks.

Miles, R. (1984) 'The Riots of 1958: Notes on the Ideological Construction of "Race Relations" as a Political Issue in Britain', *Immigrants and Minorities*, vol. 3, no. 3, pp. 252–75.

Mills, C. W. (1975) *The Sociological Imagination*, Harmondsworth: Penguin.

Moores, S. (1990) 'Texts, Readers and Contexts of Reading: Developments in the Study of Media Audiences' *Media, Culture and Society*, vol. 12, no. 1, pp. 9–29.

Morley, D. (1980) *The Nationwide Audience*, BFI Monograph 11, London: British Film Institute.

Morley, D. (1986) *Family Television: Cultural Power and Domestic Leisure*, London: Comedia.

Morley, D., Silverstone, R. (1990) 'Domestic Communication – Technologies and Meanings', *Media, Culture and Society*, vol. 12, no. 1, pp. 31–55.

Monaco, J. (1981) *How To Read A Film*, rev. edn, Oxford: Oxford University Press.

Morrison, D. E., Tumber, H. (1988) *Journalists at War*, London: Sage.

Murdock, G. (1981) 'Political Deviance: The Press Presentation of a Militant Mass Demonstration', in S. Cohen, J. Young (eds) *The Manufacture of News*, London: Constable.

Murdock, G. (1982) 'Large Corporation and the Control of the Communications Industries', in M. Gurevitch, T. Bennett, J. Curran and J. Woollacott (eds) *Culture, Society and the Media*, London: Methuen.

Murdock, G. (1984) 'Reporting the Riots: Images and Impacts', in J. Benyon (ed.) *Scarman and After*, Oxford: Pergamon Press.

Murdock, G. (1990) 'Redrawing the Map of the Communication Industries: Concentration and Ownership in the Era of Privatization', in M. Ferguson (ed.) *Public Communication – The New Imperatives*, London: Sage.

Murdock, G., Golding, P. (1984) 'Capitalism, Communication and Class Relations', in J. Curran, M. Gurevitch, J. Woollacott (eds) *Mass Communication and Society*, London: Edward Arnold.

Murray, N. (1986) 'Reporting the "Riots" ', *Race and Class*, vol. 18, no. 27, pp. 86–90.

Ousley, O., Bhavnani, R., Coke, J., Gilroy, P., Hall, S., Vaz, K. (1986) *A Different Reality – Report of the Review Panel*, West Midlands County Council.

Patton, W., Shaw, R. (1986) *Alternative Notes to the Silverman Inquiry*, Birmingham: Birmingham City Council.

Philo, G. (1990) *Seeing and Believing*, London: Routledge.

Postman, N. (1987) *Amusing Ourselves to Death*, London: Methuen.

Pryce, K. (1979) *Endless Pressure*, Harmondsworth: Penguin.

Radway, J. (1987) *Reading the Romance – Women, Patriarchy and Popular Literature*, London: Verso.

Ratcliffe, P. (1979) *Racism and Reaction – A Profile of Handsworth*, London: Routledge & Kegan Paul.

Raynsford, N. (1991) 'Housing Conditions, Problems and Policies', in S. MacGregor, B. Pimlott (eds) *Tackling the Inner Cities*, Oxford: Clarendon Paperbacks.

Rex, J. (1984) 'Disadvantage and Discrimination in Cities', in J. Benyon (ed.) *Scarman and After*, Oxford: Pergamon Press.

Rex, J., Moore, J. (1967) *Community and Conflict*, London: Oxford University Press.

Rex, J., Tomlison, S. (1979) *Colonial Immigrants in a British City*, London: Routledge & Kegan Paul.

Robins, K., Cornford, J. (1992) 'What is "Flexible" about Independent Producers?', *Screen*, vol. 33, no. 2, pp. 190–200.

Robson, B. (1988) *Those Inner Cities*, Oxford: Clarendon Press.

Rule, J.B. (1988) *Theories of Civil Violence*, California: University of California Press.

Scannell, P. (1988) 'Radio Times. The Temporal Arrangements of Broadcasting in the Modern World', in P. Drummond, R. Patterson (eds) *Television and its Audience*, London: British Film Institute.

Scannell, P. (1989) 'Public Service Broadcasting and Modern Public Life', *Media, Culture and Society*, vol. 11, pp. 135–66.

Scarman, Lord (1986), *The Brixton Disorders*, Harmondsworth: Penguin.

Schlesinger, P. (1987) *Putting 'Reality' Together*, London: Methuen.

Schlesinger, P. (1990) 'Rethinking the Sociology of Journalism: Source Strategies and the Limits of Media-Centrism', in M. Ferguson (ed.) *Public Communication: The New Imperatives*, London: Sage pp. 61–83.

Schlesinger, P., Tumber, H., Murdock, G. (1991) 'The Media Politics of Crime and Criminal Justice', *British Journal of Sociology*, vol. 2, no. 3, pp. 397–420.

Schroder, K. C. (1987) 'Convergence of Antagonistic Traditions? The Case of Audience Research', *European Journal of Communication*, vol. 2.

Scraton, P. (1987) 'Unreasonable Force: Policing, Punishment and Marginalization', in P. Scraton (ed.) *Law, Order and the Authoritarian State*, Milton Keynes: Open University Press.

Seabrook, J. (1988) *The Race For Riches,* Basingstoke: Marshall Pickering.

Searchlight (1985) 'Reporting Handsworth', *Searchlight*, no. 125 pp. 18–19.

Sigelman, L. (1973) 'Reporting the News: An Organisational Analysis', *American Journal of Sociology*, no. 48, pp. 132–51.

Sills, A., Taylor, G., Golding, P. (1988) *The Politics of the Urban Crisis*, London: Hutchinson.

Silverman, J. (1986) *Independent Inquiry into the Handsworth Disturbances*, Birmingham: Birmingham City Council.

Silverstone, R. (1990) 'Television and Everyday Life: Towards an Anthropology of the Television Audience', in M. Ferguson (ed.) *Public Communication – The New Imperatives*, London: Sage.

Skellington, R., Morris, P. (1992) *'Race' in Britain Today*, London: Sage.

Small, S. (1983) *Police and People In London*, vol. 2, *A Group of Young Black People*, No. 619, London: Policy Studies Institute.

Smith, D. J. (1983) *Police and People In London*, vol. 3, *A Survey of Police Officers*, No. 620, London: Policy Studies Institute.

Smith, D. J, Gray, J. (1983) *Police and People In London*, vol. 4, *The Police In Action*, No. 621, London: Policy Studies Institute.

Smith, S. (1989) *The Politics of 'Race' and Residence*, Cambridge: Polity Press.

Solomos, J. (1986) 'Political Language and Violent Protest – Ideological and Policy Responses to the 1981 and 1985 Riots', *Youth and Policy*, no. 18, pp. 12–24.

Solomos, J. (1989) *Race and Racism in Contemporary Britain*, Basingstoke: Macmillan.

Soloski, J. (1989) 'News Reporting and Professionalism: Some Constraints on the Reporting of News', *Media Culture and Society*, vol. 11, pp. 207–28.

Sparks, R. (1992) *Television and the Drama of Crime*, Buckingham: Open University Press.

Spencer, K., Taylor, A., Smith, B., Mawson, J., Flynn, N., Batley, R. (1986) *Crisis in the Industrial Heartland – A Study of the West Midlands*, Oxford: Clarendon Press.

Steadman-Jones, G. (1971) *Outcast London: A Study in the Relationship Between Classes in Victorian Society*, Oxford: Clarendon Press.

Sumner, C. (1982) ' "Political Hooliganism" and "Rampaging Mobs": the National Press Coverage of the Toxteth Riots', in C. Sumner (ed.) *Crime, Justice and the Mass Media*, Cambridge: Cambridge University Press.

Taylor, P.M. (1992) *War and the Media*, Manchester: Manchester University Press.

Taylor, S. (1984) 'The Scarman Report and Explanations of Riots', in J. Benyon (ed.) *Scarman and After*, Oxford: Pergamon Press.

Townsend, P. (1991) 'Living Standards and Health in Inner Cities', in S. MacGregor, B. Pimlott (eds) *Tackling the Inner Cities*, Oxford: Clarendon Paperbacks.

Tuchman, G. (1973) 'Making News by Doing Work: Routinizing the Unexpected', *American Journal of Sociology* no. 79, pp. 110–31.

Tuchman, G. (1978) *Making News: A Study in the Construction of Reality*, New York: Free Press.

Tumber, H. (1982) *Television and the Riots*, Broadcasting Research Unit, London: British Film Institute.

Tunstall, J. (1971) *Journalists at Work*, London: Constable.

Van Dijk, T. (1988) *News Analysis, Case Studies of International and National News in the Press*, New Jersey: Lawrence Erlbaum.

Van Dijk, T. (1991) *Racism and the Press*, London: Routledge.

White, D. M. (1964) 'The "Gatekeeper": A Case Study in the Selection of News', in L. A. Dexter, D. M. White (eds) *People, Society and Mass Communication*, New York: Free Press.

Williams, R. (1974) *Television, Technology and Cultural Form*, London: Fontana.

Williams, R. (1985) *Marxism and Literature*, Oxford: Oxford University Press.

Williams, R. (1988) *Keywords*, London: Fontana.

Subject index

Author index